Drug Use and Abuse among U.S. Minorities

Patti Iiyama
Setsuko Matsunaga Nishi
Bruce D. Johnson

Published in cooperation
with the Metropolitan Applied
Research Center, Inc.

The Praeger Special Studies program—
utilizing the most modern and efficient book
production techniques and a selective
worldwide distribution network—makes
available to the academic, government, and
business communities significant, timely
research in U.S. and international economic, social, and political development.

Drug Use and Abuse among U.S. Minorities

An Annotated Bibliography

PRAEGER SPECIAL STUDIES IN U.S. ECONOMIC, SOCIAL, AND POLITICAL ISSUES

Praeger Publishers   New York   Washington   London

Library of Congress Cataloging in Publication Data

Iiyama, Patti.
    Drug use and abuse among U.S. minorities.

    (Praeger special studies in U.S. economic, social,
and political issues)
    Includes indexes.
    1. Drugs and minorities—United States—Bibliography.
I. Nishi, Setsuko, joint author.   II. Johnson, Bruce D.,
1943—   joint author.   III. Title.
Z7164.N17I37 [HV5825]   016.3622'93   74-33035
ISBN 0-275-05370-9

PRAEGER PUBLISHERS
111 Fourth Avenue, New York, N.Y. 10003, U.S.A.

Published in the United States of America in 1976
by Praeger Publishers, Inc.

Printed in the United States of America

This is a bibliography of research materials on drug use and abuse among racial minorities in the United States, specifically blacks, Asian Americans, Mexican Americans, Puerto Ricans, and native Americans. It grows out of a document originally prepared by Patti Iiyama of the Metropolitan Applied Research Center (MARC), as source material for the National Conference on Drug Abuse (Washington, December 1972), which focused on narcotics addition among minorities. It was sponsored by a group of organizations including the NAACP Legal Defense and Educational Fund, the Mexican American Legal Defense and Educational Fund, the National Urban League, and the Puerto Rican Bar Association, and was coordinated by Diane E. Lacey of the NAACP Legal Defense and Educational Fund, a former consultant to the mayor of New York City's Office of Drug Use and Abuse.

Following the well-attended conference, the MARC decided that an updated and expanded version of the original bibliography would fill a critical gap in knowledge about drug use among minorities in the United States, and further, it was thought that such a bibliography, accompanied by an analytical introduction, would serve as a useful tool for policy-makers as well as students. The current bibliography includes 245 annotations, of which three out of four involve studies published within the last ten years.

"Drug abuse" in this bibliography refers primarily to opiate, in the main heroin, addiction. This restricted focus reflects in part the fact that at the time of the conference, heroin addiction was a matter of acute public concern and the subject of numerous legislative and administrative proposals. Much of the public and governmental concern had to do with the presumed incidence of drug use among minorities and youths and its association in the public's mind with crime and social protest. The focus on heroin, a "hard" drug, was also because marijuana, a so-called "soft" drug, is generally held not to be addictive, and alcohol and tobacco are not commonly considered dangerous drugs. The bibliography includes a few references to other drugs when they pertain to use among racial minorities (for example, paregoric, a tincture opiate, and glue and gasoline sniffing) and a few references from the vast literature on peyote usage. Research on the use and effects of marijuana, hallucinogens, amphetamines, and barbiturates has been omitted unless these drugs are cited as included in a multi-drug syndrome of heroin users.

The introductory essay, written by Bruce Johnson and Setsuko Matsunaga Nishi, reviews and assesses research literature and policy on drug use and abuse. It also describes the historical links between the official policies and public attitudes related to drug use, clearance, and criminality on the one hand and the governmental policies related to racial minorities in the United States on the other hand.

Dr. Johnson is project director of a study on abuse and neglect among low income families in New Jersey at the Graduate School of Social Work, Rutgers University. Dr. Nishi is associate professor of sociology at Brooklyn College and at the Graduate Center of the City University of New York and a fellow of the Metropolitan Applied Research Center (MARC).

The bibliography is organized in such a way as to group the research on drug use by five racial minorities in the United States (blacks, Asian Americans, Mexican Americans, Puerto Ricans, and American Indians) and to facilitate cross referencing. If a study pertains to several groups, it is listed under each one. Studies which refer generally to "slum inhabitants," "minority groups," and "nonwhites" are arbitrarily listed under the section on "Drug Use and Abuse Among Blacks." Within component sections, references are arranged alphabetically by author, with only the original source of publication cited. Note that there is a considerable range of definition and usage of the terms "drug abuse" and "drug addiction." The terms used to identify drug use in the annotations are those of the authors of the cited works.

The bibliography and annotations were compiled by Patti Iiyama, a MARC staff member, who was assisted by Ann Lively, a freelance researcher. Among other MARC staff who played important roles in making this publication possible were Hylan Lewis, vice president, Mary Symons Strong, editor, Adrienne Faison Davis and Joyce Marshall Nicholas, editorial assistants.

CONTENTS

PART II: ANNOTATED BIBLIOGRAPHY

LIST OF TABLES

MYTHS AND REALITIES OF DRUG USE BY MINORITIES

Bruce Johnson
Setsuko Matsunaga Nishi

THE PROBLEM OF MINORITIES AND DRUG ABUSE

Even though the estimates of addiction to narcotics by minorities in the United States vary considerably, there appears to be little doubt that blacks, Puerto Ricans, and Mexican Americans are overrepresented in the population of known addicts. A major national assessment of drug abuse sponsored by the Ford Foundation (Drug Abuse Survey Project, Wald and Hutt 1972) estimated that a majority (between 60 and 70 percent in New York City) of a possible national total of 150,000 to 300,000 active heroin addicts came from minority backgrounds. The total number estimated by the Federal Bureau of Narcotics and Dangerous Drugs (now the Drug Enforcement Administration, or DEA) for the same date (December 1971) was 559,000—more than twice the larger figure suggested by the Ford Foundation survey. The DEA estimated that there were 626,000 in December 1972 and 601,000 in December 1973. Although the proportion of minorities in the DEA estimates was not computed, blacks constituted 56 percent of the 91,750 active addicts reported in the United States Drug Enforcement Administration by police authorities by December 1974. (Addicts of Hispanic background are combined with whites in their reports) (DEA 1974*).

---

*A citation with an asterisk can be found in the list of references at the end of the Introduction.

A citation without an asterisk can be found in the main body of the annotated bibliography.

Since these racial-ethnic groups comprise less than 20 percent of the U.S. population, at first glance the extent of abuse by minorities appears to be relatively large compared to their percentage in the population. Beyond this simple conclusion, however, there is a complex situation which requires careful examination. There is room for many conflicting interpretations of the meaning of these estimates of the prevalence of drug addiction among American minorities. Some of the significant issues are: first, assessments of the magnitude and proportion of minority drug addiction; second, explanations of the nature of opiate addiction, especially the presumed susceptibility of minorities; third, effects of historical, economic, and political processes on society's perception of the problem; and fourth, development of techniques to control the use of drugs and the addicted persons.

Problems with Statistics on Drug Addiction

Prevalence and trend estimates of drug addiction as an illegal activity, particularly as they relate to racial-ethnic minorities, are fraught with difficulties. Not the least of these, as Musto (1973: 253) points out, is the problem of defining an "addict," which may range all the way from the hard-core, physiologically dependent, regular opiate user to the occasional user who could abstain without significant withdrawal symptoms, or the regular user who does not take enough for physiological dependence, but believes he does and is thus involved in the addict life style (Primm and Bath 1973*). If Primm and Bath's estimates that street bags contain only 0.5 percent or less heroin are correct, it seems probable that up to half of those considered by New York City authorities to be heroin addicts receive so little heroin per day that they would exhibit only the most minor (if any) withdrawal symptoms.

But statistics on narcotics abuse are not compiled on the basis of the nature and degree of addiction or of the self-awareness of the addicted. The DEA estimates include only addicts who have come to the attention of law enforcement agencies, primarily for narcotics law violations and secondarily for loitering or other criminal acts (De Fleur 1975). Virtually excluded from consideration are those illegal drug users who have not become involved with the police, those who obtain legal drugs from doctors, and those who are in prison (Lindesmith 1965: 102-103*; Brecher, 1972*).

Drug arrest statistics for both whites and blacks show distinct trends over time. The Uniform Crime Statistics Reports demonstrate the trends in arrests since 1933 with statistics on persons charged with violations of nonfederal narcotic laws in cities of 2,500 population

TABLE 1

Race and Black/White Ratio of Arrests for Narcotics
Laws Violations for U.S. Cities of Population 2,500 and Over,
1933-73

Year	White	Black	Black/White Ratio
1933	2,251	362	.16
1934	2,327	511	.22
1935	2,178	496	.23
1936	520	148	.28
1937	657	202	.31
1938	880	190	.22
1939	1,171	252	.22
1940	3,118	968	.31
1941	1,540	543	.35
1942	694	244	.35
1943	806	347	.43
1944	1,009	517	.51
1945	1,205	567	.47
1946	1,773	903	.51
1947	2,167	1,120	.52
1948	2,876	1,776	.62
1949	3,620	2,677	.74
1950	3,969	4,262	1.08
1951	5,873	6,697	1.14
1952	1,635	1,447	.89
1953	2,563	3,018	1.12
1954	2,371	4,154	1.75
1955	2,462	4,363	1.77
1956	2,862	4,387	1.53
1957	3,092	4,108	1.33
1958	3,807	5,740	1.51
1959	4,626	5,767	1.25
1960	8,506	7,570	.89
1961	11,371	6,742	.60
1962	11,956	8,794	.74
1963	11,725	7,134	.61
1964	12,775	9,038	.71
1965	16,869	11,816	.70
1966	22,754	14,762	.65
1967	46,011	21,672	.47
1968	85,638	27,861	.33
1969	119,154	39,491	.33
1970	177,412	55,885	.32
1971	204,817	69,616	.34
1972	239,343	77,007	.32
1973	279,191	76,672	.27

Source: John Helmer and Thomas Vietorisz, Drug Use: The Labor Market and Class Conflict, (Washington, D.C.: Drug Abuse Council, 1974) for 1933 to 1955. Calculated from Uniform Crime Reports for 1956 to 1973, (Washington, D.C.: U.S. Government Printing Office).

and over. Table 1 gives the numbers or arrests of whites and blacks
as well as the ratio between blacks and whites in the years between
1933-1973. During these years the ratio of black to white arrests for
narcotics law violations rose steadily from .16 (362 blacks to 2,251
whites) in 1933 to 1.77 (4,363 blacks to 2,462 whites) in 1955. This
increase in the ratio of black to white drug arrests happened in the
politically oppressive context of the 1950s and during an economic
slump when blacks were especially hard hit. Between 1955 and 1973,
the trend reversed: there was a steady decline from the high point of
1.77 in 1955 to .27 in 1973. During these decades the absolute number
of both white and black arrests is notable. White arrests rose more
than a hundredfold from 1955 to 1973 (from 2,462 to 279,191), and
black arrests increased 17 times (from 4,363 to 76,672). The spec-
tacular rise in white arrests since 1966 coincides with the beginning
of the counterculture movement among American youth.

The assumption that such police records of arrests for narcotics
law violation reflect the true incidence of drug use and abuse is open
to serious question. In a study of official arrest records and through
participant observations, DeFleur (1975) found systematic biases in
the operations of the Chicago police assigned to the Narcotics Division.
Due to political pressure to "do something" about narcotics in the early
1950s, the Chicago police descended on a few black neighborhoods,
arrested large numbers of "known" black addicts on loitering and dis-
orderly conduct charges, and held them for short periods. The heavy
use of minor charges and a "revolving door policy," kept drug arrest
rates for nonwhites very high.

The dramatic increase in the number and proportion of narcotics
related arrests in the fifties in Chicago was partly in response to a
public drive spearheaded by a newspaper campaign (also noted by
Hughes and others 1971*). DeFleur's analysis demonstrates that trends
in arrest records are more an indication of changes in public pressure
on the police and internal organizational responses of law enforcement
agencies than an accurate estimate of the incidence and prevalence of
drug abuse. Helmer and Vietorisz (1974) also find distorting factors
in drug arrest records, suggesting that in times of economic stress
the marginal status of minorities makes them vulnerable targets for
crusades against narcotics violators. It may be more appropriate,
then, to view drug arrest data as a measure of the way in which the
public responds to distressing problems rather than as evidence of
the true extent of narcotics addiction.

The New York City Narcotics Register has provided probably the
most accurate statistics regarding addiction from all official sources
such as arrests, hospitalizations, drug treatment programs, and
doctors. However, these estimates seem to indicate that only about
half of all addicts are listed in the Register (Larrier and others, 1972).

Thus, when addiction estimates are based on either medical or law enforcement criteria, there remain serious general discrepancies.

The high susceptibility of racial-ethnic minorities to categorization as deviant and their inclusion in inflated estimates of deviant populations has often been noted. In addition to racial-ethnic factors there are class variants in medical diagnoses, treatment, and outcome as well as in police attention, apprehension, prosecution, disposition, and correctional results (for example, DeFleur 1975), although it should be noted that Johnson and Bogomolny (1973) find only minor racial differences in the way the criminal justice system processes drug law violators. (See Criminal Justice Processing of Drug Users, p. 40.)

Another possible distortion in the assessment of the extent of dangerous drug abuse by minorities may be due to use of illegal opiates among nonwhite, non Anglo, and lower class populations. Whites and middle class drug users may be more involved with drugs that are available through legal medical sources (Chambers 1971*). As a consequence, when minorities use drugs, they may be more likely than whites to come into conflict with the law.

While these many biases inflate the number of minority addicts, the United States Census Bureau seriously underestimates the total number of minorities in the population. The most conservative estimate of minorities is the Bureau's own report of a 7.7 percent undercount of blacks (Siegel 1973*). Other reports suggest that the figure is as high as 15 percent. The U.S. Commission on Civil Rights (1974: 50*) notes that the undercount for the Spanish origin population is at least equal to that of blacks; it is estimated at 30 percent by the Cabinet Committee on Opportunities for the Spanish Speaking (U.S. Commission on Civil Rights, 1974: 48-49*).

These two factors, the undercount of minorities by the Census and the increased probability that minorities will be included in statistics on active addicts, have an important effect on calculating the percentage of addicts in a minority population. The percentage addicted is computed by dividing generally inflated estimates of the number of addicts by the undercounted number of minorities in the population. No matter how accurate the count of minority addicts may be, the overall ratio of minority addicts to minority population thus increases because of the undercount of minorities in the population.

It is evident that both the absolute and relative size of drug abuse by minorities is still unknown. Despite this, it appears that both the public and the scientific community have defined and treated the phenomenon as a socially contagious epidemic that seriously endangers society and minority populations.

Approaches to Minority Opiate Addiction

What have been the major approaches employed in investigating drug abuse among minority groups? As in so much work on behavior seen as deviating from the dominant social norms, most of the approaches have been heavily psychological. The explanation of the underlying causes of drug abuse resulting from most of the studies conducted by psychologists, social psychologists, and psychiatrists have been of two kinds: first, identifying weaknesses in the individual that presumably make him prone to abusing drugs, and second, focusing on early socialization, problems in family structure and sex role identification. Sociologists who have investigated the influences of peer groups, delinquent gangs, drug subcultures, and counterculture social movements, but have paid relatively little attention to the larger context, the racial-ethnic discrimination and economic conditions which so frequently shape this kind of collective behavior, are more likely to view socialization as a continuing process. On the other hand, most studies which do report race differences in opiate use and addiction (and its psychological and social correlates) make no analysis of how the circumstances of minority status in American society affect the differences. Research designs seldom take into account the wide variations that exist within minority populations (a notable exception is the work of Lukoff and Brook 1974).

Explaining minority drug use per se is one thing; understanding how and why American society perceives minority addiction as a major social problem is quite another matter, and one which raises a number of questions. How have minorities become associated symbolically with drugs that came to be seen as dangerous and requiring control? How has public support been generated by "moral crusaders" (Gusfield 1963*) to protect America from the evils of drug abuse? How have stresses in the larger society, such as depressions and domestic and international power conflicts, affected perception of minority drug abuse? These questions have a close bearing on the nature of crusades for narcotics control.

Traditionally, the United States has emphasized a law enforcement approach to drug abuse, with some medical considerations at times. In the broadest sense, however, drug abuse is a sociopolitical problem, linked historically to America's treatment of ethnic and racial minorities, particularly in times of social crisis. This is a major theme of Musto's (1973) and Helmer and Vietorisz' (1974) work tracing the history of narcotics control in the United States. It is a perspective which has particular importance for this bibliography. In the following analysis of the social history of minorities and opiates, the political exploitation of racial attitudes will be emphasized.

Minorities and Drug Abuse as a Problem in
Collective Behavior

Though drug addiction is usually examined as behavior deviating from institutional norms of either health or law, in our view, another analytic dimension—that of collective behavior—is necessary. It is crucial to examine from the perspective of both the user and the society the social processes by which drug addiction becomes a problem. For example, the works of Becker (1963*), Goffman (1963*), Lukoff (1974*), Johnson (1973*), and others describe the induction of an individual into the outlooks and daily routines of drug users during the course of his becoming a drug user himself. What happens is the transformation of how the person views himself and the rejection of and withdrawal from respectable society. This transformation of self-image and perception of society by the drug user are referred to as the "moral career" of the drug user (Becker 1963*). Similar changes occur in the lives of participants in other forms of collective behavior such as in social movements (Kanter 1968*, Blumer 1951*). But drug addiction has been interpreted as resignation and as expressive release rather than as the social protest that is characteristic of participants in social movements (Forman 1963*). As Gusfield (1970*: 85) suggests, it is one of the ways in which men respond to change, conflict, and deprivation. It is a "solution"—one of the alternative "modes of rejecting the established social order," the others being protest, reform, and revolution.

Another interpretation of society's definition of the problem of drug addiction among minorities and its attempts to control minorities suggests that it is similar to other American social reform movements. Frequently such movements for reform use the vulnerability of minorities to associate them symbolically with the particular social evil which is under attack. In the case of the Women's Christian Temperance Movement, a drive for reform against what was believed to be a specific societal wrong developed into an attack against a whole status sector (Gusfield 1963*). Alcohol consumption, already considered as evil in itself, also became a symbol of the "immorality" of both upper middle class women and urban immigrant Catholics. Anti-alcohol legislation was a convenient means for lower middle class rural Protestant women to express their resentment of other status groups. In this way, the "moral crusade" against saloons and drinking at the turn of the century had its roots in widespread status conflict.

Analogously, throughout the history of what also may be termed "moral crusades" against drug abuse, nonwhite or immigrant minorities and other elements considered undersirable (for example, "hippies") have become the objects of attack. In these drives, drug addiction has become a convenient symbol of the worst in the alien, primitive, hostile, anti-establishment lifestyle of these lower-status groups. From this perspective historical episodes of minority drug use as well as society's efforts at narcotics control can be seen as recurring specific social movements in the context of broader currents of change, conflict, and discontent in American society.

SOCIAL HISTORY OF OPIATES AND MINORITIES

Opium and the Chinese

The opium problem began in China. Opium smoking became commonplace around 1800 when opium, produced by a British opium monopoly in India, was smuggled into China despite Manchu edicts against it. Although many issues were involved, two Anglo-Chinese conflicts, called the Opium Wars by anti-opium crusaders (Rowntree 1905*), provide early examples of the symbolic aspects of opium. To the Chinese government, opium smuggling epitomized the essential evil of white foreigners. They believed that the British wanted to inflict this harmful drug on the Chinese people to weaken their ability to resist foreign imperialism (Fairbanks 1953*). To the British, China's opposition to opium stemmed from her desire to protect silver supplies and to keep foreigners and Western trade out of China (Fairbanks 1953*, Johnson 1975 a*, b*). To Protestant missionaries in China and to some other Americans, the opium trade was a moral outrage because governments of primarily Christian peoples were forcing immoral behavior upon the Chinese (Rowntree 1905*; Johnson 1975 a*, b*).

In the United States opium smoking and opium dens first acquired evil connotations because of anti-Chinese and anti-criminal prejudices. For example the early labor leader, Samuel Gompers, was savagely racist in the expression of this opposition to the hiring of non-union Chinese coolies. "There are hundreds, aye, thousands, of our American girls and boys who have acquired this deathly habit [opium smoking] and are doomed, hopelessly doomed, beyond the shadow of redemption" (Hill 1973*: 52). To the temperance worker, opium was more harmful and evil than alcohol, and alcohol was very, very evil (Crafts 1906*). Opium eating and morphine use were condemned because the lower classes were believed to use them—despite the fact that most studies of the era emphasize the middle class status of such users (Terry and Pellens 1928*; Helmer and Vietorisz 1974).

When the United States took over the Philippines in 1928, missionary and temperance organizations in the U.S. eventually secured a prohibitionary policy there despite recommendations for a temporary opium monopoly by responsible officials (Taylor 1969*; Musto 1973). Opium was a convenient political tool for Theodore Roosevelt's Open Door policy in China. After the Boxer Rebellion, and with increasing Chinese government hostility towards American missionaries and merchants (partly due to the maltreatment of Chinese immigrants in the U.S.), Roosevelt proposed an international opium conference in 1909 and sided with the Chinese against the British (Musto 1973). The first federal law against narcotics imports—in this case, opium smoking—was passed as a gesture of American concern. The result was that Sino-American political tensions were diffused while no major shifts in American treatment of Chinese immigrants occurred.

Cocaine and Blacks

It was not merely by chance that popular post-Reconstruction ideas about blacks were increasingly fear-provoking, and one of these was the idea of the "cocaine crazed" Negro. Stories in the press on this theme were not unusual (Musto 1973). Col. J. W. Watson of Georgia is quoted in the New York Tribune of June 21, 1903, as decrying the prevalence of cocaine sniffing among the "colored" and asserting that "many of the horrible crimes committed in the Southern states by the colored people can be traced directly to the cocaine habit" (Musto 1973: 254). In an article in the Atlanta Constitution of December 27, 1914, Negroes and cocaine use were associated, and the police chief of Atlanta was quoted as blaming drug use for "70 percent of the crimes."

Dr. Christopher Koch of the State Pharmacy Board in Philadelphia, identified as spearheading an anti-cocaine drive, testified before a Congressional committee on anti-narcotics legislation, and referred to southern Negroes' use of cocaine. Musto (1973: 255) notes that Koch is quoted in a 1914 article in the Literary Digest as stating, "Most of the attacks upon white women of the South are a direct result of a cocaine-crazed Negro brain." Another lurid tale reported in Good Housekeeping of March 1914 (Musto 1973: 255) described "old colored men hiding cocaine under their pushcart wares and spreading the drugs throughout America's cities."

Though there was evidence of cocaine use among both whites and blacks and it was commonly available in a new soda fountain drink called Coca Cola, the common belief fostered was its link with Negroes. It was thus in the context of the widening disfranchisement and subordination of the Negro at the turn of the century that the "dope fiend" image

developed around cocaine. It became symbolically linked to the widely
held fears about violence and sexuality among blacks. Attempts to control cocaine, in effect, were attempts to control and repress blacks.
Numerous state and local laws were passed to make cocaine use illegal
except in patent medicines, and in 1914 the Harrison Act was enacted,
requiring that producers and distributors of narcotics be registered
and taxed and that medical users obtain prescriptions through physicians. The campaign for drug control fully exploited foreign, alien,
and racist imagery to gain support among "decent" Americans.

Mexican Americans and Marijuana

Another instance of the exploitation of popular beliefs connecting
a drug's use with a racial minority was the campaign for the passage
of the Marijuana Tax Act of 1937. Primarily because of the opposition
of pharmaceutical houses, cannabis was not included in the drugs regu-
lated under the Harrison Act of 1914 (Musto 1973: 216-19). Marijuana was not viewed as a serious problem until about World War I,
and then was seen as affecting only very small populations such as
the Syrian colony in New York, the "Hindoos" in San Francisco, and,
increasingly, Mexican Americans of the Southwest. Despite developing pressures, primarily from labor and nativistic interest groups,
the Federal Bureau of Narcotics at first declined to become involved
in federal marijuana controls (Helmer and Vietorisz 1974).

However, the belief that marijuana was a major cause of violence
and crime committed by Mexican Americans grew persistently. Although they had been a significant part of the agricultural work force
in the Southwest for several decades, it was not until the Depression
years of the 1930s (Daniels and Kitano 1969*; Helmer and Vietorisz
1974: 22; and McWilliams 1939*), that Mexican Americans became
surplus labor. At this time campaigns for restricting their immigration and encouraging their deportation were launched in full scale in
a movement spearheaded by the American Federation of Labor. It
was in this context that Congress passed the Marijuana Tax Act in
1937, under heavy onslaught from local political leaders who, urging
control, often cited fears of violent crimes which would be caused by
marijuana use among Mexican Americans.

Heroin Enters the Ghetto

During World War II, heroin addiction in the U.S. reached one
of its lowest points (Lindesmith 1947*; Helmer and Vietorisz 1974)
as smuggling patterns were disrupted. In response to wartime industrial needs, black laborers migrated to the urban North. They continued
to do so in the postwar years even as the labor shortage came to an
end. By the 1950s, unemployment among blacks reached notably high

levels due to the convergence of a number of circumstances exacer-
bating discrimination: first, the recession of 1949-53 reduced the
number of jobs, increasing competition; second, a disproportionate
number of black youth turned sixteen in 1950—due to a record low
white birth rate in the depression year of 1934, the black birth rate
was 45 percent higher than the white (Helmer and Vietorisz, 1974);
third, black teenagers were in need of jobs because they had dropped
out of high school at a higher rate than that prior to World War II,
while white teenagers increasingly stayed in school until their twentieth
birthdays.

In the 1950s, what Claude Brown (1965*: 193) called the "shit
plague" hit Harlem. Any one interested in knowing official reaction
to this plague can consult the "scientific" literature of that decade
(see abstracts of articles written in the 1950s; Chien and others 1964;
Brecher 1972*). As heroin use in black urban neighborhoods increased,
a new belief—cultivated by longstanding racial attitudes—grew among
whites that blacks were peculiarly susceptible to heroin addiction.
(Even today this belief exerts an enormous influence on drug policy,
and an examination of this idea is a central focus of this introductory
essay.)

This was the McCarthy era, when witch-hunting for subversive
elements became a popular preoccupation and was fanned by the new
communications medium of television. In this atmosphere of suspicion,
racial minorities, along with labor organizations and politically liberal groups, were considered by many to be under the influence of an
international Communist conspiracy, using drug addiction as one means
of subversion.

The identification of blacks with heroin use in a toughening political atmosphere was a significant component in the increasing punitive-
ness of drug control legislation in this period. In 1951, the Boggs
Amendment to the Uniform Narcotic Drug Act fixed mandatory minimum sentences, increasing the prison term to ten years for repeated
offenses and to two years for first convictions of narcotic possession (Lindesmith 1965*). Many states passed their own laws to make
punishable the sale and distribution of heroin and even addiction itself.
The 1956 Narcotic Drug Control Act permitted the death penalty for
sale of narcotics to minors.

The Counterculture

Drugs outside the ghetto became a "problem" only after 1965,
with the emergence of the counterculture exemplified by Timothy
Leary, the Beatles, and Allen Ginsberg. As patterns of behavior
among college students changed from relatively conventional towards
hippie and/or politically radical values, drug use also increased.
The most striking and long lasting change in the last half of the 1960s

was the increasing use of a spectrum of illicit drugs, a fact which has been well documented. In 1967 a Gallup poll reported that 5 percent of U.S. college students had tried marijuana; by 1971 51 percent had tried it (Johnson 1973*). In 1967, one percent had tried hallucinogens, and in 1971, 18 percent. This remarkable increase in drug use was mainly drugs other than heroin. However, some of the studies emerging from the Haight-Ashbury clinics (Newmeyer and Gay 1972) indicate that some of the Flower Chidren became addicts. Scare stories about middle class white heroin addiction in suburban and small towns were circulated (Brecher 1972*), but its true extent is undocumented. Probably the best attempt to analyze the recent trend towards increasing heroin addiction is the work of Hunt (1974) who finds that decreases in major cities are offset by increases in smaller cities with a predominately white population. This upward trend of white addiction can be seen in Table 1 (discussed previously).

There are two opposing theories to explain the increased use of heroin by whites. The first of these—which might be called the official position—holds that involvement with drugs like marijuana, hallucinogens, and pills, leads to experimentation with other drugs and increased probability of heroin addiction. The second explanation—which emphasizes the role of the subculture (Johnson 1973; Goode 1969*)—holds that it is the illegality of marijuana that increases the probability of dealing in drugs and making contact with heroin dealers, who are predominately black.

The increase of drug use among whites has meant that it is no longer seen as solely a minority problem. After middle class whites became involved with drugs, especially marijuana, some whites began to see the need for fundamental changes in government policy towards marijuana and eventually argued for less punitive laws regulating heroin and opiate use (Kaplan 1970; Brecher 1972*; Zinberg and Robertson 1973*). It is difficult to predict whether actual changes in the laws on either drug will be effected, but if cannabis laws are changed the pressure for shifts in heroin control may gain ground. Meanwhile, if it is true that large numbers of whites are becoming addicts, then with very few exceptions they have succeeded in staying out of addict-processing institutions.

The social history of drug control efforts in the United States indicates that in every major drive for legislation, minorities are symbolically linked with "evil" drugs in order to build highly emotional campaigns to "protect" American morality. The popular concepts of both the minority and the drug are thus combined and seen as a double threat to society which justifies a need for control. The facts of minority drug use and abuse, insofar as they have been ascertained, either bear little relationship to the basis of historical attempts at control or contradict it. The social and economic crises that created the context of discontent in which moral crusades against so-called outsiders and drug users have been conducted (Becker 1963*; Hofstadter 1965*) stand in sharp contrast to society's tolerant response to the drug use of millions of Americans with tranquilizers, amphetamines, and barbiturates.

The Social Science Frankenstein: Racist Misconstructions
of the Social Research Reality

As Frankenstein was a monstrous distortion of mankind, so also does racism monstrously misconstrue the reality (if there is any) of minority addiction. In this bibliography few of the abstracted articles are openly biased, but interpretations and policy applications of this research have at times been outrageous. From both black and white perspectives, potentially virulent racism has supported efforts to explain and understand drug addiction. It is important to draw attention to the way that the public selectively misunderstands and misconstrues information about racial differences reported in drug studies. Although this problem is still little investigated, the meaning of the information frequently seems to be distorted to fit the frames of reference of the people receiving it.

The mental gymnastics employed by laymen to misconstrue research findings on drugs into a reality acceptable to racist views of drug addiction include the following:

● Statistical findings that blacks are overrepresented among institutionalized addicts in comparison with their proportion in the population are transformed by slippery logic into "blacks are more likely to be addicts." The narrow population base (institutionalized addicts) and the selectivity of the recruitment into this population are ignored. The basis for comparison and percentage calculation is also converted: institutionalized addicts versus total population becomes blacks versus whites.

● The generalization that "about twice as many blacks as whites have tried heroin" (Johnson 1973*) is actually based on a very small difference, seven percent of blacks versus four percent of whites. If the low percentages (seven percent and four percent) for both groups are forgotten and if the terminology is changed slightly from "have ever tried heroin" to "are addicted," the statement becomes both menacing and racist.

● Racial comparison is sometimes skipped altogether: instead of quoting the findings that "blacks are more likely than whites to become addicts," the assertion is transformed into "blacks are more likely to be addicts."

● The qualifying words, such as "more likely," are dropped and the statistic is shortened to blatant racism: "blacks are addicts," or "addicts are black."

• Any kind of experimentation with heroin or other hard drugs is equated with addiction.

Such racist deductions, though supposedly based on scientific evidence, are almost completely false. But these simplified, unqualified assertions are easier for the layman to understand and are readily embraced to suit his prejudices.

Ironically, racism may be compounded by attempts by social scientists to explain addiction by factors other than race. The drug control and research establishment avow that race in itself is not a significant factor in drug addiction. They often emphasize other conditions and variables in their research designs. One such way of explaining addiction is what may be called classism, the hypothesis that because most blacks are lower class, social class background rather than race determines addiction. Unfortunately, class explanations of addiction do not stand up under scrutiny; most relevant studies indicate that racial differences in addiction and drug use are not explained away when class is held constant, and frequently the racial factor is more important than the class (Crowther 1972; Johnson 1973*; Lukoff and Brook 1974; see discussion of class below).

Social scientists have also done extensive research on the relationship of addiction to conditions such as broken homes, female-dominated families, poor family relationships, lack of masculine identity, poor housing and environments, and poverty. In much of this research the inadequacy of the evidence and the tendency to simplify the exceedingly complex connections between these conditions and addiction have been rightly criticized (Robins and Murphy 1967). Many common assumptions about the ill effects of matriarchy, father-absence and the "culture of poverty" have been challenged effectively (Herzog and Lewis 1971*; Lewis 1967*; Billingsley 1968*; Ladner 1971*).

Despite criticism by social scientists of this kind of explanation of addition, the end result of such research may serve as further justification for a recent interpretation of addiction. Explanations like those mentioned above reinforce existing beliefs that blacks and addicts lack values considered important by the middle class (such as stable family structure, sufficient income, steady work) . Furthermore, blaming addiction on non-racial factors tends to distract the public from the importance of institutionalized racism in creating such conditions . It also fails to call attention to the wide variations in these characteristics (such as family structure and housing) among minority families, poor or not.

Unfortunately, racist misconstructions of the reality of drug addiction are rather widely believed in both white and black communities. Whites imagine that ghettos are filled with black men mugging whites for money to pay for heroin and then injecting this evil drug

so that they can spend the rest of the day nodding away in a blissful
vacuum. Many blacks, aware of the damage done by addiction subcultures to their community, also   create a racist Frankenstein.
They embrace a genocide theory which both imputes to white elites a
control over smuggling which they actually do not have, and proposes
that whites, despite all the propaganda to the contrary, actually want
to continue enslaving blacks to opiates. Some believe that the white
power structure works covertly with the Mafia to encourage heroin
distribution in the black community and that the purpose of the methadone maintenance program is to emasculate, enslave, degrade, and
kill off blacks. At the National Conference on Drug Abuse and Minorities held in 1972 sociologist J. Herman Black stated:

> The widespread abuse of drugs in communities of peoples
> of color stands the possibility of becoming the newest form
> of social control. . . . We do not here assert that there is
> some conscious design to get drugs accepted in our commun-
> ities for the purpose of containing us, but we firmly believe
> that one of the possible consequences of the continued spread
> of heroin addiction is that it will be seen as another way of
> keeping the masses in line. . . .

There has been a rising tide of criticism of the results, both
intended and unintended, of a predominantly white point of view in
social science research on racial minorities. Black and radical
caucuses of sociologists, psychologists, social workers, and other
professionals have emphasized criticism of the theories and research
methodologies that focus blame on the victims of racism (Ryan 1970*).
Ladner's (1973*) compilation of criticism from the minority perspective, The Death of White Sociology, outlines the need both for correct-
ing the biased effects of the white social science establishment and for
developing the work of black scholars on racism and the minority condition.
    The racist misconstructions of reality which may stem from
research on drug abuse are partly a consequence of a serious imbalance
in the thrust of investigation. Much research on minorities by social
scientists working from the dominant societal perspective emphasizes
that the negative features of minority values and social organization
govern individual behavior. It gives relatively little attention to the
processes by which a discriminatory society fosters conditions for
negative behavior among minorities, but it defines both the behavior
and the population as deviant, and claims it should be brought under
control. Drug addiction, like other deviant behavior, is heavily bur-
dened by public moral concern. It is this convergence of moral anxieties with racial fears that makes social scientific work in this field
particularly vulnerable to misconstruction.

THE FUNCTION OF THEORIES:
CONCEALING MORAL ENTERPRISE

In his famous discussion of moral enterpreneurs, Becker (1963*) suggests that social reformers frequently influence the passage of legislation and the enforcement of laws intended to regulate private morality. When deviant or elite groups oppose such legislation the reformers claim they are working for the good of others, not for their own self-interest. Indeed, the mark of a moral entrepreneur is to insist that his "superior" morals become the law of the land.

The history of narcotics policy presents a case study of conflict among moral entreprenuers representing various positions. In the 1910s, users of opiates and cocaine acquired a public image as "dope fiends" through the efforts of reform groups. Labeled as moral lepers, drug addicts were unable to represent their case to the public effectively. Reformers, pharmaceutical interests, and especially the medical profession did not have this problem. Zealous campaigners for anti-drug legislation had to make compromises with drug and medical interests in order to achieve the passage of the Harrison Act in 1914. In the new drug control legislation, private physicians were permitted to provide opiates "in the course of professional practice for legitimate medical purposes" (Musto 1973; Reasons 1974*). Despite this provision, when the Treasury Department's narcotics division began work in 1915 they threatened prosecution and brought some indictments against doctors for providing opiates to patients. This quickly deferred most general practitioners from treating addicts. The few that continued to provide this kind of medical treatment were soon labeled "dope doctors" by the press and the narcotics division.

The Criminalization of Addiction and the
Decline of Medical Treatment

In 1919 the Treasury Department used a trick indictment to get the U.S. Supreme Court to interpret the Harrison Act. The Court held that the medical treatment of the addict did not include "a sale to a dealer or a distribution intended to cater to the appetite or satisfy the craving of one addicted to the use of the drug" (King 1972*: 42).

In response to court cases, several localities set up clinics to care for addicts and/or to reduce their habit. Some clinics provided addicts with controlled dosages and were relatively successful, but the poorly organized and administered New York City clinic was easily attacked by prohibitionists. All clinics were closed by the Treasury Department in 1923 (King 1972*; Musto 1973). Addicts could not longer

legally obtain supplies, doctors prescribing to addicts faced prosecution. Addiction had been successfully criminalized. The two narcotic
hospitals in Lexington and Fort Worth—the one federal symbolic attempt
to provide "treatment"—fooled no one. The bars on the windows and
locked wards reminded doctors, psychiatrists, and patients that addicts were really criminals in a special prison.

The Psychological Model of Addiction

Though prevented from treating the addicted by prescribing
drugs, members of the medical profession, psychiatrists in particular,
and clinical psychologists, continued to describe addiction as a disease
that needed treatment. The definitions of "disease" and "treatment"
were changing, however. Psychological terms were now used instead
of biological or physiological terminology to describe the disease of
addiction. There were many schools of thought among the doctors
and clinicians who espoused the psychological model of addiction, but
in general they looked at the problem as follows: first, those who become addicted were psychologically disturbed (inadequate, pathological,
and so on); second, addiction further harmed their psychological states;
third, sufficient psychological and/or psychiatric therapy or support
would eventually "cure" addicts (by enabling them to abstain from
drugs). Until the 1950s and early 1960s, the major proponents of such
views were psychologists at the federal hospitals, a few psychologists
at local or state hospitals or prisons, and academic psychologists
(Milton 1944; MacFarland and Hall 1953; Gerard and Kornetsky 1954,
1955; Brummit 1963; Chein and others 1964; Laskowitz and Einstein
1963; Bender 1968; Cole, Fisher, and Cole 1968; Johnston 1968). However, in the late 1960s and early 1970s the Synanon-Phoenix House
type of "therapeutic communities" became the major advocates of this
psychological model of addiction (Casriel and Amen 1971; Yablonsky
1965*; Densen-Gerber 1973*).

Unfortunately, whether propounded by professionals or by ex-
addicts, each of these three propositions is of dubious validity. The
first two propositions, that addicts are psychologically disturbed and
that addiction intensifies their psychological problems, are doubtful
because of the post hoc reasoning employed to support them. The third
proposition, that abstinence can be effected through psychotherapy,
also rests on shaky ground (a discussion of this assertion is presented
in the section on treatment).

In order to demonstrate a relationship between psychological
disturbances and addiction, much more rigorous research is needed.
Studies have frequently reported a rather unsystematic set of clinical

observations about the psychological states of a few addicts in treatment (Bailey 1922; Gerard and Kornetsky 1954; Brummit 1963; Chein
and others 1964; Fort 1955; Vaillant 1966; Bender 1968; Cole, Fisher,
and Cole 1968). While some reports show that addicts are comparatively maladjusted according to various diagnostic tests standardized on
general populations (Hill, Haertzen, and Glaser 1960; Laskowitz and
Einstein 1963) the fact that the research subjects are usually hospitalized, imprisoned or institutionalized addicts weakens the general
validity of such findings.

Studies employing control groups are particularly lacking. The
few studies which do employ control groups in their research designs
provide little support for psychologically based theories of addiction.
Gasser and others (1974) found no differences between new and long-
term methadone patients and college students on the Eysenck Personality Inventory and on a lie scale. Robins and Murphy found in their
1967 study of black males in St. Louis that much to their surprise,
the father's presence or absence during adolescence was not correlated
with drug use of any kind. However, among those young people who
smoked marijuana, dropped out of high school, and had been arrested,
heroin addiction was correlated with the father's absence from home.
Glaser, Lander, and Abbott's 1971 study of New York City slum siblings
found that before addiction addicts were not in conflict with their parents more often or more alienated from them than their non-addict
siblings were.

Several recent surveys of drug use in a normal student population find various psychological measures to be relatively unimportant
in explaining drug use, especially when sociological factors are held
constant (Kandel and others 1974*). Mellinger and others (1975*) find
that changing drug use patterns are not systematically related to psychological impairment.

The relative infrequency of psychoses and other organic brain
or physical damage, even in long-term addicts, make the second proposition—that addiction intensifies existing psychiatric disorders—
particularly suspect (see Brecher 1972*: 25 for summaries of over
twenty studies: Malzberg 1949). If there are causal links between the
use of drugs and the deterioration of the individual's psychological
condition, they remain to be documented.

The psychological model of addiction often harbors the subtle
racism and classism which are implicit in the clinical studies and
analyses of institutionalized addict populations that form a significant
part of the literature in the field. Although most psychologists and
psychiatrists may be relatively unprejudiced, the psychological model
which they employ embodies class bias in favor of white middle-class
values (Goode 1972*) and race bias against various minority lifestyles.
The result is a value-laden terminology which clinicians use to de-

scribe their addicted patients (Bailey 1922; Dai 1937; Zimmering 1951; Fort 1955; Gerard and Kornetsky 1955; Roebuck 1962; Chein and others 1964; Fiddle 1967; Cole, Fisher, and Cole 1968). Unfortunately many professionally untrained people, such as workers in prisons and probation systems, have picked up this psychological terminology and used it glibly, thus concealing their prejudiced and moralistic judgments (Blumberg 1965*).

Perhaps the most important aspect of the psychological model of addiction is that it is the most generally accepted one, and most treatment is based on it. While police and prison custodial staff are detaining and punishing addicts, psychologists or social workers are hired to provide "evaluation," "treatment," and "rehabilitation" of addicts in all parts of the criminal justice system.

Therapeutic communities, although they replace professional psychologists with successful ex-addicts, propound and operate according to a similar psychological model of treatment. In methadone maintenance programs counselors employ therapy techniques for rehabilitation. The frequent result of the acceptance of psychological models in explaining addiction and justifying treatment by virtually all authorities is addict resentment and hostility towards "shrinks."

Another effect of the psychological model of addiction is its success in concealing from the public the real treatment being given to addicts. As interpreted by addiction personnel, it effectively hides the extent to which societal morality rather than therapy is forced upon addicts while making minimal adjustments to the addict's real needs. Nice sounding terminology - "strengthening ego structure," "building personality," "rational authority," "providing individualized treatment," (Brill and Lieberman 1969*) is employed to conceal from the public and even from treatment personnel themselves the real message which addicts are coerced to learn from relevant authorities: "Thou shalt not use opiates ever again." With all the legal pressure on them and with all the well-intended efforts of massive treatment programs, addicts have been notably successful at evading the moral message transmitted. The remarkably high rate of relapse to addiction has marked the demise of several morally exemplary treatment programs (see Waldorf 1973, and Brecher 1972*).

Sociological Explanations of Addiction

Sociological explanations of addiction and recommendations for treatment, although they are also generally inadequate, at least give more attention to racial differences in drug use and addiction and to direct observations of individuals who are in the actual process of becoming drug users. They may also be more successful at explaining through empirical data the reasons why individuals try and become regular users of illicit drugs.

Sociological explanations of addiction are derived from general sociological theories and are sometimes closely related to each other in their theoretical underpinnings. Five such closely related explanations of how addiction occurs have been employed by sociologists doing research on various phases of the problem: differential association and anomie, multiple factor, subculture, sequential drug involvement, and epidemic or contagion.

Differential association and the anomie theory derive from the work of Sutherland (1974*) and Merton (1957*) as well as from Cloward and Ohlin's (1960*) differential opportunity theory. Sutherland's theory holds that criminal behavior is learned in intimate peer groups. This proposition has received impressive support in two studies (Kandel 1973*; Kandel and others 1974*) of New York State high school student use of marijuana in which 80 percent of respondents whose best school friend used marijuana 60 or more times—versus 15 percent of those whose best friend never used it—had themselves tried marijuana. The effect of friend's use upon respondent use was maintained when a variety of other variables were held constant (Kandel 1974*; Kandel and others 1974*). It is probable (but not known) that friend's use also decisively influences respondent heroin use, and is strongly influenced by the respondent's use of other drugs (Johnson 1973*). Cloward and Ohlin's (1960*) theory holds that both legitimate and illegitimate opportunities for upward mobility are unavailable in urban slums. Those who aspire upward but fail in both opportunity structures (double failures) are disproportionately likely to seek status in heroin-using groups and to become addicted to heroin (Roebuck 1963; Abrams, Gagnon and Levin 1968; Preble and Casey 1969; Rivera and Hohlen 1973*).

Some evidence is available to support this differential opportunity theory of heroin addiction. Among black youth in St. Louis 48 percent of marijuana-using high school dropouts with juvenile arrest (double failures) became addicts, while only 20 percent or less of either the arrested high school graduates or nonarrested high school dropouts (single failures) did so (Robins and Murphy 1967). Glaser and others (1971) found that among matched pairs of siblings, addicts as opposed to non-addict siblings did poorly in school and in holding jobs but were more involved in street life, gang activities, arrests, and a hustler life style.

Lukoff and Brook's (1974) and Kleinman's (1975) studies of heroin use among families in the Brownsville section of Brooklyn may provide support for Cloward and Ohlin's theory that blocked aspirations lead to heroin use. They found that within this slum community, families with a better education and higher income were more likely to report heroin use than poorly educated or impoverished ones. Apparently those who aspired to upward mobility and found their way blocked were more likely to become addicted than those who did not have such high aspirations.

The multiple factor theory (Johnson 1973) is well represented in abstracts. This is not a true theory, but rather an agglomeration of variables related to drug use or addiction. (Fort 1954; Roebuck 1962; Bell, Bates and O'Donnell 1968; Nurco and Balter 1969; Blum 1972; Cuskey, Premkumar and Siegel 1972; Eckerman 1973; Stephens and Cottrell 1972; Callan and Patterson 1973; Johnson 1973; Kandel 1974*; Kandel and others 1974*, 1976* [forthcoming]). Extreme eclecticism in the selection of variables means that nearly everything is correlated with drug use. Some of these variables in the abstracts are age, sex, socioeconomic status, religiosity, alienation, political activity, familial instability, parental discipline, parental use of cigarettes, alcohol and drugs, respondent's cigarette and alcohol use, sexual activity, crime, prostitution, and driving safety. Such variables are related to some measure of drug use; only a few interesting tables are presented. However, as both Blumer (1956*) and Lazarsfeld and others (1972*) note, such work is unsystematic in making theoretical links and may be inadequate in other important methodological respects (see Inadequacies of Research Methods, p. 44). Further, as Johnson (1973*) notes, the multiple factor theory is probably more useful in understanding initial marijuana use and friendships with drug users than in understanding heroin use and addiction (Kandel and others 1974*).

The subculture theory of drug use and addiction provides a bridge between the two previous theories. Although several studies use part of this theory to interpret their findings and many others provide data relevant to this theory without explicit reference to it, systematic discussion of it is rare (Goode 1972*, Johnson 1973*). Subculture theory refers to the shared norms, values, role definitions and patterns of behavior governing consumption of illicit drugs. Drug subcultures are structured around norms regulating the type of drug used as well as the frequency and mode of consumption.

Among New York City college students, two relatively different drug subcultures structured along racial lines have emerged from one relatively common marijuana consuming subculture (Johnson 1973).*

These patterns are subject to change, of course. And there are recent indications that racial difference may not be large anywhere (Johnson 1973; Kandel, Single and Kessler 1976*; Robins, Davis, and Goodwin 1974*).

Blacks begin with marijuana, then progress to cocaine and heroin but avoid using hallucinogens or methedrine. Whites begin with marijuana and progress to hallucinogens, amphetamines, barbiturates, and methedrine, but have tended to avoid using heroin . Similar racial differences in non-opiate drug use are found among institutionalized heroin addicts (Chambers and Moldstad 1970; Langrod, 1970). Single, Kandel, and Faust's (1974*) Guttman scaling of drug use patterns are slightly different for blacks and whites. However, Callan and Patterson (1973) find nonwhites more likely than whites to use amphetamines and barbiturates at midwestern army facilities.

What might be called a theory of sequential drug involvement is a generalized and refined version of the "marijuana leads to heroin" hypothesis. The sequential drug involvement theory does not imply that the use of one drug inevitably leads to the use of another, but does claim some degree of predictability. Guttman scaling of drug use data among a normal high school population (Single, Kandel, and Faust 1974*) suggests that drugs are probably begun in the following sequence: liquor, tobacco, cannabis, pills (amphetamines, barbiturates, and tranquilizers), psychedelics, cocaine, and heroin. This means that virtually everyone who uses cannabis has also tried alcohol and tobacco, but has not necessarily tried pills, psychedelics, cocaine, or heroin. However, the probability of trying a particular drug, cocaine for example, is quite high if respondents have used psychedelics, intermediate if cannabis has been used, and low if only alcohol has been used.

It is implicit in this theory that if a respondent is using a particular drug at a given time, pills for example, the probability of his using an advanced level drug, psychedelics for example, at a somewhat later time is quite high. When the regularity of use of any particular drug is combined with the type of drug or drugs previously used, predictability is further increased. However, such emphasis on progression may be misplaced. Many users may not progress; there may be as much regression (giving up psychedelics while continuing pills) as there is progression.

In a recent paper, Kandel and others (1974*) provided data showing that patterns of previous drug consumption were highly correlated with the use of marijuana and polydrugs. Other factors such as race, religion, family instability, and parental liquor and drug use had little influence independent of previous drug use and best friend's drug use. If these data are correct, it would appear that a sophisticated version of "marijuana leads to heroin" comes close to being empirically most correct. However, best friend's use (peer pressure) is equally important, and much of this evidence could be reinterpreted to fit subculture theory. But the data of Kandel and others (1974*) do effectively minimize the importance of psychological variables and multiple factor variables.

Epidemic or contagion models of drug use are generally the contribution of public health oriented researchers. De Alarcon's (1969*)
classic study of the spread of heroin in an English new town has been
replicated in a white suburb, a black public housing project, and a
major 'copping' area† in Chicago's South Side (Hughes and others
1971*, see all of Hughes and others' papers in annotations). Through
careful observations by ex-addicts, interviews with addicts, searches
of official records, and other means, it is possible to determine, within a given geographical area, what the chains of initiation and drug
distribution are, and to obtain reasonably accurate information about
trends of the incidence of drug addiction over a period of time. Such
information can be used to motivate addicts to join treatment groups
(see all of Hughes and others' papers in annotations).

This model assumes that heroin addiction is analogous to an
epidemic of smallpox: if the drug dealer (diseased person) can be
captured or moved into a program (quarantined), then the spread of
infection to a larger group can be prevented. In many respects the
evidence provided by these studies gives additional support and descriptive material both for a subcultural explanation of drug use and
for the assertion that the black market provides the integrating mech-
anism—that is, the connecting functional links necessary to drug subcultures (Johnson 1973*).

Like the officially predominant criminal and psychological models
of drug addiction, these sociological explanations contain strong elements of moral enterprise. Their proponents are criticizing and ten-
tatively suggesting other solutions which are perhaps no more work-
able than present government policy. Differential association, double
failure, and multiple factor explanations suggest that transforming
the economic inequalities of American society is the way to prevent
and ultimately to eliminate addiction. One implication of the subculture
and epidemic models may be that providing opiates to addicts legally
and under very restrictive conditions, as in England (Judson 1974*),
is the most efficient way to contain addiction, since "cure" is highly
improbable. The sequential theory may mean that little can be done
to break progression from one drug to another. But all of these sociological theories are minority viewpoints which are unlikely to affect

---

†A copping area is a small geographical area in which there is
a fairly well developed market system involving all those people in
a small group who know each other and purchase drugs from dealers
in that particular locale.

official policy in the near future in any major way because of two conditions, the widespread acceptance of treatment programs based on psychological models and strong public backing for a policy of criminalizing addiction. In short, the objects of society's blame and punishment are the addicts themselves.

STATE OF KNOWLEDGE REGARDING MINORITIES AND DRUGS

The literature on the subject of the use of drugs by American racial and ethnic minorities, and especially on the use of drugs by blacks, is increasing rapidly, but it would be wrong to conclude that minority drug use is better understood simply because more data about it are now available. In fact, the extensive amount of research seems to have contributed relatively little to a realistic understanding of minority drug use. All of the research effort and fact gathering so far has yielded only meager results barely beyond the descriptive level.

It seems worthwhile, however, to look for some elements of consistency which can be extracted from the research and then discuss the findings critically. By drawing together some of the common threads of evidence in the literature, the state of knowledge regarding minorities and drugs can be summarized and assessed in several areas: first, the extent of minority involvement in opiate/heroin addiction; second, the variability in the characteristics of minority drug users; third, the processing of minorities in the criminal justice system; and fourth, the results of various drug treatment modalities on minority patients.

Minority Opiate Use and Addiction

The literature on drugs suffers from a lack of agreement on the definition of terms which are critical to building a solid body of knowledge about the field. There is confusion over the exact meanings of the terms use, abuse, and addiction, especially when heroin is the drug under consideration (National Commission on Marijuana and Drug Abuse, 1973*).

When referring to alcohol consumption, laymen generally have a clear understanding that "use" means a few (one to four) drinks on social occasions or even a relatively regular basis, "abuse" may mean getting drunk occasionally or going on sprees, while "addiction" means constantly consuming a large quantity (a pint) of alcohol on a regular basis. But moral condemnation is so strong regarding the use of heroin that any consumption is defined as abuse and equated with addiction.

It is widely believed that heroin can be used only in excess, and not in moderation like alcohol. To add to the confusion, people do not realize that even the most regular heroin-user (the "addict") may seldom be physiologically addicted. Rather he suffers from "pseudo-heroinism," as Benny Primm (1973*) so aptly calls it. Because of the infinitesimal amount (0.5 percent) of heroin in the average street bag, an addict spending $30 to $40 daily on heroin believes himself to be—and the public treats him as if he is—physiologically addicted. Yet if forced to undergo "cold turkey" he might suffer only minor withdrawal symptoms, a slight cold and a bad night's sleep.

Regardless of how addiction is defined, most of the papers abstracted in the bibliography present evidence demonstrating that blacks, Puerto Ricans, and Mexican Americans are overrepresented in the institutionalized addict populations in comparison with their proportions in the total population, while whites and Asian Americans are under-represented. As discussed previously, interpretations of such "facts" (emphasizing the magnitude of ethnic differences, converting the base for calculating percentages omitting the racial comparison, ignoring qualifications) lead easily to the belief that minorities are susceptible to heroin/opiate addiction. This idea that minorities are particularly susceptible to heroin addiction is contradicted when international and historical comparisons are made, and where careful distinctions between use, regular use, and addiction are made in general or special surveys of noninstitutional populations.

Minorities in Historical and International Comparisons

In earlier periods of American history, racial minorities were much less heavily represented in the addict population than they are at present. Terry and Pellens (1928*), Musto (1973), Helmer and Vietorisz (1974) and Reasons (1974) note that blacks were apparently underrepresented among the users of opiates in the nineteenth century. This was also true in the first two decades of the twentieth century. In one of the earliest (1913) narcotics clinics in Jacksonville, Florida, for example, 77 percent of the patients were white and 23 percent were black, while the city's population was 49 percent white and 51 percent black. There were similar conditions in Tennessee and in Shreveport, Louisiana around 1920 (Terry and Pellens 1928*: 28). But in post-World War I days things began to change. Some studies between 1920 and 1948 indicate that blacks and Chinese were overrepresented among addicts during those years (Treadway 1930; Ball and

Law 1966; Helmer and Vietorisz 1974). At New York City's narcotics
clinics 14 percent were black while nine percent of the city's population was black (Hubbard 1920*; Waldorf, Orlich, and Reinarman 1974*).
However, it was mainly after World War II, when the "plague" (Brown
1965*) hit the newly expanding black ghettos in non-Southern metrop-
olises, that minority addiction became more prevalent.

Recent research on epidemics of drug abuse traces the enormous
rise of heroin addiction among urban blacks, among New York City
Puerto Ricans, and among Mexican Americans in the West (Chein and
others 1964; Ball and others 1966; O'Donnell and Jones 1968; Chambers
and Moffet 1970; Hughes and others 1971*, 1972; Newmeyer and Gay
1972). Although little hard evidence exists on drug use in the rural
South, opiate addiction has apparently been very uncommon among
blacks who live there. All this suggests that the urban ghetto experience rather than minority group status may be the more significant
variable to focus on. As for whites, the increase in addiction occurring
among youths in San Francisco in the sixties (Gay 1972) has also occurred in smaller cities since that time (Hunt 1974*). Addiction subcultures may thus develop in certain urban minority ghettos but not
in other impoverished communities. Thus, Lander and Lander (1967)
found addiction quite common in a Puerto Rican community in New
York City but completely absent in a black Washington, D.C. ghetto.
Although they searched diligently in Chicago, Short and Strodtbeck
(1965*) could not locate heroin addiction or retreatist subcultures
among black and white gangs. Nor did large addiction subcultures
necessarily develop among minority populations in other countries.
In cities in England, for example, when there was a considerable
postwar immigration of Caribbean, African, Indian, Pakistani, and
Chinese, these minority groups are not overrepresented among
British addicts (Josephson 1973*). Though they are perhaps not as
ghettoized as American minorities are, the living conditions of these
groups are not much better than those of their American counterparts.

As for addiction in the Orient, China clearly had the most extensive opiate addiction in the world throughout the nineteenth century
and the first half of the twentieth century. Under the Communist government this addiction problem has apparently been eliminated (Lowinger 1973*), although it should be noted that independent evidence to
support Communist government claims is unavailable. Hong Kong,
where the authorities have tried to suppress addiction, still has one
of the highest incidences of heroin/opiate addiction in the world (Hess
1965*). Before 1920 (Ball and Law 1966) Chinese emigrants, especially
coolie laborers, to the United States, Australia, and the Philippines
were heavily addicted to opium smoking. As far as we know, however,
their descendents are relatively unlikely to be addicted to opiates (see
section in bibliography on Asian Americans; Kandel and others 1974*).

Comparing Minorities in Institutional Populations

Are minorities overrepresented in institutionalized addict populations when compared with the general population? If so, by how much? Most studies find minorities considerably overrepresented: for example, blacks are 20 percent more common in addict population than in general population and Hispanics are more than ten percent overrepresented (Zimmering 1972; Fort 1954; Hunt and Odoroff 1972; Brummet 1963; Royfe 1965; Abeles and others 1966; Ball and Bates 1966; Cherubin 1967; Abrams, Gagnon, and Levin 1968; Ball, Chambers, and Ball 1968; Helpern and Rho 1969; Kova 1969; Langrod 1970; Dupont 1971; Bernstein 1973; Brown and others 1973; Callan and Patterson 1973; Helmer and Vietorisz 1974). At the same time, some studies in California (Lemert and Rosberg 1948; Duster 1970; Ramer 1971) find that blacks are not overrepresented but Mexican Americans are. None of the abstracts indicates a significant heroin or opiate addiction problem among American Indians or Asian Americans since 1950, although some community leaders have noted a rise in addiction among the latter (see abstracts on Asian Americans and Native Americans). Unfortunately, the majority of institutional studies, while providing some information about the ethnic distribution of addict populations in institutions, fail to provide any comparisons with the general population living outside of institutions.

Surveys of General Populations

It is among the general population that the hypothesis of minorities' susceptibility to addiction must be tested. Many studies of general and selected non-institutionalized populations of students, youth, and adults in the United States have reported the prevalence of use—whether once, occasionally, or regularly—of heroin (NCMDA, 1973*). The National Commission on Marijuana and Drug Abuse found that about 2.0 percent of the college population (Gallup, 1972*), 1.3 percent of adults 18 years old and over, and 0.6 percent of youths (12-17 years old) had tried heroin in 1972. However, only a few of these studies have attempted to identify and count respondents who might be classified as addicted as distinguished from those who use drugs less frequently (Chambers 1971; Johnson 1973; Kandel, Single, and Kessler 1976*).

The famous Chambers (1971) study found that one percent of adults in New York State had tried heroin, but only 0.2 percent reported using it regularly (six or more times in the past 30 days). Minorities were overrepresented among regular heroin users (34 percent white, 38 percent black, 28 percent Puerto Rican) when compared to the New York State population (81 percent white, 11 percent black, and 7 percent Puerto Rican). When these data are recomputed for each ethnic group, 0.1 percent of whites, 0.8 percent of blacks, and 0.9 percent of Puerto Ricans are regular heroin users. Since these findings are based on a household survey which did not include street addicts or institutionalized addicts, it probably underestimates the extent of regular use.

Whether these data support the hypothesis that minorities are susceptible to addiction depends upon what is emphasized. Since in this study blacks are eight times and Puerto Ricans nine times as likely as whites to be regular heroin users, the hypothesis may appear to be supported. However, given the finding that less than 1.0 percent of any ethnic group uses heroin regularly, it could more accurately be said that no ethnic group is particularly susceptible. In any case, such small differences (of less than 1.0 percent) could easily be due to sampling error and for this reason fail to be statistically significant.

Other than the Chambers' (1971) study, few surveys of the general population report racial differences in regular heroin use or addiction however it is defined. But previously unpublished data from Johnson's (1973) survey of college students showed that blacks were twice as likely as whites (7.7 to 3.9 percent) to try heroin, and over twice (2.4 percent to 1 percent) as likely to use heroin regularly (monthly or more often). However, among those who had ever tried heroin, the proportion becoming regular users was roughly equal for both races (31 percent for blacks, 26 percent for whites).

Kandel, Single and Kessler's excellent 1976* study of New York State high school students found that while two percent had ever tried heroin, only one percent had tried it 10 or more times, one percent were current users (had used it in the past 30 days) and fewer than .5 percent were regular users (six or more times in the past 30 days). Of those who had ever tried heroin, only 17 percent were using it regularly. Significantly, a larger proportion—eight percent of the sample—reported some non-heroin opiate (such as opium, morphine, methadone) use for non-medical reasons, but only four percent of these non-heroin opiate users were currently using these drugs regularly.

By far the most interesting finding is the detailed ethnicity breakdown reproduced in Table 2. Because of the large sample size, it is possible to calculate the percentage of small racial minorities who have ever tried various drugs (Native Indians and Asian Americans). American Indians have by far the highest incidence of use of all drugs except heroin, a finding which is not reflected in the abstracts of drug research on Native Americans. Asian Americans have by far the lowest levels of use. While blacks (seven percent) and Spanish (five percent) are more likely than whites (two percent) to use heroin, whites are somewhat more likely (eight percent) to try non-heroin opiates than the blacks or persons of Spanish origin (six percent and five percent).

TABLE 2

Adolescent Drug Use by Ethnicity in New York State Sample, Fall 1971
(percent)

Drug	Black	White	Spanish	American Indian	Oriental
Hard liquor	59	68	50	74	18
Beer or wine	77	84	65	96	53
Cigarettes	74	73	60	93	39
Marijuana	26	30	25	40	7
Hashish	13	23	9	31	5
LSD	3	9	7	22	6
Other psychedelics	2	9	4	18	6
Methedrine	2	7	4	12	3
Other amphetamines	7	15	11	22	6
Barbiturates	9	13	11	23	5
Tranquilizers	5	8	7	20	5
Cocaine	4	3	6	13	3
Heroin	7	2	5	5	—
Other narcotics	6	8	5	17	4
Inhalants	3	8	6	12	6
Total N =	(782)	(6123)	(514)	(48)	(63)

Source: Kandel, Single, and Kessler 1976*.

Surveys of Special Populations

Unfortunately most surveys of general populations fail to include enough heroin users to make detailed analyses of addiction possible. There is however some research by Lukoff of Brownsville and by Robins and others of Vietnam veterans to provide a glimpse of heroin use in presumably addiction-prone populations. Lukoff's 1974 study of four ethnic groups in the Brownsville section of Brooklyn found that 21 percent of Puerto Ricans, 14 percent of blacks, 9 percent of British West Indian blacks, and 8 percent of whites reported a family member using heroin. According to these figures it seems that West Indian blacks were as unlikely as whites to use heroin, American blacks were intermediate in their use, and Puerto Ricans were most likely to be heroin users. These ethnic differences in heroin use reported by family members were not eliminated when social class, recency of migration to the city, age, sex, and other factors were held constant. In short, there seemed to be something in the social experience of American blacks and Puerto Ricans rather than in their race which made them "susceptible" to heroin use. In addition, Lukoff and Brook (1974) indicate that first generation males under thirty years of age were much more likely to use heroin than other residents of Brownsville.

In a follow-up of the 1971 study (Lukoff and Brook 1974), Kleinman (1975) provided further evidence of the absence of racial differences in drug use in a ghetto community. In a quota sample of 883 respondents from the Bedford-Stuyvesant ghetto in Brooklyn, they found that heroin use (three percent) and cocaine use (five percent) were equal for both blacks and whites, and that whites were more likely to use marijuana, psychedelics, and pills, and to be multiple drug users (see Table 3). Of the recent migrants to the city those over 50 years of age and the British West Indian blacks were quite unlikely to try marijuana and/or hard drugs. Among males born in the city who were between the ages of 18 and 29, the patterns of drug use were predominately dictated by friendship with other drug users. The more drug using friends and the wider the variety of drugs used by such friends, the more experimentation with and use of several drugs occurred.

Kleinman and Lukoff's data showed that for each ethnic group class differences, while not statistically significant, were positively related to drug use. That is, among whites and American blacks, the higher the socioeconomic status the higher the experimentation rate and use of hard drugs; this is just the opposite of what the class explanations of racial differences in drug use would predict. It is middle class whites in this ghetto neighborhood who are most likely to use drugs. Unfortunately, the "marijuana plus/other drugs only"

TABLE 3

Ethnic Groups Who Have Ever Tried Various Drugs,
Bedford-Stuyvesant/Fort Greene, Brooklyn, New York, 1974
(percent)

| | | Ethnic Group | |
Drugs	Whites (N = 69)	American Blacks (N = 534)	British West Indian Blacks (N = 200)
Marijuana	28	16	6
Cocaine	5	5	2
Heroin	3	3	1
Psychedelics	10	1	2
Amphetamines	10	2	2
Barbiturates	12	1	1
Drug Use Pattern			
No drug use	70	83	94
Marijuana only	10	10	4
Marijuana plus/			
other drugs only	20	7	2
Total	100	100	100

Source: Kleinman and Lukoff 1975.

category does not exclude heroin use, so white use of hard drugs
(mainly pills and psychedelics) other than heroin is being compared
with the predominately cocaine and heroin use of blacks. It should
also be noted that the frequency of heroin use in this black ghetto
community (Table 3) is not significantly higher than that reported by
Kandel, Single, and Kessler (1976*, Table 2) for high school students,
and was somewhat lower than that reported among Johnson's 1973 New
York area college students. In short, Kleinman and Lukoff's data
challenge the assumptions that race, class, and ghetto residence are
linked to heroin. Much more careful work is needed to explain the
vast discrepancy between addiction in ghetto communities and in the
penal and treatment systems.

Robins and Murphy's 1967 study of St. Louis black males found
that 12 percent had tried and 10 percent were addicted to heroin,
but made no comparison with white males. In a general sample of
Vietnam veterans, Robins (1973) found that 44 percent reported narcotics use and 20 percent considered themselves addicted, but only

TABLE 4

Drug Use Patterns by Ethnicity and Socioeconomic Status,
Bedford-Stuyvesant/Fort Greene, Brooklyn, New York, 1974
(percent)

| | Socioeconomic Status[a] | | | | | | | | |
| | Whites[a] | | | American Blacks[a] | | | British West Indians[a] | | |
Drug Use Patterns	Lower-Lower	Lower-Middle[b]	Middle[c]	Lower-Lower	Lower-Middle[b]	Middle[c]	Lower-Lower	Lower-Middle[b]	Middle[c]
No drug use	100	66	60	87	82	78	96	95	92
Marijuana only	0	7	15	7	11	12	4	2	6
Marijuana plus/ other drugs only	0	27	25	6	7	10	0	3	2
Total	100	100	100	100	100	100	100	100	100
N =	14	15	40	243	143	148	55	63	82

[a] class differences within each ethnic group are not significant.
[b] ethnic group differences within the lower-middle class are significant.
[c] ethnic group differences within the middle class are significant at .01 level.
Source: Kleinman and Lukoff 1975.

34

eight percent had injected narcotics. Among veterans providing drug-positive urine samples when leaving Vietnam, 97 percent reported narcotics use, but only 69 percent had had four major indicators of addiction. Among those drug-positive in Vietnam, 33 percent had used narcotics (mainly injectable heroin), seven percent felt addicted, but only two percent had opiate-positive urines at the date of interview a year after leaving Vietnam (Robins 1973). Thus the vast majority of veterans who used opiates in Vietnam did not take up heroin upon returning to the U.S., and even among those who did, a quarter or less were addicted at the time of the interview. In a later paper Robins, Davis, and Goodwin (1974*), found that racial differences in various measures of narcotics use relatively minor, and occasionally whites were more likely than blacks to be users. This Vietnam veteran study is the best one available that measures addiction in a reasonably normal population. It tends to disprove the hypothesis of minority susceptibility to heroin addiction. Such research also demonstrates that what is really needed in heroin abuse studies is a careful selection of opiate-using populations which is then matched with a general sample with roughly equivalent characteristics.

Variability in Characteristics

There are undoubtedly many factors which are relevant to an understanding of drug use and abuse. Information on the variations in the demographic characteristics of drug users such as sex, age, social class and geographic location are commonly obtained and presented by researchers. Unfortunately, it often happens that findings are reported about minorities as though members of these groups were all alike. Studies of drug use by Native Americans, for example, usually fail to supply detailed information about the variability within this complex minority. Japanese Americans and Chinese Americans, who constitute only about 1 percent of the United States population, are normally lumped together in surveys or combined with other categories such as white, non-black, or non-Hispanic. Consequently, very little is known about the background characteristics of Asian Americans who are drug users.

Much more is known about such differences in the black and Hispanic populations. The available information about variability by sex, age, social class, and geographic location among drug users of minority background is summarized below.

Sex. Although most studies note that 70 to 80 percent of addicts are male, it is uncommon for subsequent analysis to control for sex. However, several studies have concentrated on female addicts' patterns of criminality, prostitution, disease, drugs consumed, sexual dysfunction, length of habit, legal difficulties, and so on. (See index: female addicts—Chambers, Hinesley, and Moldestad 1970; Williams and Bates 1970; Cuskey, Premkumar, and Sigel 1972). Consequently perhaps more is known about female addicts, especially black, than about male addicts.

Four findings seem particularly interesting. First, in urban addict institutions, minority overrepresentation is about the same or even greater among females than among males (Brummit 1963; Hunt and Odoroff 1962; Ellinwood, Smith and Vaillant 1966; Chambers and Moffet 1970; Chambers and Inciardi 1971). Second, there has been a decline in the sex ratio of addicts from ten or eight males to one female in the 1950s to about six or three males to one female in 1970. (See index: sex ratio—Treadway 1930; Wieland and Chambers 1970; DuPont 1971). Third, when sex comparisons are made, female addicts seem as disturbed or more seriously disturbed than males (Malzberg 1949; Ellinwood, Smith, and Vaillant 1966; Cherubin 1967, 1968; Helpern and Rho 1967; Lucas, Grupp, and Schmitt 1972; O'Donnell 1969*). Fourth, in the Lexington sample, female addicts are about as likely as males to have engaged in five or more illegal activities prior to admission (males 31 percent, females 27 percent). Comparison by sex of type of felonies committed reveals similar behavior for armed robbery (males 19 percent, females 15 percent), forgery (males 40 percent, females 46 percent), drug sales (males 63 percent, females 55 percent), and theft (males 77 percent, females 66 percent). Females were more likely to engage in prostitution (60 percent) than males in pimping (31 percent), but less likely to commit burglary (males 60 percent, females 36 percent). (Voss and Stephens 1973).

Age. Very few studies provide much detailed information about the age of drug addicts by race (see index: age), but when it is studied, the modal age (roughly 26-32) of minority addicts appears to be the same as for white addicts. A few studies suggest that blacks may be somewhat older than whites due to recent heroin use creating a new generation of young white addicts (Newmeyer and Gay 1972). The median age at which addicts begin addiction careers is 16 for whites and 20 for blacks. (See index: age at onset).

Social class. So pervasive is the assumption that minority addicts are lower class and ghettoized that few of the abstracted studies bother to present detailed data on social class background, and class comparisons with white addicts and/or non-addicted neighborhood peers are rare (see index: income, socioeconomic status). Usually the current occupation of addicts (never employed, unemployed and lower class mainly) is given, but no data about parental background are furnished. In the few studies where parental status or other measures of class are given, social class is a relatively unimportant factor and frequently disappears when other factors are held constant (Abrams, Gagnon, and Levin 1968; Robins and Murphy 1967; Glaser, Lander, and Abbott 1971; Crowther 1972; Waldorf 1973; Lukoff and Brook 1974).

To some extent, the empirical basis of class-linked addiction theories seems to be based upon the ecological fallacy. The Road to H (Chein and others 1964) has been particularly influential in promulgating this undocumented "fact." Chein found that addict arrests were most common in neighborhoods where minorities lived and where rates of crime, poverty, low educational achievement, crowding, and disrupted families were highest, and thus implied that the lower the class, the greater was the probability of heroin addiction. But the superior design and methodology of Lukoff and Brook's (1974) research have produced findings that undermine this class-linked hypothesis. In the slum community of Brownsville (in Brooklyn) higher status families were significantly more likely to report heroin use than lower status families. Specifically, 18 percent of white collar versus ten percent of blue collar families reported heroin use by a family member. The same was true for families with higher education and income, except for immigrants where the class differences in reported heroin use by a family member virtually disappeared. Furthermore, those most likely to report heroin use among family and friends were the native born respondents under age 30 who had adopted middle class values of permissive child rearing. John O'Donnell's (1969*) study found that the occupational status of the fathers of Kentucky addicts was comparable to that of the state population but that the addicts were somewhat downwardly mobile in comparison. Data from other studies can be also interpreted as challenging the linking of addiction to very low class slum status (Abrams, Gagnon, and Levin 1968; Robins and Murphy 1967; Glaser, Lander, and Abbott 1971; Rivera and Hohlen 1973*; Johnson 1971*, 1973b*).

Even though most addicts in various treatment programs have lower status occupations and, disproportionately to non-ghetto neighborhoods, come from urban ghetto neighborhoods, the evidence suggests that factors such as age and city-origin-blocked aspirations for upward mobility may be responsible for the effects attributed to lower class status. When social class is held constant, racial or ethnic group differences in drug use hold up well. Thus "classist" theories, which are frequently invoked to explain stubborn "racial" factors, are generally inadequate. While it may be ideologically desirable to explain racial group differences by class factors, this does not prevent the man on the street from converting class explanations back into racist ones. The reasoning is that if addicts are predominantly lower class and the lower class is mainly black, then blacks are likely to become addicts.

Geographic Location. Geographic location introduces far more variability than the other demographic characteristics of sex, age, and
social class. Studies at the Federal Drug Rehabilitation Hospital at
Lexington find that among Southern addicts, blacks are greatly underrepresented in comparison with their presence in the total population;
addicts from the South are mainly older whites addicted to paregoric
and other medicinal opiates (Ball 1965; Bates 1966; Ball, Chambers,
and Ball 1968; Williams and Bates 1970).

Among addicts from non-Southern metropolitan areas, overrepresentation of minorities is common but great variability still
occurs. In New York City and State, blacks constitute about one-half,
Puerto Ricans about one-quarter, and whites about one-quarter of the
addict population (see index: New York City). Among California and
Texas addicts, Mexican Americans are greatly overrepresented while
blacks apparently are present in proportion to their percentage in the
state population (Duster 1970; Ramer 1971; Chambers, Cuskey, and
Moffet 1970; Crowther 1972).

In almost every other major city, black addicts are overrepresented. Whites seldom constitute even 20 percent of the addict population in Chicago (Abrams, Gagnon, and Levin 1968; Hughes and others
1972; McFarland and Hall 1953), Detroit (Lerner and Oerther 1967),
Baltimore (Wilson and Fisher 1969; Nurco 1969), Washington, D.C.
(Brown and others 1973; DuPont 1973), Philadelphia (Royfe 1965),
New Orleans (Louisiana Commission 1969), and New Haven (Kleber
1969). Where there are very few blacks but sizable Hispanic populations, Chicanos are heavily overrepresented, as in Colorado (Abramowitz and Pantleo 1972), Phoenix (Aumann and others 1972), Albuquerque (Scott and others 1973; Crowther 1972) and Texas (Chambers,
Cuskey, and Moffett 1970; Redling and Michel 1970; Crowther 1972).

Non-Opiate Drug Use

Many of the abstracted studies deal with the use of non-opiate
drugs by whites, blacks, and Hispanics. Two related themes are
frequently treated: the progression from marijuana to other drugs
and multiple drug use. The following are findings that emerge in the
abstracts: First, among southern addicts, marijuana is seldom used
and is only infrequently a precursor of addition to non-heroin opiates;
opiate addiction is generally a white phenomenon (Ball 1965; Bates
1966; Ball, Chambers, and Ball 1968; Williams and Bates 1970; O'Donnell 1969). Second, outside the South, heroin addicts who are black
or Hispanic typically begin with marijuana and progress within two
to three years to heroin and/or cocaine (see index: marijuana, re-

lationship to heroin—Robins and Murphy 1967; Ball, Chambers, and
Ball 1968). Third, among younger whites (those under 21), marijuana
use precedes experimentation with a variety of drugs, and several
drugs are commonly used in conjunction with opiates (see index:
multiple drug abuse—Langrod 1970; Crowther 1972; Lucas, Grupp,
and Schmitt 1972; Weppner and Agar 1971; Shephard, Smith and Gay
1972).

In urban areas, most evidence supports the idea that blacks
and Hispanics are much more likely than whites to begin with marijuana and progress to heroin, and that they avoid or use less regularly
than whites, methedrine or hallucinogens. This difference between
minorities and whites drug use remains even when class, delinquency,
and family stability are controlled (Langrod 1970; Crowther 1972).

A recent attempt to incorporate racial differences in hard drug
use into subculture theory is Johnson's 1973b* study of New York City
college students. He maintains that since 1965 a drug subculture
structured around the consumption of marijuana has become widely
and equally diffused in both the white and black youth subcultures.
Due to the illegality of marijuana, patterns of consumption and distribution are roughly similar for both blacks and whites. Involvement
in this marijuana subculture is generally the prelude to the use of
other drugs, although this is not so clearly the case in minority populations (Weppner and Agar 1971).

As marijuana use and involvement in the illicit market increase,
marijuana users make friends with people using other drugs who intro-
duce them to these drugs. But the hard drug users encountered by
whites are different from the hard drug users encountered by blacks
or Hispanics. For historical reasons that are not clear, marijuana-
using minorities are likely to befriend opiate and cocaine users. It
is also not clear why, prior to 1965 lower class whites in urban areas
used pills such as barbiturates and amphetamines (Klein and Phillips
1968*). Since 1965 marijuana-using whites have used pills and hallucinogens in larger proportions and more frequently than blacks. The
result is that white addicts report much more extensive multiple drug
use patterns than minority addicts (Weppner and Agar 1971; Langrod
1970; Crowther 1972; Johnson 1973; Single, Kandel, and Faust 1974*).

It seems that separate white and black/Hispanic drug subcultures
have developed along parallel lines. Among minority marijuana users,
experimentation with heroin and possible addiction is a common pattern
of behavior. Among marijuana-using whites hallucinogens, pills, and
methedrine are typically encountered. Johnson (1973) further suggests
that it is mainly white drug sellers who are exposed to heroin and
black dealers who are exposed to methedrine. Both black and white
drug subcultures are apparently structured around illicit selling
patterns (Hughes 1971*): marijuana sales provide the basis for contact

between dealers from the respective subcultures. The frequency of marijuana use and differences in race are relatively unimportant factors in themselves in generating hard drug use.

Criminal Justice Processing of Drug Users

It is known that minorities are sent to jail and drug treatment facilities at a much higher rate than whites. Some researchers suggest that racial prejudice by policemen and departmental investigatory police may strongly affect the racial composition of institutional populations. (Piliavin and Briar 1964*; Werthmann 1967*; Wolfgang, Figlio, and Sellin 1972*; DeFleur 1975). Hughes and others (1972) and DeFleur (1975) found that narcotics arrests in Chicago were disproportionately located in certain black census tracts, as compared to white census tracts. After the deliberate policy of harrassment of blacks was put to an end in 1965, the proportion of blacks among total drug arrests declined steadily from 88 percent in the years 1950-54 to 68 percent in the years 1965-76. When blacks began fighting back in the ghettos, the Chicago police made fewer black arrests for drug violations than they had in the mid-1950s (DeFleur 1975).

No doubt police discrimination against minorities on drug charges varies widely from time to time and from city to city. Two major studies of arrestees for drug violations are by Eckerman (1971) and Johnson and Bogomolny (1973). The second study provides much detail about how non-marijuana drug arrestees were processed by the criminal justice system in six cities: 42 percent were arrested for "opiates only," seven percent for multiple drugs including opiates, and 22 percent for ancillary offenses (needle, paraphernalia, intoxication). Thus almost 70 percent of the arrestees were involved with the opiates. Of the "opiates only" arrestees, 36 percent were convicted, 38 percent were dismissed, six percent proceeded on a non-drug charge, seven percent skipped bail, and 13 percent had charges still pending. The dismissed cases apparently included many persons diverted to drug treatment programs during early phases of court processing. Another conclusion was that police concentrated on arresting users, not disrupting dealing patterns.

Minorities were generally overrepresented among arrestees in all cities studied except Dallas. The vast majority of non-marijuana drug arrests occurred in blue collar and slum neighborhoods (implicit in Johnson and Bogomolny's data on occupation and employment status of arrestees.) The overrepresentation of minorities in arrests was probably not much greater than would be expected given the neighborhoods in which they resided. This study indicated that processing patterns within the court system were relatively blind to sociologically important but legally irrelevant variables such as race, sex, age, and class. Blacks, Spanish, and other minorities did not fare much worse than whites as cases were processed through the criminal justice system, but it should be noted that when the sentences were handed out to those convicted or pleading guilty to a drug offense they varied by race: 38 percent of the whites, 48 percent of the blacks and 51 percent of the Spanish speaking were incarcerated. Legally important variables such as type of offense, previous contact with the courts, and number of charges were not strongly related to the outcome either. Thus, the criminal justice system appeared to dispense justice in very unpredictable ways: arrest for a serious drug offense (selling) did not carry a much higher probability of conviction than a minor drug offense, (possession), although sentences might be more severe when such a conviction did occur.

The most striking finding of the study was the massive difference in the probability of conviction and sentence encountered in different cities. In Chicago only 13 percent of non-marijuana drug arrestees were convicted, and only one-fourth of the convicted spent time in jail. In Miami, on the other hand, almost 60 percent of non-marijuana drug arrestees were convicted, with 40 percent spending time in prison. Regardless of race, the typical street addict fared much better in Chicago than in other cities analyzed. The real injustice of the criminal justice system may be less its racial prejudice than its unsystematic character. Each area of jurisdiction processes its many cases in very different ways.

Minorities in Drug Treatment Programs

Almost all evidence contradicts the belief held by many Americans that addicts can be "cured" of their opiate addiction. Both whites and minorities seem about equally immune to long-term abstinence from opiates regardless of treatment modality.

Federal Hospitals (Lexington and Fort Worth)

During the three decades from 1935-65, almost the only alternatives to prison for addicts convicted of various offenses were the federal narcotics "farms" at Lexington, Kentucky and Fort Worth, Texas. Because these institutions hired professional researchers to analyze and publish papers about addicts, the best studies of treatment effects came from these institutions. Studies of various subgroups of Lexington patients (Hunt and Odoroff 1962; Duvall and others 1963;

Vaillant 1966; Stephens and Cottrell 1972; Zahn and Ball 1972) typically
found that from 80-98 percent of addicts relapsed within a year, the
majority within the first six months. Voluntary abstinence increased
with the passage of time, however: 40 percent were abstinent after
five years and about 50 percent after 10 years (Duvall and others 1963;
Vaillant 1966; Waldorf 1972). Those over age 30 who had been steadily
employed and had relatively few arrests and had volunteered for admission to Lexington were disproportionately likely to be abstinent at
follow-up studies. There were few significant racial or sexual differences in abstinence. Vaillant (1966), Diskind and Klonsky (1964*),
and Brill and Lieberman (1969*) report that patients carefully paroled
after release from prisons or Lexington do better than the non-paroled.

Local Hospitals and Civil Commitment

Before 1965 only New York State had seriously tried to provide
treatment for addicts. In 1952 a generously staffed program for adolescent addicts failed to have one abstinent addict five years later
(Brecher 1972*, 1973). In the 1960s a detoxification program for addicts was begun at the Bernstein Institute. This program probably
treated more addicts in the 1960s on a voluntary basis than any other.
A follow-up study by Richman and others (1972) found that 13 percent
were "allegedly abstinent" eight to ten years after their first detoxification at Bernstein—a success rate lower than Lexington's.

By about 1965 narcotics had become a major political issue in
New York and California. A new program was developed which made
use of an incarceration procedure euphemistically called civil commitment. As at Lexington and Fort Worth, it was originally intended to
be rehabilitative, but the facilities quickly became substitute prisons
for narcotics addicts. Addicts were confined for one to two years and
then released into aftercare, where 80 percent relapsed or absconded
(Kramer and Bass 1969*; Brecher 1972*, Stephens and Cottrell 1972).
An independent study of the New York program (Waldorf 1973: 109)
found that after one year of aftercare, about 25 percent had a "good
outcome;" that is, they had not been returned to institutions or absconded. Whites were more likely to have a "good outcome" than
Puerto Ricans (33 percent versus 16 percent).

To legitimate this program, New York State officials have argued
for the use of "rational authority" (Meiselas and Brill 1974*; Brill and
Lieberman 1969*) as a means of getting addicts to behave in a more
conventional manner. Unfortunately there is little evidence to demonstrate that the authority used by the New York State program is rational in day-to-day practice: the coercive measures employed seem
to be the most striking feature of the program (Waldorf 1972).

Therapeutic Communities

During the mid-1960s another type of treatment plan began to emerge and become part of the addiction infrastructure—the therapeutic community. New York City under Mayor John Lindsay set up several Phoenix Houses based on the experiences of Synanon and a Navy treatment program. These programs operated on an assumption of the psychological model of addiction and relied on encounter group therapy for treatment. They also provided a rigid structure of clear cut rewards and punishments reinforced by incentives for achieving upward mobility. Although they are run by ex-addicts and the patients, the programs have not been particularly successful at holding or graduating most of the addicts (Waldorf 1973: 100; Brecher 1972*; Nash 1974). The three major racial groups appear about equally successful or unsuccessful in this kind of treatment (Waldorf 1972; DeLeon 1973).

Methadone Maintenance

Since 1968 methadone maintenance has become the major treatment modality for addicts in the United States. Although it is claimed that methadone is a medication which "blockades" the euphoric effect of heroin, it is more probable that methadone is cross-tolerant with heroin. Unlike civil commitment and therapeutic communities, methadone programs generally permit a certain amount of heroin and other drug consumption without severe penalties. Rather than aiming for abstinence as the major criterion of success, declining arrest rates, declining welfare dependency, and increasing legitimate employment have become the major indicators of good outcomes.

According to the annual evaluations of the New York City methadone programs, they have been able to retain 80 percent of admissions for one year and 60 percent over five years. For unknown reasons retention rates of methadone programs outside New York City are not as high (Nash 1973). In addition, they have achieved rather striking declines in arrest rates. (Gearing 1959, 1960, 1970, 1971, 1974a, 1974b, summarized in Brecher 1972*). The decline in drug arrests is more striking than the declines in other kinds of felony and misdemeanor arrests (Lukoff and Brook 1974*). Although blacks do not improve quite as much as whites, the difference by race in any of these measures of success are not statistically significant (Gearing studies; Sells, Chathan, and Joe 1972).

INADEQUACIES OF RESEARCH METHODS

The review of various theories of minority addiction has suggested that various explanations are theoretically inadequate and unable to interpret racial differences. Much research is inadequate both in interpretation of findings and on methodological grounds. Such methodological difficulties are frequently a hindrance to making important generalizations and testing theories about addiction among minorities.

The multiplicity of disciplines and the diversity in the training of researchers on drug use contribute to the difficulty of developing unified, systematic generalizations. Psychologists utilize standardized tests to classify patients. Case studies attempt to describe addict life accurately. Investigations of street life attempt to specify roles and delineate the social structure of a "copping community." Researchers of institutionalized addicts frequently provide more information about the institution than about addicts. General surveys of normal populations locate very few heroin addicts but provide much valid information about the incidence and patterns of nonopiate drug use. Each type of study presents a slice of reality as seen from its particular vantage point. Thus we are far from a theoretically coherent understanding of addiction.

The difficulties of cumulative development are further increased because research findings on drug use are disseminated in diverse periodicals with different audiences. The two leading drug journals, the International Journal of the Addictions and the Bulletin on Narcotics, are low circulation journals read by only a few involved in drug research or treatment and are frequently impossible to obtain in all but specialized libraries. Since 1970 more than ten new drug journals have begun publication, further fragmenting the field. With the exception of Preble and Casey's 1969 study, the most important papers in the field are published in leading journals of the researcher's particular discipline rather than in a drug journal (Finestone 1957; Vaillant 1966; Robins and Murphy 1967; Hughes 1971-72; DuPont 1971, 1973; Callan and Patterson 1973; Kandel 1973*; Kandel, Single and Kessler, forthcoming in 1976*) or in books or governmental publications (Chein 1964; Duster 1970; Eckerman 1971; Josephson and Carroll 1974*; Lukoff and Brook 1974). Few book-length reports have been published; instead, the findings of many studies are reported in one or two short journal articles. This diffusion of articles in diverse publications is reflected in the following table, which classifies the abstract appearing in this bibliography according to academic discipline or program:

TABLE 5

Periodical Sources of Annotated Articles

Type of Journal	Articles Annotated	
	Number of Articles	Percent of Total Articles
Addiction	55	32.4
Medical	33	19.4
Psychological/Psychiatric	33	19.4
Sociological	17	10.0
Anthropological	10[a]	5.8
Law Enforcement	10	5.8
Miscellaneous	12	7.1
Total	170[b]	100.0

[a]Concerning the Peyote Cult

[b]Another 75 annotated items appeared in non-periodical sources: publications of government and private drug programs, academic institutions, and commercial publishers.

Source: Data compiled by the editors.

Thirty-three (19.4 percent) out of 170 articles were published in medical journals, such as the American Journal of Public Health, the Journal of Nervous and Mental Disease, Public Heath Reports, Pediatrics, and the Journal of the American Medical Association. Another 19.4 percent of the articles (33) were printed in such publications as the American Journal of Psychiatry, the Journal of General Psychology, the Psychiatric Quarterly, Corrective Psychiatry, and the Journal of Social Therapy. Fifty-five articles (32.4 percent) appeared in specialized publications on addiction such as the Bulletin of Narcotics, the Drug Forum, and the International Journal of Addictions, with the latter journal clearly the major source. Ten percent (17) of the articles came from sociological sources like Social Problems, Sociology and Social Research, and Social Forces. Five and eight-tenths percent (10) of the articles reflected the law enforcement approach to narcotics abuse in such journals as Federal Probation, the Journal of Criminal Law, Criminology and Police Science, while another 5.8 percent (10) articles, basically concerning the peyote cult, came from the American Anthropologist, the Journal of American Folklore, and similar anthropological sources. Some other miscellaneous sources were Ebony, Jet, Psychedelic Review, Yale Review, The Crisis, and City.

Survey Research

Despite the diversity of disciplines involved, survey research is the most widely used technique for investigating addiction. In the drug field, however, survey methodology is badly misused. Much of the research reported in the abstracts is conducted by non sociologists who have medical, psychological, clinical, or correctional training which does not include survey methods. The articles reporting these studies are published in obscure journals, and are often very brief and they fail to present interview forms and other methodological information. Among the inadequacies in the surveys of drug use, those that seem most important are the following:

First, conceptualization is inadequate. Theories, concepts, and hypotheses from one field are unknown to researchers in another field, so crucial variables go unmeasured. An inverse problem is also common: some studies present many variables from all branches of drug literature but fail to formulate worthwhile generalizations or theoretical explanations. Most conceptualization is done after the data are gathered rather than before: interpretations are proposed briefly in concluding sections to explain diverse statistical findings. Very seldom are theories proposed, hypotheses generated, data collected, and empirical proof or disproof of these hypotheses presented (Ball and Bates 1966; Blum 1972; Bernstein 1973).

Second, sample design and selection are inadequate for the questions to which the research is addressed. Often researchers set out to analyze some important argument, for example, that marijuana leads to heroin, or that addicts commit a disproportionate amount of crime. Usually, however, only institutionalized addicts are available for sampling. The resulting analysis is deficient because it is dependent upon the possibly inaccurate memories of forcibly abstaining addicts and because information about the behavior of crucial comparison groups (the vast majority of marijuana users, who are not addicted to heroin or the prisoners who are not addicts) is unavailable (Glaser, Inciardi, and Babst 1969; Ball, Chambers, and Ball 1968; Chambers and Inciardi 1971*; Voss and Stephens 1973.) Studies with samples appropriate for analyzing such questions generally find very few heroin addicts because there are so few addicts in the general population (Chambers 1971; Johnson 1973; Robins 1973; Lukoff and Brooks 1974; Kandel 1973*; Kandel and others 1976*). This finding is also due to the fact that addicts are absent from interview locations used to sample normal populations (Kandel 1975*). Only three studies have attempted to select a relatively normal population with a high probability of heroin use and/or to over sample opiate users when their proportion in a population is known (Robins and Murphy 1967; Robins

1973; Lukoff and Brook 1974). Studies which carefully stratify and/ or oversample those most likely to be heroin addicts are badly needed.

Third, survey instruments, either questionnaires or interviews, are frequently inadequate. Many of the abstracts reflect a lack of awareness of index information and the operationalization of concepts. They also lack sophistication in the phrasing and ordering of questions (Selltiz and others 1951*; Lazarsfeld 1972*). A related problem is the researchers' ignorance of the language and symbolic systems used by minorities and addicts; their questions may have little meaning to respondents and may not be interpreted as the researcher intends them to be.

Fourth, analysis of statistical data is inadequate. It is the most serious inadequacy of many of the surveys abstracted here. A common practice (trenchantly criticized by Johnson, 1974*, and Blumer 1956*, in another context) is the presentation of two-variable tables which relate several independent variables to one or several different dependent variables (Abeles and others 1966; Ball, Bates, and O'Don-nell 1966; Vaillant 1966; The Louisiana Commission 1969; Langrod 1970; Chambers 1971; Blum 1972; Shepard, Smith, and Gay 1972; Bernstein 1973; Callan and Patterson 1973). Most drug researchers seem to lack the statistical sophistication to make use of three-variable analysis, multivariate analysis or correlation regression analysis (for example, Lazarsfeld and others 1972*; excepting for Robins and Murphy 1967; Weppner and Agar 1971; Crowther 1972; Lukoff and Brook 1974).

A discussion of a survey research study conducted by one of the most published drug abuse investigators can serve to illustrate some of the serious methodological deficiencies in the drug addiction surveys. Probably no other drug study has been so widely cited as Carl Chambers, An Assessment of Drug Use in The General Population (1971), written when he was research director of the New York State Narcotic Addiction Control Commission. This study and its follow-up report (Chambers and Inciardi 1971*) contain major weaknesses in research design, statistical analysis, and presentations.

In this survey of 7,378 New York State residents age 14 and older, the stated purpose of the study was "to establish the dimensions of current drug use; it was not designed to document the incidence of current drug abuse in New York State" (Chambers 1971: 1*). However, although the data presented in the report provided information about the incidence of use for each drug, detailed information about sex, race, and the use of other drugs is presented only for regular (six or more times in the past 30 days) users. Table 6 presents data relevant to heroin use.

Chambers projected from his sample of 7,378 respondents to the total population of New York State by weighting stratified samples

TABLE 6

Incidence and Prevalence of Heroin Use in New York State,
August 1970

	Number	Percent
Never used	13,392,000	97.2
Former users (no use in past six months)	83,000	.6
Infrequent users (fewer than six times a month)	32,000	.2
Regular users (at least six times a month)	32,000	.2
No data	245,000	1.8
Total	13,784,000	100.0
Ethnic Distribution of 32,000 Regular Users of Heroin (at least six times a month)		
White	11,000	34.4
Black	12,000	37.5
Puerto Rican	9,000	28.1

Source: Chambers 1971.

in the general survey. The top of Table 6 shows these projections:
97.2 percent never used heroin, 0.6 percent were former users (no
use in past six months), 0.2 percent were infrequent users (fewer
than six times a month), 0.2 percent were regular users (at least six
times a month), and there were no data for 1.8 percent. These proportions when appropriately weighted give 13,392,000 non-heroin users,
83,000 former users, 32,000 infrequent users, and 32,000 regular
users. Such projections are a valid statistical procedure, and the top
half of Table 6 probably reflects patterns of heroin use among New
York adults quite accurately. By the use of careful sampling and
weighting, 7,378 completed interviews may be projected to the 13,
784,000 adults who are 14 years of age and over in New York State.
Thus, each respondent represents roughly 1,868 citizens in the state,
depending on sampling weights—a perfectly acceptable procedure.
The difficulty occurs when Chambers uses the projected population
figures at the bottom of Table 6 to indicate the ethnic distribution of
regular heroin users in New York State. The N of 32,000 which on the
face of it might seem large enough for projecting the number of whites,
blacks, and Puerto Ricans who are supposed to be regular users of
heroin was derived from only about 17 respondents, approximately
six of whom were white, six black, and five Puerto Rican. Seventeen

cases are not sufficient for making accurate projections. Combining
all the heroin users in the survey (about 79) might have been a better
statistic procedure. The results would also have been more meaningful if the percentages had been calculated in the opposite direction,
that is, by giving the percentage which had tried and regularly used
heroin for each ethnic group. When the data are recomputed (assuming
accurate measurement), 0.1 percent of whites, 0.8 percent of blacks,
and 0.9 percent of Puerto Ricans were regular heroin users—such
differences are relatively minor.

     An additional shortcoming of the study was the extremely high
completion rate of the survey—98 percent—because of quota sampling.
If a particular respondent was not at home, the interviewer tried to
obtain a replacement nearby. Absent respondents were not traced
down. Chambers recognized this shortcoming and estimated that his
count of heroin users probably underestimated by two-thirds the number of heroin users in the state.

     A third inadequacy of the study is the presentation of standard
error as if it were based upon a purely random sample (Chambers
1971*: 163). Since quota sampling was employed, the standard error
was larger than indicated. More important, the standard errors should
be based on actual sample size, not on the weighted figures.

     Fourth, the stated purpose of the Chambers' survey was to
"establish the dimensions of current drug use" in New York State,
not drug abuse. But though it included an indicator on drug abuse ("used
six times in past month"), the report failed to provide detailed data
about and various important correlates of the particular drug used.
Although racial breakdowns of the "ever-used" statistic were probably available in the original computer runs, Chambers neglected to
present them in the published report.

     Finally, Chambers does not indicate the social or theoretical
significance of his detailed findings on drug use and/or abuse. Yet
clearly the social implications are enormously important. If the incidence and regularity of use are what should be prevented, then public
policy and attention should be focused on pep pills, diet pills, and
minor tranquilizers, which are used by much larger proportions of
the adult population than heroin, cocaine, methedrine, and other illicit
drugs.

Evaluation Research

     Perhaps the major obstacle facing evaluation research in the
area of drug addiction is the lack of consensus about the goals which
the various drug programs are intended to accomplish. Although there

is agreement that long-term abstinence from opiates should be the major goal, no program has succeeded in getting a rate of abstinence much above ten percent for a period of one year. While the methadone maintenance programs of New York evaluated by Gearing in annual studies from 1968-74 have reported striking declines in arrest rates, unemployment, and welfare dependency, many critics have attacked these programs for not making addicts abstinent and/or for increasing alcoholism. They have also raised questions about whether it is an acceptable goal of treatment to make the addict dependent on another drug, methadone, in the course of producing an opiate-abstinent person.

A further problem in the evaluation of drug programs is the difficulty in measuring the results which can be mainly ascribed to treatment programs. For example, Duvall and others (1963) and Vaillant (1966) found in their studies that about ten percent were apparently abstinent one year after release from Lexington, 40 percent five years later, and 46 percent after ten years. But so much occurs in the lives of addicts following their hospitalization that it is impossible to ascribe such abstinence solely to treatment at Lexington. Related to this difficulty in connecting results to particular treatment modalities is the fact that, for reasons unknown, almost all addicts have periods of voluntarily abstinence at various times in their careers when living on their own in the communities (Waldorf 1973; Hughes and others 1972). The low rate of addiction among Vietnam veterans following their return to the United States (studied by Robins 1973) is an illustration of voluntary abstinence from the use of heroin, the reasons for which are not attributable to any known treatment program.

Aside from these problems associated with assessing drug treatment programs, the fact is that very few independent evaluations of important drug programs have ever been completed. The Columbia University evaluation of New York's Narcotic Addiction Control Commission (NACC), Phoenix House, and methadone maintenance programs (1968-69) is a classic example of the tension likely to occur between independent researchers and funding agencies. According to the Columbia researchers, their third year of funding was cancelled because the negative findings might have been politically damaging to the NACC programs. On the other hand, NACC officials claim that the Columbia researchers were not investigating what had been contracted for and were not producing creditable reports by the end of the second year (personal communications by authors with the respective parties). In view of the good quality of the reports which have since emerged from the Columbia University study (Langrod 1970; Waldorf 1971*; Brill 1971*; Waldorf 1972; Brecher 1972*: 80), the claim that political considerations influenced the termination of funding seems strong indeed.

Addiction Research in the Ghetto

Minorities have expressed a good deal of resentment at repeated studies (conducted by social scientists in their communities) which fail to result in any beneficial consequences for the residents who have cooperated in the research (Josephson 1970*). In the case of drug research, only very limited funds have been devoted to the analysis of drug addiction within a ghetto or minority community. Only five research projects have concentrated on such populations (Robins and Murphy 1967; Lander and Lander 1966; Glazer, Lander, and Abbott 1971; Burnham 1969*; Lukoff and Brook 1974; Ianni 1974*; Hughes and others 1971, 1973). Instead almost all drug research money has gone to general population surveys on research conducted in institutions such as hospitals and other treatment facilities.

At the Newark conference on drug surveys in 1972, (Einstein and Allen 1972*) a black man in the audience fervently asked the assembled drug researchers, "What do you know about heroin addiction on the streets of the black community? What are the facts?" Although the experts offered many opinions, they all admitted that they had very few facts. For all the concern about ghetto addiction and the reasonably large sums spent on analyzing addiction (probably over $50 million between 1968-74), very little has been published to show what really happens on inner city streets where drugs are pushed and used, and why and how ghetto youth become addicts.

Attempts to gather information on these questions have begun. The Ianni (1974*) and Hughes' and others (1971, 1972) studies initiated some effective approaches to research in ghetto addiction subcultures. They employed ex-addicts who worked alongside college trained researchers from minority backgrounds and maintained regular contacts with addict dealers. The program that Hughes (1972) evaluated achieved remarkable success in undermining drug distribution systems and encouraging addicts to enter methadone programs, but these techniques of gaining the cooperation of the minority community, ex-addicts, and addicts have to to be applied elsewhere on a large scale.

SOME FUTURE RESEARCH NEEDS

Many questions about addiction need exploration, but these needs are not likely to be fulfilled as long as research funds are virtually monopolized by institutions treating addicts and by a few academic researchers. Such funding patterns ensure a continuation of the repetitive "here is what our addicts are like" and "how successful we are" kinds of research. If this pattern is ever broken and funds are made available, priority should be given to a more extensive analysis of the varying social structures, processes, and patterns of drug addiction within different racial and ethnic communities. The studies by Lander and Lander (1967), Hughes and others (1972), Ianni (1974*), Liebow (1968*), and Lukoff and Brook (1974) show that ghetto communities can be effectively researched, addiction subcultures observed, and valuable information secured. While many technical difficulties must be overcome, the time certainly seems ripe for studies investigating drug use and addiction, hustling, marginal employment, and poverty as they affect each other in selected ghetto neighborhoods. As with so many other kinds of social research, the need for longitudinal research on minority addiction is in order. Fortunately, much good information (Hunt and Odoroff 1962; Duvall and others 1963; Vaillant 1966; Brecher 1972*) of a longitudinal nature through record search and interviews with institutionalized addicts exists. The main need is for longitudinal research on non-institutional populations. Robins and Murphy's (1967), Robins' (1973), and Lukoff and Brook's (1974) studies are the best available models; Hughes and others' (1972) study of trends in a 'copping' community is valuable and suggests that longitudinal studies of addicts in the field may be possible.

Much more careful evaluations of treatment programs by impartial agencies are needed. The Addiction Services Agency of New York City has made a beginning (The Journal, June-August 1974*; Amari and Winick 1974*) in the face of great resistance from the psychologically-oriented therapeutic communities whose very existence is threatened by critical assessments of their effectiveness.

Another area needing investigation, and one in which almost no research exists, is the interaction between addicts and personnel in drug treatment programs. The literature on prisons depicts two uncompromising subcultures of guards and prisoners who distrust each other, a situation which severely hampers prisoner rehabilitation. Racism is the underlying source of friction within the prison environment. Discord may also occur in civil commitment facilities for drug addicts (Waldorf 1973), the federal hospitals, and other quasi-prison treatment facilities. Therapeutic communities, in contrast, seem to have been able to bridge the racial staff-prisoner relationship gaps more satisfactorily. (Yablonsky 1965*; Densen-Gerber 1973*). Methadone maintenance programs and the British drug treatment centers studied by Judson in 1974 provide a chemotherapy model of social control which appears to avoid much of the usual conflict between addicts and social control agents while exerting a good deal of control over patient drug-consuming behavior.

A third neglected research area is the role of sociopolitical conflict and symbolic exploitation of minorities in the legislative arena. Histories of drug legislation, especially where the laws are aimed primarily at minority groups have only begun. For example, the battle to pass the repressive Rockefeller drug law of 1972 with mandatory life sentences for all drug dealers, big time or small, was a classic political conflict, with the Lindsay administration and New York City police department opposing it, and upstate and suburban Republican legislators supporting it. Not since the 1950s has a drug law with such a predictably racist effect been passed. In an investigation of the legislative history of the bill, particular attention should be paid to the role of black and minority leaders, both political and civil. If more minority politicians and community leaders had been actively opposed to the legislation, the governor might have dropped his plans. But the need felt by many blacks for more effective solutions to the drug addiction problem plaguing their communities was translated into political support for compulsory life sentences for small-time drug dealers (Bayer 1974).

Information concerning the consequences of this law cannot be readily obtained from the law enforcement agencies engaged in its administration. While the number of arrests (18,409), indictments (6,193), convictions (3,329), and life sentences (209) under the Rockefeller law (New York Times, November 10, 1974*) are available, numerous telephone calls made by the editors to relevant officials turned up no data broken down by race. By not keeping such information—or by not making it available to the public, the legal system appears to be protecting itself from charges that the enforcement of the law has been differentially applied and has resulted in the imprisonment of small-time minority dealers. Indeed, the whole history of drug legislation and mobilization of public opinion against drugs needs further examination. Musto (1973) and Helmer and Vietorisz (1974) suggest that overt racism and anti-foreign propaganda have often been employed by anti-opium moral entrepreneurs and enforcement agencies in drug control legislation. The more recent practice of associating drugs, heroin addiction, and violence with blacks in the "law and order" slogans of political campaigns in the sixties and seventies also needs analysis.

CONCLUSIONS

The major finding of this review of drug literature is that although addiction among minorities is perceived by the public as a serious social problem, many facts indicate that the extent of the problem does not warrant the amount of public concern and attention given. This is not meant to underestimate the negative impact of drug addiction on the personal lives of many who are involved or to deny

the damage that results to minority communities. But the moral filter
through which addiction is perceived grossly distorts and magnifies
the issue. Society's response to narcotics addiction has become—as
much as anything else—a major source of the problem.

One widely accepted belief is that drug addiction seriously dam-
ages the health of the user. But questions have been raised by many
drug experts as to whether this is true. The relevant literature on
physiological effects supports Wikler's view that regular heroin or
opiate consumption by itself produces "no physical traits or diseases
among opioid addicts in the United States except for those consequent
to drug abuse. . . . from use of contaminated needles and . . . neglect"
of health (Wikler 1971*: 292). Brecher (1972*) reviews a variety of
scientific sources which suggest that opium consumption is less harmful than regular use of barbiturates, alcohol, or amphetamines, and
that most of the harm attributed to heroin addiction is due to its being
illegal and sold on the black market, which makes purchase and use
of heroin a criminal act. The Drug Enforcement Administration (1974*:
24) reports more overdose deaths due to barbiturates (1,196) than to
heroin (1,017) in 1974, although this is almost never publicized. The
only direct negative consequence to the individual of opiate consump-
tions is addiction and the accompanying withdrawal symptoms. Similar
physiological withdrawal symptoms are produced by alcohol, barbiturates, and tranquilizers, and to a lesser extent by amphetamines,
nicotine, and cocaine, yet such comparisons are almost always over-
looked. For the most part, only opiates are singled out for particular
public concern.

In point of fact, the heroin problem in the United States affects
fewer people than most other social problems. Even assuming that
addicts are undercounted in general surveys, diverse studies (Chambers 1971; Johnson 1973; NCMDA 1973; Kandel, Single, and Kessler
1976*; Kleinman and Lukoff 1975) provide solid evidence that heroin
is very infrequently tried. Fewer than one percent of them use it
on even a weekly basis; other substances are more likely to be tried
and/or used on a regular basis. If it is assumed that there are 500,
000-750,000 heroin addicts in America (DEA 1974*; Hunt 1974), then
0.2 percent to 0.4 percent of 220,000,000 Americans are addicted to
heroin. Although exact statistics are unavailable for the numbers involved in other "social problems," there are many more than one
million alcoholics.

The major argument used against heroin—that addicts commit
vicious crimes—is a badly misunderstood half-truth. A proportion
of addicts (about one-third according to Hughes 1972), probably commit acquisitive crimes (burglary, theft, larceny, stolen property,
and purse snatching). A study of arrestees in six cities (New York,
Chicago, New Orleans, San Antonio, Los Angeles, and St. Louis)

found that current heroin users were much less likely than non-drug
user arrestees to be charged with serious crimes against persons
(homicide, rape, aggravated assault) although more are likely to
commit property crimes (Eckerman 1971). Eckerman's data actually
suggest that current heroin users are somewhat less likely to engage
in serious crimes against persons than current marijuana and barbiturate users. By ignoring such data, and by failing to compare heroin
users with non-heroin users, the public maintains its widespread belief about addict-inspired violent crime. In fact, our society may partially generate the crime it wishes to prevent by forcing addicts to
pay high prices for illicit heroin.

Although the data are far from complete, the few studies which
compare addicts with their non-addict counterparts in urban communities find few consistent or important differences between them in a
variety of psychological and sociological dimensions (Chein 1964;
Blumer 1967; Eckerman and others 1973; Glaser, Lander, and Abbott
1971; Hughes 1971-73; Scott and others 1973; Lukoff and Brook 1974;
Gasser and others 1974; Kleinman and Lukoff 1975). Apparently addicts only differ from their non-addict neighbors in having higher
aspirations for upward mobility which are blocked (Cloward and Ohlin
1960*; Johnson 1973b*; Lukoff and Brook 1974).

If heroin consumption is not more damaging to the user than
other commonly used substances, if addiction is a comparatively
small problem, if addicts are less apt to commit crimes of assault
against persons (when compared with non-addict arrestees), and if
addicts are not much different in social background and personality
from non-addicts in the same neighborhood, then why is there such
widespread belief that heroin addiction is a major problem and produces crime (NCMDA, 1973*)? Answers to this question can only be
speculative since systematic research on the development and consequences of public attitudes towards addiction has yet to begin. For
one thing, it may be that for the white majority these beliefs serve as
an indirect and socially acceptable way of expressing racial prejudice.
The transfer of fear and hatred to addicts is not difficult for whites
since they have been encouraged to think that drug abuse is mainly a
black phenomenon. Similarly, blacks express their racial fears and
hatred for whites by blaming the "man" for bringing the heroin plague
on the black community and by accusing the white power structure of
cooperating with the international drug traders to keep blacks down.

Stereotypes about criminals are imputed to addicts. Popular
beliefs of both races have transformed addicts into rapists, robbers,
and vicious criminals who systematically plunder the law-abiding
citizenry. People ignore the possibility that there might be many
addicts who support their habit by working (Hughes and others 1972),
or by non-theft hustles (welfare, living off relatives, drug dealing)—

the entrenched belief held by both whites and blacks is that all addicts are criminals. This is typical of the way the dominant society views deviant behavior of minorities and, in turn, of how the minorities view themselves.

Two major elites, government officials and drug abuse treatment specialists, seem to be mainly responsible for maintaining the symbolic reprehensibility of addiction. For example, public health experts and epidemiologists (Hunt 1974; Hughes and others 1972) refer to "epidemics" of heroin addiction in various populations, thus unintentionally attaching to heroin the fears commonly associated with physical illness spreading rapidly out of control. Significantly, such experts seldom refer to epidemics of marijuana or barbiturate use, which are much more common than heroin addiction.

More than any other group, officials of the Bureau of Narcotics and Dangerous Drugs (now the Drug Enforcement Administration) and officials of state governments charged with enforcement of drug laws are responsible for negative stereotypes about opiates. These agencies continue to contend in public that if only the supply of opiates could be cut off at the source and increasing amounts of money, manpower, and effort were poured into interception efforts, the problem could be solved. Despite decades of failure, such agencies constantly propagandize against heroin, addicts, and opponents of their policies.

Drug enforcement agencies learned long ago that constant appeals to the ideal of total abstinence from opiates was an effective way of gaining political and financial support. These agencies call addiction "living death," degrade the "typical" addict, and publish misleading statistics; all of these practices perpetrate an exaggerated and frightening image of addiction. These agencies also persist in ignoring studies refuting their propaganda (Brecher 1972; NCMDA 1973*), including those commissioned by themselves (Chambers 1971; Eckerman 1971; McGlothlin and Tabbush 1972*), and occasionally attack those who attempt to refute their claims (Lindesmith 1965*).

But the major responsibility for present drug policies belongs to public officials, who ignore what little evidence is available when they take to the soapbox for political reasons (Musto 1973). The classic example was the 1972 Rockefeller drug law imposing life sentences on minor dealers. In 1970 the famous Chambers (1971) study of drug use in New York State found that heroin was the least frequently used (one percent had tried) and least regularly used (0.2 percent had used it six or more times in the past month) of any drug in the survey. Eckerman's 1971 study on arrests showed that heroin arrestees in New York were committing not violent crimes but acquisitive crimes. The Lindsay administration argued—with reasonably correct data from the Narcotics Register—that addiction was declining or leveling off. But despite data from his own administration and opposition from the city government, Governor Rockefeller pressed for punitive legislation which capitalized on racial fears and anger about crime in order to win a political reputation for being tough on crime.

If public officials and agencies have run drug policy on moral rather than factual premises, the drug research establishment has not been particularly effective in contributing to more rational policy either. The rather dismal state and low quality of research on minority drug use suggests that much of it deserves to be ignored. As the abstracts herein reflect, research on minorities and drug abuse is largely inadequate. Researchers usually report racial differences (or lack of them) but make little or no attempt to interpret or relate the data to the relevant literature on the contexts in which the use of drugs thrives. Racial-ethnic differences are not consistently reported, and when they are, they are frequently contradicted by other studies. Such confusing race differences are left for the reader to interpret—a very difficult task even for the professional.

Scientific explanations of racial differences in drug use are frequently not responsibly interpreted; for example, class explanations are suggested as an interpretation of racial differences, but usually no attempts to control for class are made. Considering the lack of theoretical relevance, such post hoc explanations of racial factors invite the reader to ignore them.

Because of the lack of consistent results and adequate explanations of minority addiction, none of the research results here justifies the extremely punitive laws and enforcement policies which tend to be applied more heavily to minorities. In short, scientific information about drug addiction, while admittedly inadequate and imprecise, generally refutes public myths about such things as the criminality, physical and mental harm, and sexual deviance caused by heroin consumption. Yet these beliefs continue to be widely held (NCMDA 1973*). Knowledge and information have not been able to penetrate the ideology which dominates popular beliefs about heroin addiction.

Thus, though the real heroin problem continues unabated, the "problem" as envisioned by the public and politicians—that there is extensive addiction to heroin and that a large amount of crime is committed by addicts—remains undocumented, misunderstood, and phenomenally exaggerated. What few firm facts there are about addiction do not penetrate the political mind or public consciousness, much less public policy.

As the authors of this introduction see it, the "problem" of drugs is quite different from the public conception of it. The true problem is the symbolic transformation of a relatively small public health concern into a gigantic moral problem. With the moral indignation against addiction so strong, heroin functions as a moral lightening rod magnetically attracting negative stereotyped concepts.

Because governmental policy on drugs is seen as morally correct (Johnson 1975b*), decades of failure and billions of dollars poured down the same bottomless drain are excused. The Frankenstein of racism means that minorities continue to be the focus of blame for drug addiction as well as the objects of social control efforts. The "problem" of drug abuse has remained virtually stalled at the same place it was in the 1950s. While the substantive issues around which the debates revolve have shifted, the symbolic role of drug abuse remains unchanged. For many whites, it symbolizes their fears of the mythic violent black. To many blacks, it symbolizes their hatred for their white oppressors.

REFERENCES

Amari, Salvatore and Charles Winich
"A comparative analysis of 24 therapeutic communities, in New York City," mimeographed. Bethesda, Md: System Science Incorporated.

Becker, Howard S.
1963   Outsiders. New York: Free Press.

Billingsley, Andrew
1968   Black Families in White America. Englewood Cliffs, New Jersey: Prentice-Hall.

Black, Donald J. and Albert J. Reiss
1967   "Patterns of behavior in police and citizen transactions." President's Commission on Law Enforcement and the Administration of Justice, Studies in Crime and Law Enforcement in Major Metropolitan Areas, Field Surveys II, Vol. 2, Washington, D.C.: U.S. Government Printing Office.

Blumberg, Abraham
1965   Criminal Justice. New York: Quadrangle.

Blumer, Herbert
1951   "Collective Behavior," in Alfred McClung Lee (ed.), Principles of Sociology. New York: Barnes and Noble.

1956   "Sociological analysis and the 'variable.' " American Sociological Review 21 (December): 683-90.

1957   "Collective behavior," in Joseph B. Gittler (ed.), Review
           of Sociology: Analysis of a Decade. New York: Wiley.
           127-58.

Brecher, Edward M.
1972   Licit and Illicit Drugs. Boston: Little, Brown.

Brill, Leon
1971   "Some comments on the paper, 'Social control in thera-
           peutic communities' by Dan Waldorf." International Journal
           of the Addictions 6 (March): 45-50.

Brill, Leon and Louis Lieberman
1969   Authority and Addiction. Boston: Little, Brown.

Brown, Claude
1965   Manchild in the Promised Land. New York: Macmillan.

Burnham, David and Sophy
1969   New York Times Magazine (January 5). "El Barrio's worse
           black is not all bad," in Daniel Glaser (ed.), Crime in
           the City. New York: Harper and Row, 1970. 154-62.

Chambers, Carl D. and James A. Inciardi
1971   Drug Use in New York City and Selected Geographical
           Regions of New York State. Special Report, No. 2. Albany,
           New York: New York State Narcotic Addiction Control Com-
           mission.

Cleaver, Eldridge
1968   Soul on Ice. New York: McGraw-Hill.

Cloward, Richard and Lloyd B. Ohlin
1960   Delinquency and Opportunity. New York: Free Press.

Cooper, Eunice and Marie Jahoda
1947   "The erosion of propaganda: how prejudiced people respond
           to anti-prejudice propaganda." Journal of Psychology 23
           (January): 15-24.

Crafts, Wilbur F.
1906   Intoxicants and Opium in All Lands and Times. Washington,
           D.C.: International Reform Bureau.

Daniels, Roger and Harry H. Kitano
1969   American Racism: Exploration of the Nature of Prejudice.
         Englewood Cliffs, New Jersey: Prentice-Hall.

DeAlarcon, R.
1969   "The spread of heroin abuse in a community." Bulletin on
         Narcotics 21 (July-September): 17-22.

Densen-Gerber, Judianne
1973   We Mainline Dreams: The Odyssey House Story. Garden
         City, New York: Doubleday.

Diskind, Meyer H. and George Klonsky
1964   "A second look at the New York State parole drug experi-
         ment." Federal Probation 28 (December): 34.

Drug Abuse Survey Project
1972   Dealing with Drug Abuse: A Report to the Ford Foundation.
         New York: Praeger.

Drug Enforcement Administration
1974   Reported Narcotic Abusers, Calendar Year, 1972. Washing-
         ton, D.C.: Bureau of Narcotics and Dangerous Drugs.

Eaton, Joseph W. and Neil Gilbert
1967   "Racial discrimination and diagnostic differentiation,"
         in Roger R. Miller (ed.), Race, Research, and Reason:
         Social Work Perspectives. New York: National Association
         of Social Workers. 79-88.

Einstein, Stanley and S. Allen (eds.)
1972   Proceedings of the 1st International Conference on Students
         Drug Surveys, September 12-15, 1972. Farmingdale, New
         York: Baywood.

Fairbanks, John K.
1953   Trade and Diplomacy on the China Coast. Cambridge,
         Mass.: Harvard University Press.

Forman, Robert E.
1963   "Resignation as a collective behavior response." American
         Journal of Sociology 69 (November): 285-90.

Gallup International
1972   Special Report on College Students. Gallup Opinion Index
         80 (December 1971), Princeton, New Jersey.

Goffman, Erving
1963   Stigma: Notes on the Management of Spoiled Identity.
            Englewood Cliffs, New Jersey: Prentice-Hall.

Goode, Erich
1969   "Marijuana and the politics of reality. " Journal of Health
            and Social Behavior 10 (June): 83-94.

1972   Drugs in American Society. New York: Knopf.

Gusfield, Joseph R.
1963   Symbolic Crusade: Status Politics and the American
            Temperance Movement. Urbana: University of Illinois
            Press.

1970   "Rejections of the social order and their direction, "
            in Joseph R. Gusfield (ed.), Protest, Reform, and Revolt:
            A Reader in Social Movements. New York: Wiley. 85-99.

Herzog, Elizabeth and Hylan Lewis
1971   "Children in poor families: myths and realities. " Annual
            Progress in Child Psychiatry and Child Development.
            Stella Chess and Alexander Thomas (eds.), New York:
            Brunner Mazel.

Hess, Albert G.
1965   Chasing the Dragon: A Report on Drug Addiction in Hong
            Kong. Amsterdam: North-Holland.

Hill, Herbert
1973   "Anti-Oriental agitation and the rise of working class
            racism." Society 10 (January-February): 43-54.

Hofstadter, Richard
1965   The Paranoid Style in American Politics. New York: Knopf.

Hubbard, S. Dana
1920   "The New York City narcotic clinic and differing points of
            view on narcotic addiction. " Monthly Bulletin of the De-
            partment of Health, City of New York 10 (2).

Hughes, Patrick H. , Gail Crawford, and Noel W. Barker
1971   "Developing an epidemiological field team for drug depen-
            dence. " Archives of General Psychiatry 24 (May): 389-94. '

Hunt, Leon G.
1974   Recent Spread of Heroin Use in the United States: Unanswer-
         ed Questions. Washington, D.C.: Drug Abuse Council.

Ianni, Francis A. J.
1974   Black Mafia, Ethnic Succession in Organized Crime. New
         York: Simon and Schuster.

Johnson, Bruce D.
1971   Social Determinants of the Use of "Dangerous Drugs" by
         College Students. Ph.D. dissertation, Department of So-
         ciology, Columbia University. Privately published, June.

1973a   "Sense and nonsense in the study of drugs: An anti-com-
         mission report." Society 14 (May/June): 53-58.

1973b   "Empirical support for a 'double failure' theory of heroin
         addiction." Paper presented at the Society for the Study
         of Social Problems, New York City, August.

1974   Book review of Richard Blum, Horatio Alger's Children.
         Contemporary Sociology 316: 529-32.

1975a   "No opium policy which is morally wrong can be politically
         right." Paper presented at the American Sociological As-
         sociation, San Francisco, August.

1975b   "Righteousness before revenue; the moral crusade against
         the Indo-Chinese opium trade," Journal of Drug Issues 4
         (Fall): 304-26.

Josephson, Eric
1970   "Resistance to community surveys." Social Problems 18
         (Summer): 117-29.

1973   "The British response to drug abuse." Second Report of
         the National Commission on Marijuana and Drug Abuse,
         Drug Abuse in America. Washington, D.C.: U.S. Govern-
         ment Printing Office. Appendix IV: 176-97.

Josephson, Eric and Eleanor E. Carroll
1974   Drug Use. New York: Halsted.

Journal, The
1974   A newspaper reporting drug news. Toronto, Ontario:
         Addiction Research Foundation.

Judson, Horace F.
1974   Heroin Addiction in Britain. New York: Harcourt Brace
            Jovanovich.

Kandel, Denise
1973   "Adolescent marijuana use: role of parents and peers."
            Science 181 (September): 1067-70.

1975   "Reaching the hard to reach: illicit drug use among high
            school absentees." Addictive Diseases (January):

1974   "Interpersonal influences on adolescent drug use" in Eric
            Josephson and Eleanor E. Carroll (eds.), Drug Use. New
            York: Halsted. 207-40.

Kandel, Denise, Eric Single and Ron Kessler
1976   "The epidemiology of drug use among New York State high
            school students: distribution, trends, and changes in rates
            of use." American Journal of Public Health (forthcoming).

Kandel, Denise, Eric Single, Donald Treiman and Richard Faust
1974   "Adolescent involvement in illicit drug use: a multiple
            classification analysis." Paper presented at the American
            Sociological Association, Montreal, August.

Kanter, Rosabeth M.
1968   "Commitment and social organization: a study of commit-
            ment mechanisms in utopian communities," American
            Sociological Review 33 (August): 499-517.

Kaplan, John
1970   Marijuana—The New Prohibition. Cleveland: World.

King, Rufus
1972   The Drug Hang-Up. New York: Norton.

Kitsuse, John I. and Malcolm Spector
1973   "Toward a sociology of social problems." Social Problems
            20 (Spring): 407-19.

Klein, J. and D. L. Phillips
1968   "From hard to soft drugs: temporal and substantive changes
            in drug usage among gangs in a working-class community."
            Journal of Health and Social Behavior 9 (June): 139-45.

Kramer, John C. and Richard A. Bass
1969   "Institutionalization patterns among civilly committed ad-
         dicts." Journal of the American Medical Association 208
         (June 23): 2297-2301.

Ladner, Joyce
1971   Tomorrow's Tomorrow: The Black Woman. New York:
         Doubleday.

1973   The Death of White Sociology. Joyce Ladner (ed.), New
         York: Random House.

Lang, Kurt and Gladys Engel Lang
1961   Collective Dynamics, New York: Crowell.

Lazarsfeld, Paul F., Ann K. Pasanella and Morris Rosenberg
1972   Continuities in the Language of Social Research. New
         York: Free Press.

Lewis, Hylan
1967   Culture, Class and Poverty. Washington, D.C.: Health
         and Welfare Council of the National Capitol Area.

Liebow, Elliot
1967   Tally's Corner. Boston: Little, Brown.

Lindesmith, Alfred
1947   Addiction and Opiates. Chicago: Aldine.

1965   The Addict and the Law. New York: Vintage.

Lowinger, Paul
1973   "How the People's Republic of China solved the drug abuse
         problem." American Journal of Chinese Medicine 1 (2):
         275-82.

1974   "Issues in the evaluation of heroin treatment," in Eric
         Josephson and Eleanor Carroll (eds.), Drug Use. New
         York: Halsted. 129-57.

Lukoff, Irving
1975   Personal Communication (March).

Malcolm X
1964   The Autobiography of Malcolm X. New York: Grove.

McGlothlin, William H. and Victor C. Tabbush
1972   Alternative Approaches to Opiate Control: Cost, Benefits
          and Potential. Bureau of Narcotics and Dangerous Drugs,
          June.

McWilliams, Carey
1969   Factories in the Field: The Story of Migratory Farm Labor
[1939]   in California. Hamden, Conn.: Shoe String.

Meiselas, Harold and Leon Brill
1974   "The role of civil commitment in multimodality program-
          ming," in James A. Inciardi and Carl D. Chambers (eds.),
          Drugs and the Criminal Justice System. Beverly Hills,
          Calif.: Sage.

Mellinger, Glen D., Robert H. Somers and Dean L. Manheimer
1975   "Drug use research items pertaining to personality and
          interpersonal relations." Paper presented at the Drug
          Lifestyles Conference, St. Simons Island, Georgia, Jan-
          uary.

Merton, Robert K.
1957   Social Theory and Social Structure. Glencoe, Illinois:
          Free Press.

National Commission on Marijuana and Drug Abuse
1973   Drug Abuse in America: Problem in Perspective. Washing-
          ton, D.C.: U.S. Government Printing Office.

New York Times
1974   "209 convicted under strict drug law." November 10: 1, 72.

O'Donnell, John
1969   Narcotic Addicts in Kentucky. Public Health Service Pub-
          lication 1881. Washington, D.C.: U.S. Government Print-
          ing Office.

Piliavin, Irving and Scott Briar
1964   "Police encounters with juveniles." American Journal of
          Sociology 70 (September): 206-14.

Primm, B. J. and P. E. Bath
1973   "Pseudoheroinism." International Journal of the Addictions
          8 (2): 231-42.

Reasons, Charles
1974   "The politics of drugs: an inquiry in the sociology of social
          problems." Sociological Quarterly 15 (Summer): 381-404.

Reiss, Albert J, Jr.
1971   Police and the Public. New Haven: Yale University Press.

Rivera, Ramon and G. Hohlen
1973   "Drug use and 'double failure': an empirical assessment."
          Paper presented at the Society for the Study of Social
          Problems, New York City, August.

Ryan, William
1970   Blaming the Victim. New York: Pantheon.

Robins, Lee N., D. H. Davis and D. W. Goodwin
1974   "Drug use by army enlisted men in Vietnam: a follow-up
          on their return home." American Journal of Epidemiology
          99 (4): 235-49.

Rowntree, Joshua
1905   The Imperial Drug Trade. London: Methuen.

Selltiz, Chaire, Marie Jahoda, Morton Deutsch and Stuart W. Cook
1951   Research Methods in Social Relations. New York: Holt,
          Rinehart and Winston.

Single, Eric, Denise Kandel and Richard Faust
1974   "Patterns of multiple drug use in high school". Journal
          of Health and Social Behavior 15 (December): 344-57.

Short, James F. and Fred J. Strodtbeck
1965   Group Process and Gang Delinquency. Chicago: University
          of Chicago Press.

Siegal, Jacob S.
1973   "Estimates of coverage of the population by sex, race, and
          age in the 1970 census." Paper presented at the Annual
          Meeting of the Population Association of America, New
          Orleans (April 26).

Skolnick, Jerome
1967   Justice Without Trial. New York: Wiley.

Smelser, Neil J.
1962   Theory of Collective Behavior. New York: Free Press.

Sutherland, Edwin and Donald Cressey
1974   Criminology. (ninth edition) Philadelphia: Lippincott.

Taylor, Arnold H.
1969   American Diplomacy and the Narcotics Traffic, 1900-1939.
          Durham, N.C.: Duke University Press.

Terry, Charles E. and Mildred Pellens
1928   The Opium Problem. New York: The Haddon Craftsmen.

Thomas, Piri
1967   Down These Mean Streets. New York: Knopf.

Turner, Ralph H. and Lewis M. Killian
1972   Collective Behavior. (second edition) Englewood Cliffs,
          New Jersey: Prentice-Hall.

U.S. Commission on Civil Rights
1973   To Know or Not to Know: Collection and Use of Racial and
          Ethnic Data in Federal Assistance Programs. Washington,
          D.C.: U.S. Government Printing Office.

1974   Counting the Forgotten: The 1970 Census Count of Persons
          of Spanish Speaking Background in the United States. Wash-
          ington, D.C.: U.S. Government Printing Office.

Waldorf, Dan
1971   "Social control in therapeutic communities for the treatment
          of drug addicts." International Journal of Addictions 6
          (March): 29-44.

Waldorf, Dan, Martin Orlik and Craig Reinarman
1974   Morphine Maintenance, The Shreveport Clinic, 1919-1923.
          Washington, D.C.: Drug Abuse Council.

Werthmann, Carl
1967   The Function of Social Definitions in the Development of
          Delinquent Careers. Task Force Report: Juvenile Delin-
          quency and Youth Crime. A Report of the President's
          Commission on Law Enforcement and the Administration
          of Justice. Washington, D.C.: U.S. Government Printing
          Office.

Wikler, Abraham
1971   "Drugs: addiction, organic and psychological aspects."
          Encyclopedia of the Social Sciences IV: 290-97.

Wolfgang, Marvin E., Robert M. Figlio and Thorsten Sellin
1972   Delinquency in a Birth Cohort. Chicago: University of
         Chicago Press.

Yablonsky, Lewis
1965   Synanon: The Tunnel Back. New York: Macmillan.

Zinberg, Norman E. and John A. Robertson
1972   Drugs and the Public. New York: Simon and Schuster.

Abeles, Hans, Ralph Plew, Irving Laudeutscher and Harvey M. Rosenthal, "Multiple Drug Addiction in New York City in a Selected
Population Group," Public Health Reports 81, no. 8 (August
1966): 685-90.

An assessment of multiple drug use and characteristics of
multiple drug users admitted to three detention institutions in
New York City during July and August 1965. Of the 7,855 men
admitted at that time, 9.7 percent (759) were drug users and
480 out of 1,277 women (37.6 percent) were drug users. Adequate information on 1,231 of the drug users was obtained. Over
half of the addicts are black, 41.6 percent are white, and 6.8
percent are unstated or "other." Among the male addicts, 48.2
are white and 41.9 percent black, while female addicts are 31.3
percent white and 67.1 percent black. Since this group, appre-
hended by law enforcement agencies, is highly selective, "the
preponderance of Negro addicts in the groups studied does not
necessarily reflect the ethnic distribution of addicts in the general population" (p. 687). Over 50 percent of all drug users are
found to be addicted to more than one drug; 93 percent of all
drug users are addicted to heroin, with barbiturates the second
most common drug to which they are addicted. Combined heroin
and barbiturate addiction is more often found among male drug
users above the age of 20 than among women. Twenty percent

This section also includes references to the racial minorities
in general.

of the women drug users use amphetamines, compared to three percent of the men. The authors point out in conclusion that multiple drug use presents new problems in treatment, especially barbiturate withdrawal symptoms requiring immediate recognition and specific therapy.

Abrams, Arnold, John H. Gagnon and Joseph J. Levin, "Psychosocial Aspects of Addiction," American Journal of Public Health 58, no. 11 (November 1968): 2142-55.

An analysis of police and Federal Bureau of Narcotics records and of a sample of 400 narcotic addicts in 1957 at Cook County Jail in Chicago, Illinois. The authors summarize the psychoanalytic theories of addiction as caused by the psychopathic personality and the socio-psychological theories of addiction as an expression of underlying disorder in the social life of the individual. They cite data from Chicago to show that Chicago is second nationally to New York in the incidence of drug addiction. The characteristics of the addicted population are almost exactly the reverse of those in 1930, when Bingham Dai surveyed Chicago: the addicts are 76.9 percent black and 19.4 percent white, with 4.6 percent other, compared to a large percentage of Chinese with whites in the majority in the 1930s. The average age is 27.8 years, while in 1930 the average age was 36.9. There are nine males to every one female addict. The majority of the addicts were born in Chicago or some northern city and had completed grade 11 of school, in contrast to the average of 9.5 grades in the total Chicago population and 8.5 grades in the high addiction area. The authors contend that these data indicate that the drug addicts aggressively assault reality through drug use. The areas in which they live and their higher education only serve to heighten their awareness of the inequities between themselves as a racial minority and the white population, their lack of opportunities, and their relatively restricted avenues to social and economic success. The authors stress the high levels of aspiration and consequent frustration combined with the availability of drugs as the major factors contributing to drug use.

Agar, Michael, The Junk Novel: Addict Autobiographies As Life History Data. New York: New York State Drug Abuse Control Commission, 1973.

Agar suggests more utilization of autobiographies by drug users as a better means for squares to know a junkie's life and subcultural norms. He uses two autobiographies as cases in point: Junkie by William Burroughs, who is white and Blues Child, by George Cain who is black. Quoting passages from each he demonstrates his claim that junkies may not perceive objects, persons, and events the same as squares assume they do, and that by comparing sections from the two writers' works, he shows that the same overt behavior (for example, drug use and relapse) may have different meanings for two junkies. Not only would autobiographies teach about the junkie's own life, Agar says, but they could be enlightening in square-junkie interaction and the analysis of what junkie life does for an individual.

Agar, Michael and Richard C. Stephens. The Methadone Street Scene: The Addict's View. New York: New York State Drug Abuse Control Commission, 1975.

Interviews were inducted with 41 persons in 1974 (21 in a methadone maintenance program, 20 in an abstinence-oriented modality, 19 were black, 14 Puerto Rican, 7 white, and 1 an American Indian.

Indications were strong that street methadone is widespread: 34 reported they knew persons who had become "strung out" on the streets with methadone. Its availability and inexpensiveness as well as its satisfaction as a euphoric were given as the main reasons for its growing popularity. Nearly all the respondents reported that the main source of street methadone was methadone maintenance program patients, especially through sale of take-home doses.

The authors caution that these rather negative insights into the methadone street scene may cause concern but that the positive aspects of methadone must be kept in mind for a total perspective of the drug and its distribution.

Amsel, Zili, J. J. Fishman, Leslie Rivkind, Florence Kavaler, Donald Krug, Mary Cline, Flora Brophy and Donald Conwell. "The Use of the Narcotics Register for Follow-up of a Cohort of Adolescent Addicts," International Journal of the Addictions, 6, no. 2 (June 1971): 225-39.

An examination of subsequent drug activity and mortality (through the Narcotics Register of New York City and other agency reports over a 13-year period) of 247 young addicts admitted to Riverside Hospital in 1955 for treatment. Ages at admission ranged from 14-22 years. The group was 42 percent white, 26 percent Negro, and 32 percent Puerto Rican; predominantly male; 70 percent Roman Catholic, 24 percent Protestant and 5 percent Jewish. A psychiatric examination showed 42 percent with personality disorders and 21 percent psychotic.

As stated by the authors, the most significant finding of the
study was the group's high mortality rate. Over a 13 year period,
11 percent of the whites had died, 8 percent of the blacks, and
7 percent of the Puerto Ricans. The deaths were only those
recorded in New York City; it is possible than an even higher incidence would have been found if follow-up outside had been made.

Active drug involvement after hospital release (relapse) occurred very frequently: over half had records of subsequent
detoxification efforts, and 86 percent had arrest records. Among
reports indicating relapse, Negroes had a higher percentage
than whites or Puerto Ricans; whites were disproportionately
represented in the abstaining group. Analysis of arrest records
(conviction records unavailable) showed that 68 percent had been
for crimes against property and 32 percent against persons,
giving further evidence that crimes against property constitute
the bulk of crimes committed by addicts.

The authors conclude that the Narcotics Register is a valuable
tool in follow-up of addicts over time.

"An Alert: Narcotic Usage Among Employees in Industry," Journal
    of Occupational Medicine 1, no. 10 (October 1968): 619-20.

A short description of a group of nine males identified as
using heroin, cocaine, methadone, codeine, or barbiturates in
a medium-sized industry in an urban community on the East
Coast. They are young, ranging in age from 19-26, occupy
clerical positions with a relatively low income, and include
both blacks and whites, although blacks predominate. The
author speaks of the use of urinalyses to identify drug-using
employees, and advocates a program of rehabilitation similar
to that offered to alcoholics for narcotics users. He estimates
that more drug users in industry will be uncovered as studies
continue and warns that "we have much to learn and much to do
to cope adequately with this problem" (p. 620).

Babst, Dean V., Carl D. Chambers, and Alan Warner. "Patient
    Characteristics Associated with Retention in an Methadone
    Maintenance Program," British Journal of Addiction 66, no. 3
    (November 1971): 195-204.

The purpose of this study was to determine if it is possible
to differentiate between types of patient as to their ability to
stay in a methadone maintenance program. The study was based
on 679 admissions to the Dole-Nyswander methadone program
from its inception in 1964 until March 1968. All patients were
followed up to determine whether they were still in the program

two years later. Eighty percent of both males and females were continuously in the program for two years or longer.

Ethnic characteristics of all admissions (N = 871): 48 percent white, 33 percent black, 18 percent Puerto Rican, and 1 percent other. Sample (N = 679): 39 percent white, 41 percent black, 17 percent Puerto Rican, and 3 percent other. Percent of males in program two years after admission: of males, 82 percent of whites, 77 percent of blacks, 81 percent of Puerto Rican and 79 percent of others; of females, 80 percent of whites, 77 percent blacks, 88 percent Puerto Rican, and 100 percent other.

As expected, those patients who did less well were those who had longer conviction records, were multiple drug users, abused alcohol, were not employed at admission, were older, and were not married. Other factors that were expected to be related to the ability to stay in the program but proved to have little or no influence were: age when heroin use was started, number of previous hospitalizations, length of education, and longest job held. Patients with relatively short usage or very long usage did better than those in the middle range (8 to 19 years of use).

When several factors suggested by clinical experience were combined, interesting classifications of patients emerged. For example, the best group were those who were abusers for five years or less and had no multiple drug or alcohol abuse. This group had a 96 percent retention rate. The worst group were those who had 12-15 years of abuse and seven or more convictions. This latter group had 58 percent in the program two years after admission.

Babst, Dean V., Sandra Newman, Norman Gordon, and Alan Warner. "Driving Records of Methadone Maintenance Patients in New York State," Journal of Drug Issues, 3, no. 4 (Fall 1973): 285-92.

Because rehabilitative improvement, especially as it relates to employability, being able to obtain a driver's license and automobile insurance, the driving records of methadone maintenance patients were matched against a general driving population. (The addict population checked for driving records [N = 1573] was 42 percent white, 40 percent black, 15 percent Puerto Rican and 37 percent other or unknown). Accident and conviction rates however were about the same for methadone maintenance patients and New York City male drivers of the same age. These findings are similar to conclusions of other studies on the same subject.

Bailey, Pearce. "Contribution to the Mental Pathology of Races in the United States," Mental Hygiene 6, no. 2 (April 1922): 370-91.

An examination of cases recorded at military recruiting depots and at camps among 69,394 volunteers and draftees in the U.S. Army made in order to compare the mental pathology patterns of the various "races." Bailey divides the neuro-psychiatric cases into several clinical classifications: mental deficiency, psychoneurosis, psychoses, nervous diseases and injuries, epilepsy, constitutional psychopathic states, endocrinopathies, and alcoholism and drug addiction. Mental defect is the focus of this article, and the most mentally defective "races" are found to be the African, American Indian, Italian, Mexican and Slav. An average of three percent of the sample is found to be drug-addicted. Blacks and Mexicans are below the average, while American Indians are about average, and Jews, Italians, and Irish are above the average in their addiction rates.

Bailey, Walter C. and Mary Koval. "Differential Patterns of Drug Abuse Among White Activists and Nonwhite Militant College Students," International Journal of the Addictions 7, no. 2 (Summer 1972): 191-99.

A study of 154 white, black, and Puerto Rican activist and non-activist students made at a college campus in 1968-69 in order to determine patterns of drug abuse. Blacks and Puerto Ricans are grouped as "nonwhite." This study shows that white activist college students are markedly more involved in drug use than are nonwhite militants. White activists report much more use of heroin, LSD, and amphetamines than nonwhite militants, although they only use the drugs occasionally. Only in marijuana use is there substantial involvement of nonwhite militants. More white activists than nonwhite are involved in marijuana use however, and whites tend to use it regularly, while nonwhites report using it only occasionally.

Ball, John C. "Marijuana Smoking and the Onset of Heroin Use," Drug Abuse: Social and Psychopharmacological Aspects. Edited by Jonathan O. Cole and J. R. Wittenborn. Springfield, Illinois: Charles C. Thomas, 1969, p. 117-28.

Substantially the same article as John C. Ball, Carl D. Chambers, and Marion J. Ball, "The Association of Marihuana Smoking with Opiate Addiction in the United States."

Ball, John C. "Two Patterns of Narcotic Drug Addiction in the U.S.,"
Journal of Criminal Law, Criminology and Police Science 55,
no. 2 (June 1965): 203-11.

The identification of two patterns of opiate addiction in the
United States using medical records of 3,301 addict patients
discharged from the Lexington and Fort Worth Hospitals in
1962. One pattern consists of heroin use among Northern urban
youth who are primarily of minority group status. The other
pattern consists of opiates other than heroin or synthetic anal-
gesics used primarily by middle-aged whites from Southern
rural areas. Ball compares this record with the 1937 hospital
population of opiate addicts at Lexington Hospital. Male patients
in 1962 are an average of eight years younger than in 1937, have
increased in their use of heroin while decreasing in their use of
morphine, and come from the urban centers as opposed to the
rural South.

Ball, John C. and William M. Bates. "Migration and Residential
Mobility of Narcotic Drug Addicts," Social Problems 14, no.
1 (Summer 1966): 56-69.

An exploration of the records of 925 addict patients at the
U.S. Public Service Hospital in Lexington, Kentucky in 1962 to
determine the relationship between mobility and addiction. Over
half of the sample are black—Puerto Ricans are classified generally as white. The black addicts are second-generation migrants
to the Northern cities, while the Puerto Rican addicts are first-
generation migrants. In neither case are the addicts more mobile than their respective base populations. The white addicts
are also stable in place of residence since birth and exhibit much
intergenerational stability. In contrast to the black patients,
who move within the city, the white patients who move leave
the county. The authors conclude that "it appears that the relationship of mobility to crime and deviant behavior has been over-
simplified and ambiguously presented. . . . From the present
study there is no evidence that such a relationship exists among
drug addicts in the United States" (pp. 68-69).

Ball, John C., William M. Bates and John A. O'Donnell. "Characteristics of Hospitalized Narcotic Addicts," Health, Education and
Welfare Indicators (March 1966): 17-26.

A brief description of some of the characteristics of narcotic
addicts admitted from 1935-1965 to the two U.S. Public Health
Service psychiatric hospitals at Lexington, Kentucky and Fort

Worth, Texas. Addicts are found to be young male adults under 40 years of age, one-third of whom are black and 11 of whom are Orientals, and come from metropolitan areas in New York, Illinois, or New Jersey. There is a changing pattern of black admissions: although black admissions remain the same in the South, they rise sharply between 1935 and 1963 in New York State and Illinois, thus reflecting the migration of blacks from the South to New York City and Chicago.

Ball, John C., Carl D. Chambers and Marion J. Ball. "The Association of Marihuana Smoking with Opiate Addiction in the United States," Journal of Criminal Law and Criminology 59, no. 2 (June 1968): 171-82.

An examination of the medical records of 2,213 addict patients admitted to the Lexington and Fort Worth Hospitals during 1965 to study the relationship between marijuana smoking and the subsequent use of opiates. Two patterns of opiate use are found. One pattern of opiate addiction is associated with marijuana use and concentrated in four states (New York, Illinois, California, and Texas); the second pattern is in the Southern states and not associated with marijuana use. The addicts following the first pattern are characterized by a marked concentration in metropolitan areas with an illicit drug subculture, 87 percent male, 38 percent nonwhite (Puerto Ricans and Chicanos are classified as "white") and with a mean age of 30.4 years. They generally smoke marijuana as youths, are arrested, and then turn to opiate use. This pattern is contrasted to the second, in which addicts are more often from rural areas in the South, 75 percent male, 5 percent nonwhite, mean age 41.3 years, and use doctor-prescribed opiates rather than heroin. A study of 703 nonwhite addicts, overwhelmingly black, is also included. The addicts are all from areas outside the South. Black addicts who have used marijuana are found to be significantly different from those who do not use marijuana in their younger age involvement in deviant acts leading to arrest in terms of onset of opiate use and hospitalization for addiction. Black and white female addicts are found to have the same characteristics as the men. The authors conclude that "the incipient addict is predisposed to opiate addiction by his use of marihuana" (p. 181).

Ball, John C., Harold Graff and John J. Sheehan, Jr. "The Heroin Addict's View of Methadone Maintenance," British Journal of Addiction 119, no. 1 (March 1974): 89-95.

A comparison of patient and staff attitudes toward drug dependence. In interviews held with a sample of methadone maintenance patients in Pennsylvania in 1971 (N = 224, predominantly male) 65 percent were black, 66 percent were under 30 years old, 41 percent lived with parents, only 7 percent had less than a ninth grade education, 72 percent had worked three or more years since leaving school, 84 percent had been arrested. Staff members numbered 44 (no data other than position were given).

The outstanding finding was the lack of consensus between addicts and staff concerning the etiology of patient's problems. The staff sees patient as physically and mentally ill, and the addict sees himself as neither. The authors see this divergence as a cultural conflict, especially between ghetto addicts and middle class clinic staffs. "The staff views the patient as psychologically impaired; the patient sees himself as an unfortunate who is part of a disadvantaged group or subculture."

Two other key findings were that addicts view ex-addict counselors as the most effective staff workers and that longer-term patients tend to reflect staff attitudes more than newer patients.

Bates, William M. "Narcotics, Negroes and the South," Social Forces 45, no. 1 (September 1966); 61-67.

A delineation of the demographic and racial patterns of addict admissions to the Fort Worth and Lexington Hospitals. The data show that black addicts generally come from Northern metropolitan areas and are underrepresented in the Southern areas. The Southern drug users are usually from rural areas, white, eight years older than the Southern black addicts, and ten years older than the Northern white addicts. In the North for the past five years, the blacks and whites have been about the same mean age, 30 years old.

Bates, William M. "Occupational Characteristics of Negro Addicts," International Journal of the Addictions 3, no. 2 (Fall 1968): 345-50.

An identification of the occupational characteristics of 99 black addicts admitted to the Lexington Hospital. The data clearly demonstrate that a large number of black addicts never even begin an occupational career, which Bates feels substantiates Finestone's analysis of the "cat" culture rejecting work in favor of hustling. A large percentage of those black addicts who do start steady careers suffer extensive unemployment, which seems to

Bates to substantiate Robins' concept of low socioeconomic status as a correlate of deviant behavior. The author calls for further precise study of the relationship between deviant behavior and occupation.

Bayer, Ron. "Repression, Reform and Drug Abuse: An Analysis of the Response to the Rockefeller Drug Law Proposals of 1973," Journal of Psychedelic Drugs 6, no. 3 (July–September 1974): 299-309.

A study whose purpose was to approach analytically the public response of four groups to the 1973 "get tough" proposal of Governor Nelson Rockefeller of New York regarding narcotic addiction: professionals related to the criminal justice system, professionals associated with addiction treatment, blacks and Puerto Ricans, and political liberals. These groups were selected because the response of each "elucidates a particularly critical element in the social reaction to drug use" and "the logic of their positions should help elucidate the emerging pattern of drug abuse politics."

According to Bayer, the response also reveals "the limitations of treatment as a response to the problem of drug abuse. There is, at present, an excess of treatment capacities, both maintenance and drug-free, and yet large numbers of drug users do not use them. Liberal reform measures have not solved the problem. Large numbers of drug users are simply not interested in giving up drugs."

The author also discusses public attitudes toward heroin users and drug dealers because they "provide some insight into the strategies necessary for mobilizing public support for both repressive approaches to drug use as well as those based on non-punitive premises." Using nationwide opinion surveys as a source he indicates that the majority of the population sees the addict as sick rather than criminal and favors a treatment approach. More punitive views are held toward heroin sellers.

In one survey where socioeconomic and ethnic data were available, it was found that blacks and Puerto Ricans were more favorable to the life sentence for drug pushers than whites were. Persons of high income, higher education, and white collar occupations were less likely to favor the life sentence.

Significant black support was given to the Rockefeller proposal through black spokesmen, but that support tended to be moderate when the program was more thoroughly outlined regarding the life sentence for street addicts and the virtual elimination of rehabilitation.

A stress on compulsory treatment instead emerged as the characteristic black response. Also, according to Bayer, it was the black and Puerto Rican spokesmen who most consistently raised the issue of the social roots of addiction and the link between racism and drug use.

Following more specific analysis of the responses of the four groups Bayer summarizes that they indicate the limits of both repression and reform, "Those who opposed the repressive thrust of the Rockefeller proposal did so in the belief that a more humane solution to the problem could be developed within the confines of our social system. This analysis has indicated the diminished quality of that goal."

Bernstein, Blanche and Anne N. Shkuda. The Young Drug User: Attitude and Obstacles to Treatment. New York: Center for New York City Affairs, New School for Social Research, June 1974.

Directed to the goal of preventing drug abuse, "this study examines the attitudes and motivating factors surrounding the youthful drug abuser's decision to seek or not to seek treatment and the experience of those who have been in a program" The sample included narcotics users confined to a detention institution (Rikers Island in New York City)—426 interviews were held with heroin, cocaine, or illicit methadone users (rather than those using barbiturates, amphetamines, or hallucinogens) because "this type of drug use was still the center of public concern."

Demographically, the sample (all between 16-22 years) was 56 percent black, 32 percent Hispanic, 11 percent white, and less than 1 percent "other nonwhite." Most were born in New York and had relatively large families, and a high proportion of them were high school dropouts. First drug use of any kind was before 14 years for 42 percent of the sample; alcohol was also widely used. More than half said they had started drugs because their friends were doing it. The sample found a recurring pattern of peer pressure in initial drug use; pushers were never mentioned as the reason for first use. A high incident of multiple drug use was found.

The type of treatment programs considered were therapeutic communities (TC), drug-free day care, and methadone maintenance. Seeking treatment was positively related to self-perception of their own drug use and to previous knowledge and positive reports of treatment programs. Among the 46 percent who said they had been in some treatment at least one, race does not seem to be a crucial factor (although blacks were less

likely to seek treatment); age is more important, and the younger
are less likely to go for treatment of any kind. More restrictive
programs (such as TC) and programs which employ self-exam-
ination drew a high proportion of negative evaluative responses
(42 percent positive, 28 percent negative); methadone maintenance programs were given much more positive responses (76
percent positive, 11 percent negative).

A six-page summary makes suggestions based on the findings
of the areas to consider in improving treatment programs.

Bernstein, Rosalie. "A Profile of Narcotic Addicts on Public Assist-
     ance," Narcotic Addicts on Public Assistance. Edited by Pat-
     ricia M. Pettiford, New York City Human Resources Administra-
     tion, Department of Services Study Series 1, no. 1 (October
     1973): 1-18.

A description of the demographic characteristics of addicts
on public assistance in New York City, drawn from a sample of
469 cases in the Central Narcotics Registry of the Department
of Social Services. Addicts are only .4 percent of the entire
public assistance caseload. The average addict on public assistance is found to be male, black or Puerto Rican, living alone,
born in New York City, average age of 29 years, and a median
education level of tenth grade. Most are unskilled laborers or
office workers, and nearly 43 percent had not previously received public assistance. Nearly three-fourths had arrest records, with over half of the arrests for illegal use, possession
or sale of drugs. Over 60 percent of the clients began using
heroin by the age of 20; the average age at the time of first
arrest is 24 years. Nearly half have had previous treatment
for addiction, with most of the open cases enrolled in methadone
maintenance programs and most of the closed cases in residence
house programs. No statistical differences are found between
open and closed cases, although the average open case has been
open for 9.5 months and the average closed case only for five
months. "Perhaps there is some sort of critical period (i.e.,
six months) and if the addict is able to stay off drugs for this
period, he has a better chance of staying off for increasingly
longer periods of time" (p. 15). Bernstein points out the difficulty, however, in judging "without intensive psychological
data on the individuals" why some addicts continue successfully
in treatment while others do not (p. 15).

Bender, Lauretta. "A Psychiatrist Looks at Deviancy as a Factor in
     Juvenile Delinquency," Federal Probation 32, no. 2 (June 1968):
     35-42.

An elucidation of multiple factors which tend to occur in
certain social cultural patterns and in personal pathology patterns. The patterns she describes are pathological family situations, identity confusion (especially with minority group members), social and economic deprivation, inadequate educational
opportunities, brain damage, and mental illness (especially
schizophrenia). Bender explores these patterns of deviancy in
terms of sex offenses in children, drug usage in adolescents,
and homicidal aggression. Bender focuses on drug abuse studies
showing that rather than being passive, introverted, oral-fixated,
and dependent on their mothers, "juveniles prone to drug usage
were deviates without group status in their own ethnic, neighborhood, age, and social groups" (p. 40).

Berry, William Earl. "How Drugs Are Used to Rip-off the Black
    Community," Jet 42, no. 20 (August 10, 1972): 22-29.

The citation of statistics and vignettes to show how drugs
affect the black community economically, in mortality rates,
theft, youth addiction, police involvement, family structure and
relationships, and the effects of methadone maintenance treatment. Berry concludes by describing how black and Puerto
Rican youth have begun to fight against drug traffickers. "It is
up to black people to declare war against drug traffickers and
pushers since the federal government . . . has been unsuccessful in ridding the black community of addiction and increases in
crime" (p. 29).

"Blacks Declare War on Dope," Ebony 25, no. 8 (June 1970): 31-4,
    36, 38, 40.

An account of various organizations in the black community
which have been forced by police inaction to initiate war on drugs.
The groups discussed include Mothers Against Drugs (MAD),
WWRL educational program, Phoenix House, methadone maintenance programs, and the Upper Park Avenue Baptist Church.

Blum, Richard. "Blue Collar Black Families," Horatio Alger's
    Children. By Richard H. Blum and Associates. San Francisco:
    Jossey-Bass, 1972, pp. 140-54.

A delineation of the differences between ten black families with
a high risk of producing drug-taking children and ten low risk
black families in California in a blue-collar black community.
Blum is unable to procure a sample of real high risk black
families: few children, including the "high risk" sample in this

study, even use illicit drugs. The differences between the families are slight; all of them are intact, Protestant, have employed fathers, and vote for the Democratic Party. Blum finds that high risk parents are married longer than low risk ones, have a boy as the first child, have more children, have more cases of alcoholism and medication use, lower educational levels, less religious activity, more tendency to use drugs themselves, less disciplining of children, less of an egalitarian relationship with each other, and more permissive values, and that they generally contribute to a negative home atmosphere. It is suggested that "in certain ways the low risk blue collar [black] family resembles the middle-class [white] high risk one" (p. 151).

Blumer, Herbert. "The World of Youthful Drug Use." Mimeographed. Berkeley, California: School of Criminology, University of California, January 1967.

An evaluation of a project to develop abstinence among youthful drug-users of marijuana, amphetamines, barbiturates, heroin, crystal, and LSD in Oakland, California. A "good cross section of the juvenile population in the underprivileged groups" (p. 1) is represented, including blacks, Mexican Americans, and whites, from youths using facilities in churches to the Neighborhood Youth Corps and street gangs. Blumer outlines the history of the project, the method of study, the composition of the world of youthful drug use, recruitment into drug use, and career orientation. He shows that youthful drug use in Oakland, although rooted in the lower class, is expanding into the middle and upper classes. Drug use is a natural way of life for its users and is not a pathological phenomenon. The use of heroin in the adolescent drug-using world is very narrowly limited: "it is inaccurate to view adolescent drug use in the imagery of heroin use or opiate addiction" (p. 78). Since adolescent drug use is a collective practice with a supporting set of justifying beliefs, users reject the conventional methods used to prevent or eliminate it. Blumer distinguishes between four types of drug users—the rowdy, the pot head, the mellow dude, and the player—who belong either to the rowdy or cool style. Rowdy people are excluded from the world of youthful drug use. The main way to enter the drug-using world is to join a cool crowd which is using drugs; people are recruited to drug use as part of accepting the entire mode of life of the cool set. "The character of this process of recruitment throws the gravest doubt on current notions that the use of drugs is an 'escape from reality,' or a retreatist form of defeat, or an inability to live a normal life, or an expression of personal

pathology" (p. 80). In addition, as youthful drug users age, they
have different career orientations and career lines, thus opposing the conventional notion of a single line of progression towards
heroin addiction. Only the players are most likely to move in
the direction of opiate addiction, since they are most likely to
associate with heroin users. The pot heads and mellow dudes
are most likely to become ordinary conforming citizens in conventional society, while the rowdies are most likely to adopt a
career of crime. "This picture of differential career orientations and career lines in the world of youthful drug use suggests
the feasibility of a program designed to help youngsters move
in a conventional direction and away from a criminal direction"
(p. 80) through intervention at critical turning points.

Brotman, Richard E., Stephen L. Suffet, and Rasik Shah. "Genera-
    tional Differences Among Drug Abuse Patients," International
    Journal of the Addictions 7, no. 2 (Summmber 1972): 219-35.

A discussion of the generational differences among 167 out-
patients in the drug abuse treatment program of the Division of
Community Mental Health (DCMH), Department of Psychiatry,
New York Medical College. One group consists of patients who
are 16-24 years of age at the time of their screening by the
DCMH; the others are between 25 and 46 years of age. Both
groups tend to be unemployed, native-born, New York-bred,
male Catholics who come from a broken home. The recogniz-
able generational differences indicate that the younger group
"(1) contains a greater proportion of middle class [white] persons and (2) is more volatile than the older [i.e., began a wide
variety of socially disapproved modes of behavior at an earlier
age]" (p. 234).

Brown, Barry S., Robert L. Dupont, Urbane F. Bass III, George
    W. Brewster, Sara T. Glendinning, Nicholas J. Kozel, and
    Marilyn B. Meyers. "Impact of a Large-Scale Narcotics Treat-
    ment Program: A Six Month Experience," International Journal
    of the Addictions 8, no. 1 (February 1973): 49-57.

A study of the impact of the Narcotics Treatment Administration (NTA), a multimodality program established in 1970 in
Washington, D.C., regarding the functioning of 450 of its adult
clients and 150 of its youth clients. The NTA clients are 95 percent black and 83.5 percent male, with a median age of 25.9
years and a median tenth-grade education. Nearly three-fourths
have a record of previous arrests, and 46 percent have previous
convictions; two-thirds are voluntary admissions. Over a period

of six months, 85 percent of the clients on high-dose methadone
maintenance stay in treatment, while only 37 percent on low-
dose methadone and 18 percent in the abstinence program remain. Over half of the adult clients remain in treatment. Most
of the youth are in the abstinence program, so their rate of
retention is much lower. Overall, 34 percent of the clients
remain in treatment. In terms of arrest, only 11 percent of
the adults on high-dose methadone maintenance are arrested
during treatment, compared with 20 percent on low-dose maintenance and 39 percent on abstinence; 42 percent of the youths
are arrested during treatment. There are no significant differences between treatment modalities in terms of employment
or illicit drug use among clients retained in the program. The
authors conclude that methadone maintenance is effective in
retaining people in treatment but that additional techniques are
necessary to help change the clients from anti-social to pro-
social functioning.

Brown, Barry S., Robert L. DuPont, and Nicholas J. Kozel. "Heroin
    Addiction in the City of Washington," Drug Forum, 2: no. 2
    (Winter 1973): 187-90.

    A discussion of the relation of various measures of social
disorganization to the rate of addiction by census tract for the
city of Washington, D.C. Significant correlations were established between addiction and various crime categories as well
as between addiction and poverty, overcrowding, and quality of
family life. Addiction has spread throughout the city, beyond
the inner city confines. The authors see heroin addiction as
part of the problems of urban life. It cannot be seen only as a
symptom: it is part of the disease itself.

Brummit, Houston, "Observations on Drug Addicts in a House of De-
    tention for Women," Corrective Psychiatry and Journal of Social
    Therapy 9, no. 2 (Second Quarter 1963): 62-70.

    A description of drug addicts at the House of Detention for
Women in New York City. The author cites statistics showing
the increase in drug addiction among women and reversal of the
1938 pattern, when whites outnumbered blacks two to one.
Brummit estimates that in 1962, 73 percent of the drug addict
population is black, 16 percent Puerto Rican, and 11 percent
white. Brummit stresses a rejecting home environment and the
the addict's consequent turn to underworld society for a satis-
factory life as the most common factors contributing to addiction.
He feels that drug addicts can function adequately in well defined

situations, and urges prisons and psychiatric hospitals to provide intensive vocational programs to prepare addicts to function in society. Ninety-five percent of the addicts are between the ages of 20 and 40; after 40 there appears to be a "maturing out." The author also discusses ways in which the House of Detention uses psychotherapy to release the unconscious hostility which drug addicts, especially blacks, feel about their parents and other authority figures. Black inmates are found to be less trusting of the therapists than whites or Puerto Ricans, who are both more verbally communicative than blacks.

Bullington, Bruce, John G. Munns, Gilbert Geis, and James Raner, "Concerning Heroin Use and Official Records," American Journal of Public Health 59, no. 10 (October 1969): 1887-92.

A criticism of Robins and Murphy's finding that "no heroin addict fails to come to police attention" in their study of drug use in a normal population of black men in St. Louis. The authors of this critique show that St. Louis law enforcement officials concentrate disproportionately, in terms of other cities, on blacks and narcotics. They give three case histories of undetected Mexican American addicts and discuss the accuracy of official statistics on heroin addiction. They conclude that, contrary to Robins and Murphy, "an unknown number" of street addicts, as well as middle class and medicine addicts, use heroin intensively for prolonged periods and avoid official recognition. They recommend more intensive efforts to take a reliable census of heroin addicts and to gauge the extent of undetected addiction, rather than relying simply on police records.

Callan, John P. and Carroll D. Patterson. "Patterns of Drug Abuse Among Military Inductees," American Journal of Psychiatry 130, no. 3 (March 1973): 260-4.

A survey of 19,948 men who entered the Army at a large training center in the Midwest from January 15, 1971, through June 30, 1971, and who were administered a questionnaire concerning drug abuse. Nearly one-third, or 6,203, have used drugs, but most are casual users or experimenters, using any particular drug no more than five times. However, 15 to 20 percent of the drug users are hard-core confirmed drug-users, using drugs 15 times or more. Although there is little racial difference in overall drug use between whites and blacks, blacks, Hispanics and American Indians were overrepresented in terms of their proportion to the population. Whites are 84 percent of the total enlisted men, with a 32 percent usage rate; blacks are 7.1 percent of the total, but have a 31 percent usage rate; Spanish

Americans are 3.8 percent of the total but have a 21 percent usage
rate of drug abuse, while Native Americans who are only .78 percent of the total have a 35.89 percent drug usage rate. The nonwhites also differ markedly from the whites in terms of drugs
used; nonwhites' use of amphetamines, barbiturates and heroin
is twice that of whites, but whites tend to use more marijuana,
LSD, and hashish. There is a higher rate of drug use among men
who are college drop-outs from urban areas, from unstable
families, and from families with high income. Age at onset of
drug use ranges from 11-25 years, with most users beginning
at 17 or 18. Glue sniffing has the earliest average age at onset
of use, 14 years. "One of the startling finds of the study is that
99 percent of the users indicated that they were first introduced
to drugs by friends. . . . These figures reinforce the concept of
the importance of peer relationships in drug abuse" (p. 264).

Casriel, Daniel and Grover Amen. Daytop: Three Addicts and Their
Cure, New York: Hill and Wang, 1971.

The life stories, as revealed through interviews, of three
ex-addicts who live at Daytop, a therapeutic community where
addicts cure each other through intensive group therapy. Two
of the addicts are white men; one is a black woman from the
West Indies whose middle class family must cope with her
alcoholic father. She turns to drugs and prostitution in order
to escape from her family life. The book, and Daytop itself,
are predicated on the assumption that people turn to drugs to
avoid their emotions and their feelings of isolation and fear.
"It is precisely the society itself, and, on a smaller scale, the
family, with its absence of close relationships, the sense of
isolation, the inability to communicate emotionally, which directly leads to a void in which chemicals become a substitute
for human feelings, emotional pleasure: love" (p. x). The
cure is, therefore, a psychological process which prevents the
individual from withdrawing and individuals communicate and
interact with others through group therapy.

Chambers, Carl D. "The Detoxification of Narcotic Addicts in Out-
patient Clinics," Major Modalities in the Treatment of Drug
Abuse. Edited by Leon Brill and Louis Lieberman. Boston:
Little, Brown, 1969.

Chambers states a case for outpatient detoxification: the
program is comparatively inexpensive. Rehabilitation occurs
while the patient is still part of a community setting with normal
responsibilities, stresses, and temptations. He provides

statistical data on a voluntary outpatient detoxification clinic
in Philadelphia. In June and July 1969, admissions (53 total)
were 28 years median age, 81 percent male, 68 percent employed, with 49 percent indicating that their primary source of financial support was illegal. Twenty-eight percent had been
arrested before age 16 and 25 percent had spent five years or
more in prison. Daily drug costs were $51 or more for 23 per-
cent, $31-50 for 21 percent, and below $30 for 57 percent.

A two year census showed that of 321 patients, 25 percent
were successful detoxifications and 24 percent were found to
be unsuited to the modality and transferred to a methadone maintenance program. The characteristics most associated with
dropping out of a sample of 86 addicts showed being married at
time of admission and quitting school early as significant factors.
Race, age, sex, and employment were not related to dropping
out. Analysis also suggested that relapse is highest among
younger addicts with short addiction records who detoxified
over a relatively short period of time, but further study is required for reliable verification.

Chambers, Carl D. An Assessment of Drug Use in the General Population. Special Report No. 1, Drug Use in New York State.
New York: New York State Narcotic Addiction Control Commission, May 1971.

Subsequently, A statewide (New York) epidemiological assessment of drug
use, not drug abuse, in 1970. This report gives results for
the total state; other reports refer to various geographical areas.
Primary emphasis was drug use in general population, with
secondary emphasis on an assessment of the accuracy of pre-
vailing beliefs about drugs and on awareness of and attitudes
towards persons abusing drugs. Data were obtained by interviews from a sample of persons 14 years and over.

Specific information was collected for 17 different drug
groups (such as barbiturates, tranquilizers [major and minor],
pep pills, diet pills, LSD, methedrine, heroin, cocaine, inhal-
ants). Users of all types were related to sex, employment, age,
ethnicity, socioeconomic status, education, place of use, and
if used with other drugs. Blacks and Puerto Ricans were either
underrepresented or proportionate to their distribution to the
general population among all types of drug use except heroin.
Blacks constitute the largest proportion of heroin users (37.5
percent). Generally, white females represent a disproportionate
number of users of legal drugs in comparison with males, and
white males predominate among the users of illegal drugs other

than heroin. (The only exception to these generalizations is among cocaine users, where the proportion of blacks and Puerto Ricans was found to be higher than their proportion in the total sample, but not nearly to the same extent as among heroin users.)

Chambers, Carl D. Differential Drug Use Within the New York State Labor Force. New York: New York State Narcotic Addiction Control Commission, July 1971.

A study of the use of various drugs by members of the labor force and within various occupational groups. The source of data was a statewide assessment of drug use in New York in 1970 through a representative sample of persons 14 years or over; this sample was used for projections for the total state population.

Of persons who had used heroin at least once (projected N = 149,000), 69 percent were currently employed. Of the regular users (at least six times a month) (N = 41,000), 83 percent were regularly employed. Sales and clerical workers had a higher incidence of regular heroin use than other occupational groups, while nonwhites predominated among the heroin users in most groups, but among sales workers the identified heroin users were exclusively white.

Chambers emphasizes that the incidence of heroin use determined in this survey is undoubtedly underrepresentative of the actual situation. The sample procedure drew subjects from among persons in regular residence; it did not include transient or institutionalized populations. Study procedure required only two "call-backs," and addicts are frequently out "taking care of business." Therefore, even those with regular residence were likely to be missed. Chambers estimates that the survey identified only about one-third of the heroin population—the least "dysfunctional" portion of it.

Chambers, Carl D., Walter R. Cuskey and William F. Wieland. "Predicators of Attrition During the Outpatient Detoxification of Opiate Addicts," Bulletin on Narcotics 22, no. 4 (October-December 1970): 43-8.

An assessment of the significant characteristics of addicts remaining in treatment which is based on a survey of 86 addict patients, 77.9 percent black, admitted to an outpatient methadone clinic between August and November, 1968. Fifty-nine of the patients (68.6 percent) terminated the detoxification process against medical advice. Only two variables were found to be significant: the more formal education the patients had, the

more likely they were to remain in treatment; and those addicts
who were married when they began treatment were more likely
to terminate treatment before detoxification. Those addicts who
were concurrently abusing other drugs as well as heroin at the
beginning of treatment were more likely to remain in treatment
than those abusing heroin alone. The authors surmise that this
happened because "addicts who concurrently abuse multiple
drugs will correctly perceive of their detoxifications as being
more difficult and requiring more time," whereas "heroin-only
addicts . . . would experience fewer physical and psychological
changes and would perceive of their detoxifications as being less
difficult and requiring less time" (p. 47).

Chambers, Carl D., R. Kent Hinesley and Mary Moldestad. "Narcotic
   Addiction in Females: A Race Comparison," International Journal of the Addictions 5, no. 2 (June 1970): 257-78.

   A statistical account of the social, addiction, and other deviancy characteristics of female addicts, based on the medical
records of 168 female addicts admitted to Lexington Hospital
between June and December, 1965. Two-thirds are white and
one-third is black. Significant race differences are found in all
three areas. In terms of social characteristics, black women
addicts are more likely than whites to come from broken homes
or from homes where the mother has an outside job and where
the father has a blue-collar job. They are more often found in
urban regions outside the South and more often support themselves through illegal activity. They also are more likely to
have intact marriages and are much younger than the whites. In
terms of their addiction characteristics, black women first use
marijuana, then experiment with opiates in the company of their
peers. They use heroin as their first opiate and prefer it to all
other drugs. They are currently addicted to heroin, which they
purchase illegally from pushers. In contrast, white female addicts do not use marijuana, begin using opiates for medical or
quasi-medical reasons, and use and prefer the legally manufac-
tured drugs, which they purchase from doctors or drugstores.
There is no racial differentiation on recidivism, although black
patients are more often admitted as prisoners than as voluntary
patients. In terms of history of other deviancies, black women
are more frequently prostitutes and pushers and therefore have
longer arrest records than white women. Black women are diagnosed as having personality trait disorders or sociopathic disturbances, whereas white women addicts are diagnosed as having
either "personality pattern or trait disorders."

Chambers, Carl D. and James A. Inciardi. "Some Aspects of the
    Criminal Careers of Female Narcotic Addicts," mimeographed,
    paper presented to the Southern Sociological Society, Miami
    Beach, Florida, May 1971.

A comparison of two separate interview studies revealing behavior patterns of female addicts, especially focusing on drug
selling and prostitution. The first study is of 168 females admitted to Lexington Hospital for addiction in 1965 (see Carl D.
Chambers, R. Kent Hinesley and Mary Moldestad, "Narcotic
Addiction in Females: A Race Comparison"). The second study
involves 52 females admitted to the New York State Narcotic
Addiction Control Commission during 1970. This comparison
reveals that while the incidence of drug selling among female
narcotic addicts has significantly increased from 25 percent to
38.5 percent, the incidence of selling as the only means of support among all female addicts has decreased from 17.7 percent
to 7.7 percent. Both incidence of prostitution and reliance upon
prostitution as complete support for the drug habit have decreased
significantly. The percentage of female addicts who admit en-
gaging in both prostitution and drug selling has remained constant,
between 13-17 percent. The data also suggest that there is no
significant change in the percentage of those female addicts who
neither sell drugs nor prostitute, around 45 percent of the total.
Approximately 50 percent of the female narcotic addicts in New
York City are black, 25 percent white, and 25 percent Puerto
Rican. Some of the preliminary findings on ethnic differences
are that Puerto Ricans sell drugs more frequently than either
whites or blacks, although whites are significantly more liable
to be arrested than blacks by 25 percent to 10 percent, and arrests
among Puerto Rican females are almost nonexistent. Approximately 40 percent of both white and Puerto Rican female addicts
prostitute, compared to 25 percent of the blacks. Black prostitutes, however, more frequently rely on this activity as their
primary or only means of support and consequently are more
often arrested for prostitution. White addicts more frequently
combine drug selling and prostitution to support their habits
than do black and Puerto Rican women. Some of the general
characteristics of the female addict are also summarized
briefly.

Chambers, Carl D. and Arthur D. Moffett. "Negro Opiate Addiction,"
    in The Epidemiology of Opiate Addiction in the United States.
    Edited by John C. Ball and Carl D. Chambers. Springfield,
    Illinois: Charles C. Thomas, 1970, pp. 178-201.

A documentation of evolutionary patterns associated with black opiate addiction and a description of the characteristics of the contemporary black addict. In the first part, the records of 26,674 black addicts admitted to Lexington and Fort Worth Hospitals between 1935-1966 are examined. Blacks have been overrepresented in the opiate addict population since shortly after World War II and have remained so to the present. Females have always been underrepresented in the black addict population, increasing from 10 percent before 1950 to 20 percent and remaining constant to the present. Recidivism (readdiction and then readmission to the hospital) has always been high: around one-third of all black admissions are recidivist. Between 1935 and 1945, 95 percent of all black admissions were prisoners, but since 1945 the number of voluntary admissions increased until by 1966 three-fourths of black patients were voluntary. Black opiate addicts are generally young adults, decreasing in mean age from 36 to 26 between 1935 and 1950 and then increasing from 26 to 30 between 1951 and 1966. Black addicts are concentrated in Northern urban areas, mainly New York and Illinois. In part two, the records of 832 blacks admitted to the two hospitals in 1965 are augmented by interviews with 155 of the admittees. The homogeneity of the contemporary black addict is revealed. Compared with normal black groups, the black addict is more likely to come from a broken home, more likely to drop out of school, more likely to have been married and then divorced or separated, and less likely to have legal employment. Black addicts turn to illegal and criminal activity for their economic support and are consequently arrested by law enforcement authorities. The pattern of marijuana use also appears to be an important independent variable in the age of onset of opiate use and the likelihood of the addict selling drugs, being arrested, and experimenting with other drugs.

Chambers, Carl D., Arthur D. Moffett and Judith P. Jones. "Demographic Factors Associated with Negro Opiate Addiction," International Journal of the Addictions 3, no. 2 (Fall 1968): 329-43.

Essentially a recapitulation of the article by Chambers and Moffett entitled "Negro Opiate Addiction."

Chambers, Carl D. and Mary Moldestad. "The Evolution of Concurrent Opiate and Sedative Addictions," The Epidemiology of Opiate Addiction in the United States. Edited by John C. Ball and Carl D. Chambers. Springfield, Illinois: Charles C. Thomas, 1970, pp. 130-46.

A presentation of the pattern of concurrent opiate and sedative addiction, revealed through the records of 400 voluntary
admissions to Lexington Hospital who live in urban areas and
were admitted in 1944, 1948, 1957, and 1966. The incidence
of concurrent sedative abuse has increased among opiate abusers
and has become the prevalent pattern of abuse. The incidence
of sedative addiction has increased among opiate abusers, while
addiction liability for sedative users has increased. Although
in 1944, 1948, and 1957, sedative abuse and addiction were more
frequent among white opiate abusers, by 1966 significant race
differences between white and black sedative abuse and addiction
had disappeared. Whites are still more likely to become addicted
to sedatives than blacks, however. In large urban centers, both
races tend to prefer and use the same drugs, to buy the drugs
from the same illegal sources, and to administer them in the
same manner and setting. The authors conclude that "the data
suggest the hypothesis that, given continuity of the current
circumstances surrounding opiate use, the incidence of sedative
abuse and addiction among opiate users may not significantly
increase beyond the 1966 level" (p. 146).

Chambers, Carl D., W. J. Russell Taylor and Arthur D. Moffett.
"The Incidence of Cocaine Abuse Among Methadone Maintenance
Patients," International Journal of the Addictions 7, no. 3 (Fall
1972): 427-41.

An examination of the abuse of cocaine among 173 heroin
addicts participating in the Philadelphia General Hospital outpatient methadone maintenance program during December, 1969.
There are 101 whites and 72 blacks. Through urinalysis, 32
are found to be using cocaine while still in the program and 141
are found not to be. The characteristics associated with cocaine
abusers in the program are that the majority are over 35 years
old, black, divorced or separated, unemployed, and have been
abusing drugs for a minimum of ten years, with continued involvement in illegal activities. Comparisons which do not produce statistically significant differences are sex, arrest histories,
previous treatment histories, and treatment and adjustment
characteristics. The urinalysis also revealed that 15 percent
of the 173 patients supplement their daily doses with methadone
purchased illegally, 84.2 percent are cheating with heroin, 60.8
percent with amphetamines, and 32.2 percent with barbiturates.
When confronted with the findings on cocaine, the addict patients
decrease use of cocaine; by 16 months after the experiment, the
incidence of cocaine abuse is 2.3 percent as revealed by random

urinalysis. "If the interpretation is accurate—that such confrontation can produce a decline in drug abuse behavior among methadone maintenance patients—it would be the most significant result
from this research effort" (p. 436).

Chappel, John N., Vickie M. Hayes and Edward C. Senay. Death and
the Treatment of Drug Addiction: A Five-Year Study of Deaths
Occurring to Members of the Illinois Drug Abuse Program
Chicago: Illinois Drug Abuse Program and the University of
Chicago Department of Psychiatry, 1973.

A report on deaths among 8,564 (71 percent black, 21 percent
white, 7 percent Hispanic, 1 percent other) addicts in
treatment at the Illinois Drug Abuse Program (IDAP), 1968-72.
Sources of information included in IDAP records, medical and
coroner reports, interviews with friends and relatives of the
deceased, and "street talk." Masking (covering-up) of the precipitating cause of death was prevalent among all sources.
The proportion of deaths among addicts was higher among
those in treatment (8.5/1000) than those out of treatment (2.8/
1000) because programs did not screen out those with medical,
psychiatric or alcohol problems. Death from drug overdose
(the most frequent cause of death among addicts) was much more
common among addicts out of treatment (55 percent) than those
in treatment (13 percent). Homicide was the second most frequent cause of death (19 percent of those out of treatment, 23
percent of those in) and cardiovascular causes the third most
frequent (7 percent among those not in treatment, 23 percent among those in). Differences in death rates by racial-ethnic
classification were not significant.

Chein, Isidor. "Narcotics Use Among Juveniles," Social Work 1, no.
2 (April 1956): 50-60.

A summary of the findings of his book, The Road to H, on
various aspects of drug addiction among teenage males: the
characteristics of the neighborhoods in New York City with
high incidence of heroin use, the relationship between rates
of drug addiction and other forms of delinquent activity, the
characteristics of home life and other behavioral and attitudinal
differences between heroin users and non users, drug use patterns in street gangs, and the attitudes, values and drug knowledge of teenage males. He finds that Puerto Rican and black
youths have the least amount of information on drugs and the
most favorable attitudes about heroin users among all teenage
males. Chein feels that the social and physical environment

influences the likelihood of drug addiction occurring and the
specific forms it takes. The kind of environment that is most
likely to breed drug addiction is characterized by widespread
poverty, low educational level, and a high proportion of broken
families. Individuals who "do not have strong internalized re-
straints and who, on the other hand, have various neurotic and
other needs such as an accumulated hostility against man and
society" (p. 59) are more likely to turn to drugs within the context of that environment. Chein perceives drug use among juveniles as only one stymptom of that breakdown and therefore
proposes a program for all personally damaged and culturally-
deprived youth, not just for drug abusers.

Chein, Isidor, Donald L. Gerard, Robert S. Lee and Eva Rosenfeld.
The Road to H: Narcotics, Juvenile Delinquency, and Social
Policy. New York: Basic Books, 1964.

A frequently cited classic study of patterns of juvenile drug
use in New York City in the early 1950s. Among the factors investigated are the characteristics of communities with a high
incidence of heroin use, the relationship between drug addiction
and other forms of delinquent activity, familial and attitudinal
characteristics of heroin users and non users, drug use patterns
in streetgangs, the personality of the addict, and the attitudes,
values, and drug knowledge of teenage males. Analyzing court,
police, and hospital records, the authors demonstrated that
juvenile drug use was heavily concentrated in the most economically and socially deprived neighborhoods. These areas of high
drug use were characterized by high proportions of blacks and
Puerto Ricans, low educational attainment, the highest poverty
rates, the most crowded living conditions, the highest incidence
of disrupted family life, and a dense population of teenagers,
especially juvenile delinquents.

In a questionnaire administered to classes of all eighth grade
boys in four junior high schools and seven parochial schools in
three areas widely differing in drug abuse incidence, the authors
found three interwoven strands in delinquent orientation: one
emphasizing the mood of pessimism, social isolation, futility,
and undependability of the future; one reflecting negative attitudes
to authority figures and to middle class values of behavior; and
one centering on the drug using subculture and reflecting much
of the delinquency orientation that was part of it.

The most famous part concerns drug use patterns in street
gangs. The authors studied 305 members of 18 delinquent
gangs in New York City with an exceptionally high rate of gang

warfare. Seven of the gangs were Puerto Rican, six black, two Italian, one Irish, and two Irish-Italian. In four gangs, there was no heroin use at all; in eight, less than half of the members use heroin; in six, more than half use heroin. About 80 of the gang members used marijuana only; those were exclusively black and Puerto Rican. The authors found that street gangs are not a major factor in the spread of heroin use. The gangs merely provide an environment in which use of drugs could develop, although they tended to discourage incontinent use and to satisfy needs that might otherwise lead to heroin use. "They offer a sense of solidarity and belonging, and they provide inadequate individuals with channels of achievement and recognition that enable such boys to avoid confronting their own inadequacy in the normal channels of legitimate competitive endeavor. It is apparently precisely at the point where the ganges become relatively inadequate in satisfying such needs and at the point where the threatening onset of adulthood becomes imminent that many of these individuals turn to narcotics. The Schiff study indicates that, for such individuals, the use of narcotics helps to preserve their self-esteem, presumably by freeing them of the obligation to confront their responsibilities as adults" (p. 192).

The pathological personality of the addict is discussed in terms of ego pathology, narcissism, and disturbance of sexual identification. The addict is seen as passive and with a low frustration tolerance, fatalistic, dependent, lacking self esteem, effeminate, fearing latent homosexuality, and with a peculiarly close relationship with his mother. The authors also describe in detail studies on psycho-physical factors in addiction, such as craving rather than dependence as the primary force in maintaining the cycle of addiction, and the family of the addict contributing to addiction, especially through the lack of a father figure and the lack of a spontaneous, warm, and flexible atmosphere.

In studying 20 females, eleven black, three Puerto Rican, and six white, admitted to the Riverside Hospital in New York City, they found that females are proportionately less involved with drugs than males. The female addicts begin to use drugs in the context of serious difficulties in terms of relationships and behavior at school, work, and home. Usually introduced to heroin by their female peers, they begin using heroin out of curiosity, They came from the same socioeconomic neighborhoods and families as the male adolescent addicts.

In the second part of the book, the authors offer suggestions on prevention and treatment of drug addiction among adolescents.

Cherubin, Charles E. "Clinical Severity of Tetanus in Narcotic Addicts in New York City," Archives of Internal Medicine 121, no. 2 (February 1968): 156-8.

A description of the clinical features of a new form of addict tetanus. The unusual features of this tetanus are the high frequency with which it occurs among black women (mainly from the Harlem area), the relative youth of the addicts infected, and its strikingly high mortality rate of 90 percent. The site of injury for most patients is the subcutaneous route. The symptoms of this new disease, its progress while the patient is hospitalized, and suggestions for further future treatment are discussed.

Cherubin, Charles E. "Investigations of Tetanus in Narcotic Addicts in New York City," International Journal of the Addictions 2, no. 2 (Fall 1967): 253-58.

A survey of tetanus among addicts and non-addicts in New York City from 1950-65. Cherubin cites his findings in "Urban Tetanus: The Epidemiological Aspects of Tetanus in Narcotic Addicts in New York City." Addict tetanus cases are likely to be black women in Harlem, while non-addict tetanus cases are likely to be white males distributed throughout the city. Compared to addicts in general, addict tetanus cases involve many more women, somewhat more blacks, and more Harlem dwellers. Cherubin also describes another study of 100 men and 100 women admitted to Morris J. Bernstein Institute for narcotic detoxification in 1966. The majority are in their twenties and thirties; 70 percent are Black, 15 percent white and 15 percent Puerto Rican. Nearly twice as many addicted women are unprotected from tetanus as addicted men. Cherubin suggests that a reaction to quinine, which is used by dealers to dilute heroin, and the greater female use of skin-popping instead of intravenous injection explain the concentration of tetanus in black women addicts in Harlem. Prevention of tetanus among addicts is a simple matter of immunization of all addicts seen in medical facilities and public institutions.

Cherubin, Charles E., "Urban Tetanus: The Epidemiological Aspects of Tetanus in Narcotic Addicts in New York City," Archives of Environmental Health 14, no. 6 (June 1967), 802-8.

A description of the characteristics and distribution of tetanus cases in New York City between 1937 and 1965 using records from the New York City Department of Health, Narcotics Registry Department and Department of Hospitals and three Manhattan

Municipal Hospitals. Cherubin compares tetanus in addicts to tetanus in non-addicts as revealed by these statistics and then compares addicts with tetanus to the addicted population. He finds that between 1955 and 1965 nearly 75 percent of all known tetanus cases in New York City occurred among narcotic addicts. Addicts differ significantly from non-addict tetanus cases who are predominantly white males over 50 years of age, whose incidence of illness is concentrated in the summer and who have a 38 percent fatality rate that is similar to the national rate. The addicts with tetanus are usually black women between 20 and 39 years of age who have no seasonal concentration of incidence and a case fatality rate of 87 percent and who live in Manhattan, particularly central and east Harlem. Although there are estimated to be four times as many men as women addicts, tetanus occurs two to three times more frequently among women addicts. There is a higher proportion of blacks and a lower proportion of Puerto Ricans and whites among addicts with tetanus than among the general addict population. Cherubin suggests reasons for this higher incidence of tetanus among women addicts and concludes by calling for tetanus immunization programs in all institutions treating addicts.

Cherubin, Charles E., Elaine Palusci and Mario Fortunato. "The Epidemiology of 'Skin Popping' in New York City," International Journal of the Addictions 3, no. 1 (Spring 1968): 107-12.

A report on the pattern of skin-popping heroin in New York City on the basis of an interview survey of 285 addicts in the detoxification wards at Morris J. Bernstein Institute in New York City. There are 58 whites, 92 Puerto Ricans, and 145 blacks in this survey. Whites and Puerto Ricans are overrepresented in terms of their proportions in the addict community; the results are really only statistically significant for blacks, since they are the only numerically accurately represented group. A much larger proportion of black women skin-pop than men. Furthermore, skin-popping seems to be more concentrated in Harlem than in other areas. One-fourth of the black women living in Harlem use this method compared to six percent from other areas. Nine percent of the male addicts in Harlem "skin-pop" compared to two percent elsewhere. Skin-popping is also found to increase with age. The authors conclude that "these findings help to explain the observed increased risk of tetanus among addict women and particularly in the Harlem area" (p. 111).

Clark, June S., William C. Capel, Bernard M. Goldsmith and
 Gordon T. Stewart. "Wives, Families and Junk: A Comparative
 Study of Wives of Heroin Addicts Maintained on Methadone,"
 Journal of Drug Issues 2, no. 1 (Winter 1972): 57-65.

 A study of wives of addicts in methadone maintenance clinics
of New Orleans in 1971-72 which uses interviews, home visits,
psychological tests (Eysenck) for introversion-extroversion and
neuroticism-stability, and IPAT (measure of anxiety) was a
source of data. The racial distribution of non-addicted wives
(N = 51) was 39 percent white and 61 percent black; among addicted wives (N = 22), 59 percent were white and 41 percent black.

 Results of the study included the following: appearances and
location of the homes of both groups were similar (neat, working
class); neither group was either especially religious or non-re-
ligious, most wives were not ignorant of their husbands' drug
use at the time of marriage; differences in psychological patterns (slightly more introversion and anxiety among the addicted
wives) did not seem sufficient to play an important role in family
life.

 The authors state that "none of the measures in this study
pointed to any startling differences between the family life of
heroin addicts maintained on methadone and the family which
would be expected of other persons in the same socioeconomic
condition who are not concerned with the problem of addiction."

Clinger, Orris W. and Nelson A. Johnson. "Purposeful Inhalation of
 Gasoline Vapors," Psychiatric Quarterly 25, no. 4 (October
 1951): 557-67.

 A detailed delineation of two cases of adolescent boys who
habitually inhale gasoline vapors. One male is a 16-year-old
black who lives in a rural area; the other is a 13-year-old white
from another neighborhood. Both use the inhalation of gasoline
vapors as a means of creating fantasies that blot out unpleasant
reality. They are both maladjusted individuals, with the black
displaying definite schizophrenic symptoms and the other a schizoid personality. The authors theorize that gasoline addiction
may be more prevalent than currently believed and that it occurs
among people with pre-existing defects in personality.

Coddington, R. Dean and Robert Jacobsen. "Drug Use by Ohio Adolescents: An Epidemiological Study," Ohio State Medical Journal
 68, no. 5 (May 1972): 481-4.

 An evaluation of the pattern and extent of drug use among
5,299 junior high and high school students in Ohio (some college

students are also included). The subjects are 50 percent male and 50 percent female, between the ages of 12 and 24, 80 percent white and 20 percent black, 32 percent urban and 28 percent rural, with the rest suburban. The use of alcohol and marijuana is seen to increase with age, leveling off during the college years. The peak incidence of heroin use is 16 years of age. Males show consistently greater use of all drugs than females. Total drug use is the same for both blacks and whites. Blacks, however, use less alcohol and more drugs other than marijuana. The authors feel that "the difference reflects the availability of drugs rather than a racial pattern" (p. 483). The urban and suburban youth are quite similar in their patterns of drug use, but the rural population is not yet feeling the impact of drugs. Those adolescents who do not identify with any religion show a greater use of all drugs. Most of the drug abuse occurs among 20 percent of the adolescent population, but the authors conclude that it is "a significant health problem requiring early case finding and educational as well as therapeutic programs" (p. 484).

Cole, K. E., Gary Fisher and Shirley S. Cole, "Women Who Kill: A Sociopsychological Study," Archives of General Psychiatry 19 (July 1968): 1-8.

A definition of operational behavior patterns of 112 females convicted of murder: the masochistic, the overtly hostile violent, the covertly hostile violent, the inadequate, the psychotic and the amoral. Variables of race, age, I.Q., the act of killing, use of alcohol or drugs, type of victim, type of weapon, previous criminal record, and brain dysfunction are found to be differentially associated with these behavior patterns. The behavioral pattern most involved with narcotics is the inadequate personality: half of these inadequate personalities are white, one-third are black, and one-sixth are Puerto Rican. The inadequate person kills by indirect action the most frequently of any other group; she uses a wide assortment of methods and her victims are her children, casual acquaintances, and strangers. Others who have some involvement with narcotics are the hostile violent overt and the psychotic.

Coles, Robert. "Drugs: Flying High or Low [Drug Addiction on Two Scenes: The Middle Class Youth and the Negro and Puerto Rican Poor]," Yale Review 57, no. 1 (Autumn 1967): 38-46.

A contrast between the reasons why black and Puerto Rican poor take drugs and why middle class white youth do. The ghetto poor take heroin and marijuana to escape from the reality of

tenements, poverty, and disease, whereas the whites take acid
and marijuana for self-actualization, a retreat into the self
from the hypocritical morality of the world in which they live.
Coles prefers the silent honesty of the black youth to the wordy
denunciations of property by white youth on drugs. He reveals
the irony that black youth on drugs aspire to the same material
possessions which the white youth on drugs renounce.

Collier, Walter V. "An Assessment of Prior Methadone Use by Residents of a Drug-Free Therapeutic Community," Journal of Drug
Issues 3, no. 4 (Fall 1973): 332-33.

Along with the increase in methadone treatment programs,
there has also been an increase in on-the-street use of methadone. One of the effects of these statistical trends has been an
increase in the numbers of previous methadone users and abusers
among individuals entering drug-free treatment programs. This
study sought to profile former methadone users within Daytop
Village's drug-free therapeutic community. The study also included a subinvestigation on the outcome of treatment within the
treatment community as a function of previous involvement within a methadone maintenance program.

Of all the residents in Daytop at the time of the study, 247—
or 51 percent—indicated they had used methadone previously.
Of these, 24 percent had been involved in a methadone maintenance
program and 76 percent had used methadone obtained on the
streets. Blacks (N = 85) were more likely to have used illegal
methadone than whites.

Cuskey, Walter R., T. Premkumar and Lois Sigel. "Survey of Opiate
Addiction Among Females in the United States Between 1850 and
1970," Public Health Reviews 1, no. 1 (February 1972): 5-39.

A review of the available published literature on the patterns
of female drug abuse. The authors summarize the history of female addiction from 1850-1970 and some definitions of addiction.
The behavioral and social characteristics of the female addict
during these different periods are described in terms of age,
regional distribution, race, religion, patterns of drug use, deviancy, and personality disorders. Family background, the addict couple, and marriage, divorce, and separation are examined,
as are complications in maternity, precipitate labor, premature
birth, low birth weight, dead babies, and addicted babies. A
brief prognosis of future drug patterns is also presented. By
1970 the authors find that "the developing patterns of opiate addiction, particularly heroin, become manifest and intense in

blacks before whites, in the poor before the well-to-do, and in
males before females. It is also true that . . . the whites and
females have been catching up more rapidly in the past decade
than ever before" (p. 20). The pattern for female addiction has
been evolving, like the men's, from the rural Southern white
who gets her drugs from medical sources and prefers codeine,
morphine and paregoric to the urban black who obtains her drugs
from illegal sources and prefers heroin. Another emerging
pattern of concern to the authors is that of legal sedative-hypnotic
and stimulant abuse among middle class women.

Dai, Bingham. Opium Addiction in Chicago. Montclair, New Jersey:
   Patterson Smith, 1970. (First published in 1937.)

   A pioneer analysis of the demographic characteristics, social
situations, and personality factors related to opium addiction in
Chicago in the early 1930s which uses data from the Federal
Bureau of Narcotics, Cook County Psychopathic Hospital, and
the Narcotics Division of the Chicago Police Department and
examines concentrations of addicts and conducts intensive interviews with selected addicts. He uses a sociological approach,
studying the opium habit in terms of the total personality of the
male addict and and his social and cultural context. He gives
a brief history of opium addiction in the United States and a
description of some pharmacological and cultural aspects of
addiction. He then proceeds to some general characteristics of
opium addicts in Chicago and their geographic distribution within
Chicago and to more detailed descriptions of social situations
and personality factors related to opium addiction; he uses many
excerpts from interviews. The social situations which breed
addiction are characterized by a marked absence of social control. Opium addicts are found to feel inferior or inadequate.
Although blacks and Chinese are addicts out of proportion to
their number in the population, Dai concludes that "opium addiction cannot be considered as a purely physical disease or a
vice that is inherent in the individual or race; it is essentially
a symptom of a maladjusted personality, a personality whose
capacity for meeting cultural demands has been handicapped by
inadequate emotional and social development, for which . . . the
general cultural chaos and social disorganization that is characteristic of modern society is mainly responsible" (p. 191). In-
terestingly, none of the interviewed addicts quoted is black or
Chinese.

Dale, Robert and Farley Ross Dale. "The Use of Methadone in a
    Representative Group of Heroin Addicts." International Journal
    of the Addictions 8, no. 2 (April 1973): 293-308.

A study of a representative group of heroin addict patients
admitted into a methadone maintenance treatment program. At
the end of two months, 199 of the original 814 were inactive
(no longer in the program); at the end of eight months, 322 were
inactive. In both cases, the majority were discharged for failure
to keep appointments. Blacks were more likely to become inactive
than Puerto Ricans or whites.

The longer persons stayed in treatment the more likely they
were to show "perfect" urine (urine without heroin or quinine).
A persistent ethnic difference appeared in urinalysis. Blacks
consistently showed a lower frequency of "perfect urine" than
Puerto Ricans or whites. After eight months, 35 percent of the
blacks showed a perfect record, as did 50 percent of the Puerto
Ricans and 86 percent of the whites. Twenty-four percent of the
blacks, 13 percent of the Puerto Ricans, and no whites failed
all urine tests. Yet blacks were less likely to say they would
have to use methadone maintenance as a lifetime treatment and
45 percent of the Puerto Ricans and 37 percent of the whites felt
the same way.

Social rehabilitation (measured by success at obtaining or
staying in school or on the job [30 percent of blacks, 33 percent
of Puerto Ricans, and 64 percent of whites]) showed that length
of time spent in the program increased the rate of success. A
decline of arrests was found with "prolonged" methadone maintenance: of the total group, those arrested 12 months prior to
treatment were 34 percent black, 37 percent Puerto Rican, and
40 percent white. After eight months on methadone, 15 percent
of blacks had been arrested, 13 percent of the Puerto Ricans,
and 9 percent of the whites.

The authors comment that "since black patients made up the
largest proportion of the addict population, it is admittedly dis-
appointing that they appear to do less well on methadone maintenance than other groups at least in these early studies. . . . It
should be pointed out that the long years of social, economic,
and political neglect of the Black ghetto have led to narcotic
addiction becoming an almost accepted way of life there; with
little more social stigma than that associated with the use of
alcohol in most other communities."

DeFleur, Lois B. "Biasing Influences on Drug Arrest Records: Im-
    plications for Deviance Research," American Sociological Re-
    view 40, no. 1 (February 1975): 88-103.

Official statistics are often used to identify deviance trends over time or in other types of deviance research. Distorting factors affecting the statistics can be either random or the result of systematic bias. This report deals with this problem and concludes that three decades of arrests for drug abuse by Chicago police reveal systematic bias for both whites and nonwhites on a varying basis over time.

Four areas which are sources of bias are discussed: first, the nature of the deviant activity (for example, street crime versus white collar crime); second, the climate of social control (for example, what the public expects or demands); third, the organization of agencies (for example, the number and attitudes of personnel); and fourth, the interaction between the offender, the public, and the control agency.

Data on arrests (1942-70) included information on place of arrest, type of charge, offender's residence, age, sex, and race (the nonwhite category is primarily black, but did include a small number of Asian Americans, American Indians, Puerto Ricans, and Mexican Americans).

Several trends were apparent. In the 1940s arrests of whites were few, but by the 1960s large numbers were being arrested for drug offenses, primarily in areas of changing populations. Among nonwhites, arrests in the 1940s were primarily in the near South Side (the inner-city area). In the 1950s there was a dramatic increase in arrests, with the center shifting farther to the south (a transition area). In the 1960s there was a drop in the number of arrests. Observations and interviews with police officers suggest that police attitudes and public demands at that time—rather than the actual incidence of drug abuse—explain the arrest figures of nonwhites in the 1950s. (Generally in the 1940s there was a lack of public concern, and only a small number of law enforcement officers were assigned to drug work.) A public drive in the 1960s against the use of hallucinogens is seen as affecting the increased number of white drug arrests during that period.

Other factors included in the analysis are: first, the passage of tighter legal search laws (leading, for example, to fewer arrests of nonwhites under the guise of loitering, which had previously been used); second, police fear of nonwhite community hostility (leading to fewer arrests); and third, the demeanor of the potential arrestee (the militant, both black and white, is more likely to be brought in, while the older addict plays it cool).

DeFleur concludes that bias does occur in arrests, and that when official statistics are used in research or otherwise the sources of bias, especially those which change over time, must be understood and assessed.

deLemos, Gaston. "Outpatient Treatment of Heroin Addiction: Patterns and Problems," Journal of Drug Issues 2, no. 4 (Fall 1972): 21-28.

A follow-up study at the end of a year of clients of an outpatient, walk-in treatment facility using methadone detoxification and psychotherapy. The discouragingly low number of "rehabilitated" persons (black and white) leads the author to consider that "no methadone treatment for heroin addiction should exist in a vacuum." Instead methadone should be used as an intervening agent of support along with extensive and intensive counseling, group therapy, and social and vocational rehabilitation.

DeLeon, George, Sherry Holland and Mitchell S. Rosenthal. The Phoenix Therapeutic Community: Changes in Criminal Activity of Resident Drug Addicts. Phoenix House Research Unit, Phoenix House: Studies in a Therapeutic Community (1968-73), MSS Publications Information Corporation, New York, 1974. A shortened version of this paper appears as "Phoenix House—Criminal Activity of Dropouts," Journal of the American Medical Association 222, no. 6 (November 1972): 686-89.

The purpose of this study was to explore the relationship between residency in a therapeutic community and criminal activity. Two samples were compared: 254 addicts (30 percent white, 39 percent black, 31 percent Spanish) who had been in a Phoenix facility but failed to complete the program, and 104 persons (43 percent white, 38 percent black, 18 percent Spanish) who had remained.

An analysis of arrests from a period of one year prior to residence to one year following residence showed a decrease in arrests for all categories of age, voluntary status, and length of residence (with the decrement increasing with longer residence). There is some indication of ethnic effect in the degree of decrease: Spanish addicts showed the smallest decrease, blacks came second, and whites had the greatest decrease. Ethnic differences, however, were considerably reduced among subjects remaining longer in the program. The authors hypothesize that the seeming reduction in drug-related criminal activity is related to the socialization aspect of the Phoenix programs.

DeLeon, George and Harry K. Wexler. "Heroin Addiction: Its Relation to Sexual Behavior and Sexual Experience," Journal of Abnormal Psychology 81, no. 1 (February 1973): 36-38.

An examination of the relationship between sexual disturbance and addiction to heroin by interviews of 31 male addicts residing

at a Phoenix House therapeutic community in New York City.
Nearly half are black; 12 percent Puerto Rican, and 40 percent
white. Their median age is 25 years. Median age at onset of
addiction (not use) is 16, and median age of first heterosexual
intercourse is 14. It is found that during addiction, the addict
experiences a "loss" of sexuality in terms of decreased frequen-
cies of intercourse, masturbation, and nocturnal emissions.
The proportion of orgasm drops; the sexual desire and quality
of orgasm are low, and the time to ejaculation is long. Sexuality
recovers in the post-addiction phase with all of these factors
reversed. "In view of these changes, it may be hypothesized
that any discomfort related to sexual arousal presumably would
be mitigated in the addiction period. This suggests that one of
the reinforcements in the use of heroin is its reduction of discomfort which may relate to experiences of sexual inadequacy
(e.g., performance failure, weakness, unmanliness)" (pp. 37-8).

Dembo, Richard. The Ex-Addict on After Care: An Employment Pilot
    Study. Phase II: The Personal Correlates of Job Response. New
    York: New York State Narcotic Addiction Control Commission,
    1970.

    An examination of the personal characteristics of 183 ex-
addicts who were clients of the employment unit of the Cooper
Community-based Center showed that marital status, physical
disorders, and frequency of drug arrests were significantly related to completing employment referral interviews and to beginning work or work training. Race and ethnic group membership, however, were not significantly related to ex-addicts'
response to employment counseling, job training, and work.

Drug Abuse Council. Survey of City/County Drug Abuse Activities,
    1972, MS-8. Washington, D.C.: Drug Abuse Council, Septem-
    ber 1973.

    A documentation, based on questionnaires sent to local gov-
ernmental bodies throughout the country, of the broad involvement of local governments in drug abuse prevention, treatment,
and control. Special attention was given to methadone maintenance programs, since this form of treatment has become widespread but remains controversial. Of approximately 14,000
methadone maintenance patients reported in 72 cities and 15,000
in 60 counties, the ethnic composition was 50 percent black, 38
percent white, 10 percent Mexican American, and 1 percent
Puerto Rican. The North Central region is the most reliant on
methadone maintenance as a treatment modality and is even

more dominated by black patients (75 percent). In the West, 48 percent of methadone patients were white, 36 percent Mexican American, 15 percent black, and 1 percent other. Ethnic analysis was not given on other aspects of drug abuse and treatment: employment, law enforcement, and so forth.

Drug Abuse Programs: A Directory for Minority Groups. Report
      Series 10, no. 3. Rockville, Maryland: National Clearing
      House for Drug Abuse Information, June 1973.

A list of Drug Abuse programs. Of the 322 programs listed, the majority offered treatment or rehabilitative services, which have at least 50 percent clients from minority groups (American Indian, Asian American, black, Mexican American, Puerto Rican).

Dupont, Robert L. "Coming to Grips with an Urban Heroin Addiction
      Epidemic," Journal of the American Medical Association 125, no.
      1 (January 1973): 46-48.

A report on the Narcotics Treatment Administration (NTA) program in Washington, D.C., which initiated a massive multimodality program in 1970 aimed at treating all of the city's heroin addicts within three years. He comments that the epidemic may have been stabilized, but that it was not ended. Several lessons had been learned through the first two years: first, the size of the addict population was grossly underestimated (original estimate of 5,000 was upped to 18,000): second, the unimodality clinic within a multimodality program is more appropriate than a multimodality clinic: third, careful monitoring (financial, managerial, and service) of contract agencies is necessary: fourth, developing contact with addicts through other means (such as courts and schools) is necessary—voluntary seeking out of treatment by the individual is not enough: fifth, recent "success" reports of treatment centers can be misleading; and sixth, law enforcement directed to reducing the supply of drugs must accompany treatment programs which are directed to reducing the demand for drugs by addicts.

DuPont, Robert L. "Profile of a Heroin-Addiction Epidemic," New
      England Journal of Medicine 185, no. 6 (August 5, 1971): 320-4.

An account of the rising epidemic of heroin addiction in Washington, D.C. Evidence for the epidemic is drawn from the rate of incarceration of narcotics offenders, the rate of heroin overdose deaths, the rate of narcotic-related arrests, and figures of addicts treated through the Washington heroin addiction treatment programs. According to these estimates, there are about 17,000 addicts, 2.2 percent of the total population of the city. Two-thirds of the addicts are under 26 years of age, 91 percent of them are black, and 74 percent are male. Over half of them began using heroin between 1966 and 1970. The concentration of addicts in the black community, the cost of the heroin epidemic to the community, and a possible solution through methadone maintenance are explored.

Duster, Troy. "The Moral Implications of Psychic Maladjustment in the Deviant," The Legislation of Morality: Law, Drugs, and Moral Judgment. New York: The Free Press, 1970, pp. 153-92.

A study of the resident addict population of the California Rehabilitation Center (CRC) from early 1964 through the spring of 1965 which includes a random sample of 103 males and 52 females who were interviewed (half had their files checked), and summary census data on the total CRC population of 1,303 in the last months of 1964. The ratio of males to females is nearly six to one and the median age is 25 years, with 45.9 percent of the total population under 25 and 75 percent under 30 years of age. Half of the males are Mexican Americans: blacks appear in proportion to their number in the population, ten percent. Among the females, nearly two-thirds are white, while 23 percent are Mexican American and 16.8 percent are black. Over 90 percent of the inmates have either working class or lower class occupations or a history of no employment. One of the most important findings is that 93 percent of the male inmates and 96.8 percent of the females have no jail history prior to offenses for the use of drugs. "This figure refutes the often heard claim that the drug addict population is a criminal population before it turns to drugs" (p. 170). The median age at which they first use drugs is 20 years. Duster's findings indicate that "the prospective addict sees himself as an exception to the pattern of addiction around him" (p. 180). Over 80 percent of those interviewed stated that although they knew narcotics were addictive, they did not believe that they themselves would become hooked. Typically, the prospective addict knows or knows of people who use narcotics but are neither addicted nor known to the police. The first contact with drugs is usually through a friend; "the addict seems to be drawn into a normal set of social relations and normal kinds of social behavior when he experiences the drug for the first time" (pp. 181-182). The female usually is drawn into drug use by her close emotional attachment to a lover or husband who uses heavily or is addicted.

"These findings suggest that the social dimension of the early
experimentation with narcotics is more than a simple desire to
conform to a deviant subculture or to rebel against middle-class
authority and morality. . . . It achieves its insidious anti-bour-
geois, anti-authority character from the response that later comes
from the authorities, agencies, and institutions committed to a
different moral-legal view of drugs" (p. 183). Duster points out
that most addicts feel morally inferior to non-addicts and feel
anger, resentment, and hostility towards others who are addicted. He concludes that society's reaction to addiction must be
changed, as must the addict's moral conception of himself, because the essence of the narcotics problem "does not lie within
the structure of the individual psyche, but in the prevailing social interpretation and social meaning of narcotics use" (p. 213).

Duvall, Henrietta J., Ben Z. Locke and Leon Brill. "Followup Study
of Narcotic Drug Addicts Five Years After Hospitalization,"
Public Health Reports 78, no. 3 (March 1963); 185-93.

An assessment of the social characteristics and addiction
status of 453 addicts five years after they were discharged
from Lexington Hospital between 1952 and 1955 and became residents of New York City. Over 97 percent become readdicted, but
by the fifth year of discharge only 46 percent became readdicted,
while 49 percent are abstinent, either voluntarily or involuntarily.
White males over 30 years old have the highest rate of voluntary
abstention, while black females have the lowest rate. Black males
have the highest rate of involuntary abstention, white males the
lowest, and Puerto Rican males are in the middle. There are
not, however, significant statistical differences among the groups
with respect to factors of age, sex, and race in terms of the
pattern of abstinence. Age is the important factor in voluntary
abstinence: dischargees over 30 years of age have a significantly
higher rate of voluntary abstinence compared to the younger
ones, and also a significantly greater ability to remain drug-free.
Readdiction rates decrease with the passage of time. While 70
percent of the sample have been arrested at least once in the
five year period, the under-30 age group has a higher arrest rate
than the older ones. The overwhelming majority of the arrests
are due either to narcotics law violations or illegal means of
supporting their habit. "This adds impetus to the conjecture that
it is the influence of narcotics which makes the criminal and not
the criminal which makes the narcotics addict" (p. 193). The abstinent addicts show a significantly higher rate of full employment. The authors conclude by proposing the need for systematic
community aftercare.

Eckerman, William C. Drug Usage and Arrest Charges: A Study of
  Drug Usage and Arrest Charges Among Arrestees in Six Metro-
  politan Areas of the United States. (Final Report). Washington,
  D.C.: Drug Control Division, Office of Scientific Support, Bu-
  reau of Narcotics and Dangerous Drugs, U.S. Department of
  Justice, (December 1971).

A study whose purpose is to provide data on the actual crime
pattern among drug users, and especially to determine whether
there has been a shift in recent years from less serious to more
serious crimes (particularly those involving personal violence).
The data were collected by an outside research organization.
The scope of study is approximately 1,800 arrestees, 300 each
from six metropolitan areas (New York, Los Angeles, Chicago,
St. Louis, San Antonio, and New Orleans). The racial-ethnic
background of the arrestees varied by area, but the largest
group among the total was Negro (57 percent). This reflects
the fact that the study locations were in central cities with large
Negro populations. Caucasians represented 25 percent of the
total, Mexican Americans 12 percent (largely in the Los Angeles
and San Antonio areas), Puerto Ricans 5 percent, and others
1 percent.

For analysis, the arrestees were divided into categories of
drug user and non-drug user based on urinalysis, questionnaire
data, and crime and drug registers. The findings were that non-
drug users had a higher representation among those currently
charged with serious crimes against the person (homicide, forc-
ible rape, kidnapping, and aggravated assault) than drug users.
This pattern held true for all types of drug users, but was especially true of heroin users.

Arrest rates for drug users were higher than for non-drug
users over time, and for three time periods (prior to 1960,
1960-63, and 1964-67) the rate of crimes against persons was
higher for the drug user group than non-drug users. In the period
1968-71, there was a downturn in the arrests for serious crimes
against persons among drug users. Arrestees currently using
heroin were less likely (7 percent) to commit serious crimes
against persons (homicide, rape, aggravated assault) than non-
drug users (24 percent) or than current amphetamine users (10
percent) or barbiturate users (13 percent). However, drug
using arrestees were more likely to commit property crimes
than non-users. Among arrestees, robbery charges are more
common among drug users (18 percent) than non-users (11 percent).

Edmondson, William R. "The Narcotics Addiction Epidemic," The
  Crisis 74, no. 3 (March 1972): 79-82.

   A brief article summarizing some statistics about drug addiction, the nature of addiction to various opiates, hallucinogens,
   and the use of marijuana, and some of the solutions to heroin
   addiction, such as day care centers, methadone maintenance
   and therapeutic communities. Edmondson favors the therapeutic
   communities, which are based on attitudinal and behavioral
   change. He does not mention race at all as a factor in addiction,
   although he is black and a significant number of readers of The
   Crisis are black.

Edmundson, Walter F., John E. Davies, James D. Acker and Bernard
  Myer. "Patterns of Drug Abuse Epidemiology in Prisoners,"
  Industrial Medicine 41, no. 1 (January 1972): 15-19.

   A health survey of 470 prisoners in the Dade County Jail in
   Florida in April and May, 1970, with a population that is 92 percent male and 8 percent female, 60 percent black and 40 percent
   white. More whites (58 percent) than blacks (43 percent) use
   illicit drugs. Only one regular drug user is over 40 years of
   age. In contrast, regular alcohol use is distributed equally
   among all age groups of both races. Heroin is the preferred
   drug of 35 percent of the white and 18 percent of the black drug
   abusers. The patterns of drug use by 209 prisoners reveal that
   multiple drug use is common, although heroin and marijuana
   usually are the most preferred. Over 80 percent of the regular
   drug users first begin using illicit drugs when under 21 years
   of age, while 20 percent experiment with drugs before they are
   16. No difference in initiation patterns is found between males
   and females, whites and blacks. Some of the socioeconomic,
   health and criminal charges patterns are described. Drug users
   are found to have nine times more frequent a history of hepatitis
   than non-drug users, thus demonstrating a health risk directly
   associated with the injection of illicit drugs.

Einstein, Stanley. "The Future Time Perspective of the Adolescent
  Narcotic Addict," Drug Addiction in Youth. Edited by Ernest
  Harms. Oxford: Pergamon Press, 1965, pp. 90-98.

   Three studies on 98 male and female adolescent addicts'
   future time perspective, compared with non-drug using delinquents and non-using, non-delinquent adolescents. The adolescents are black, white, and Puerto Rican. Ethnicity and sex
   are other variables tested for differentiation. It is found that

sex, ethnicity, and non-drug using delinquency are not associated with significant differences in future time perspective. The future time perspective of both the adolescent addicts and the non-drug using delinquents, however, is significantly shorter than that of their non-using, non-delinquent peers. Einstein explains some of the factors influencing these results, such as mistrust of the future due to lack of success in the past and narcotic usage as heavily oriented to the present, and reinforcing the inability to postpone immediate gratification.

Einstein, Stanley and David Laskowitz. "Attitudes Toward Authority Among Adolescent Drug Addicts as a Function of Ethnicity, Sex and Length of Drug Use," Drug Addiction in Youth. Edited by Ernest Harms. Oxford: Pergamon Press, 1965, pp. 86-89.

Examination of the role of ethnicity, sex, and length of drug use in influencing attitudes toward authority among 235 adolescent addicts entering Riverside Hospital in New York City from September, 1960 through June, 1961. As a partial control, 28 male non-drug using delinquents from Rikers Island are compared to the first group. Both groups are white, black, and Puerto Rican, range from 17 to 21 years of age, have a minimum of eighth grade education and an I.Q. range from 83 to 112. With the exception of ethnicity, none of the other factors tested are found to be significant variables influencing attitudes toward authority; nor is there any significant difference between adolescent male addicts and adolescent male non-using delinquents. The Puerto Ricans are found to be the most accepting of authoritarian attitudes, while the blacks are intermediate and the whites are the least accepting.

Ellinwood, E. H., Jr., W. G. Smith and G. E. Vaillant. "Narcotic Addiction in Males and Females: A Comparison," International Journal of the Addictions 1, no. 2 (June 1966): 33-45.

A comparison of the patterns of narcotic addiction among male and female patients admitted to Lexington Hospital. A psychiatrist interviewed 81 men and 30 women. The chief difference noted was that four times as many men were addicts as women. Three-fourths of the patients were from urban areas. Both males and females were an average age of 31; 60 percent were white and 40 percent were black. The general pattern of drug use was also similar, with two-thirds of both sexes revealing a subcultural motivation, such as curiosity or "kicks," and both sexes overwhelmingly using heroin. Women appeared to manage longer habits and experienced less legal difficulty than

men; more women than men were married or living with someone
of the opposite sex. Family backgrounds were similar, except
that men tended to come from larger families. Differences in
family dynamics and cultural factors were also noted.

Feldman, Harvey W. "Ideological Supports to Becoming and Remaining
a Heroin Addict," Journal of Health and Social Behavior 9, no.
2 (June 1968): 131-9.

A challenge to the traditional explanations of drug addiction
resulting from psychological predisposition and emotional problems or from a retreatist adaptation to slum life. Feldman uses
his personal observations as a social worker for six years in the
Lower East Side of New York City and data from the drug addiction ward of an eastern hospital. The author sees drug experimentation arising within a context "where rewards of high status
and prestige are confered upon action-seeking youth who strive
to become stand-up cats by becoming involved in behavior that
is exciting, daring, tough and dangerous" (p. 137). Slum youth
turn to drugs in order to achieve high status within their community. Whether or not they become confirmed users of heroin
depends on whether they experience pleasure from heroin use.
If they begin a career in drugs then they renounce the routine
activities of the "stand-up cat" and become involved in a drug
consuming subculture.

Fiddle, Seymour. Portraits from a Shooting Gallery: Life Styles
from the Drug Addict World. New York: Harper and Row, 1967.

A description of the unity and diversity of the lifestyles of
drug addicts, based on the work with addicts that Fiddle conducted for several years at Exodus House, a therapeutic community. The book points out some of the myths about drug addiction, six life patterns of the addict (the pseudo life of the
husler, the passive life, the obsessional life, the paranoid life,
the depressed life, and the retreatist life), and various aspects
of the heroin subculture. Fiddle suggests that addiction is an
exaggerated state of the existential existence of modern man:
alienated, free, and without direction, and founded in existential anguish. The main part of the book is devoted to transcripts
of three lengthy tape-recorded interviews with male addicts.
One is black and characterized by paranoic tendencies. Another
is a 39-year-old Puerto Rican whose rigidity has led "progres-
sively, if not continuously, [to tendencies] toward more and more
dependence on sharply defined frames of reference, one of which
was the addict culture" (p. 240). It also contains eight cameo

portraits of other drug addicts, six of whom are black or Puerto
Rican, to indicate through a synopsis of their lives the diversity
among addicts. Fiddle concludes with recommendations for treatment, focusing on the value of therapeutic communities like
Synanon and Exodus House in treating this existential problem.

Finestone, Harold. "Cats, Kicks and Color," Social Problems 5, no.
1 (July 1957): 3-13.

A discussion of the characteristics of young black drug users,
based on intensive interviews between 1951 and 1953 with over
50 male black users of heroin in Chicago. He portrays the "cat"
(black male drug addict) as representing an indirect attack against
central conventional values, through use of manipulative techniques rather than an overt attack to get his way; through his rejection of planning for the future and his emphasis on the importance of the "kick." Finestone shows that the generic features
of the social orientation of the "cat" are those of play, as defined by Johan Huizinga in Homo Ludens. Many of the interests
of the "cat" are seen as an extreme form of the adolescent youth
culture, while the social type of the "cat" represents " a reaction to a feeling of exclusion from access to the means towards
the goals of our society," due to his color and tradition (p. 13).
This article is often cited as depicting the prototype of the black
male addict.

Fort, John P., Jr. "Heroin Addiction Among Young Men," Psychiatry
17, no. 3 (August 1954): 251-59.

An analysis from a psychiatric point of view of 100 male
heroin addicts, mainly in their twenties, at Lexington Hospital
in 1951 and 1952. They are from big cities; over half are black
and there are a "large number" of Puerto Ricans from New York
City. The blacks are Protestant; the whites are more often
Jewish and Roman Catholic than Protestant. Although there is
great variation in their economic background, few come from
conditions of real poverty. Most of them are introduced to
heroin by friends who are already addicts. Fort attacks the
concept of the psychopathic personality of the addict, finding
instead that most addicts exhibit neurotic character disorder.
They are particularly characterized by a striking lack of good
masculine identification and by the all-embracing presence of
the mother, which results in mixed feelings of love and violent
hostility toward the mother. This pattern is especially prevalent
among black patients, whose families are matriarchal, that
is, mother-dominated. In order to cover up their basic lack

of masculine identity and their dependency, they often turn to violent aggression; drugs are a means of escaping from the unhappiness caused by these aggressive feelings, since a noteworthy characteristic of heroin addiction is its inhibition of aggression. Heroin use serves many purposes: it vanquishes addicts' doubts, fears, and guilt, inhibits their frightening aggression, and provides a ceremonial group association. Fort calls for group and individual psychotherapy to treat these deviants and counsels toleration and moderation in treatment for those using drugs as an attempt to solve their problems.

Fort, John P. "The Psychodynamics of Drug Addiction and Group Psychotherapy," International Journal of Group Psychotherapy 5, no. 2 (April 1955): 150-6.

Observations of personality features of the addict and progressive stages in group therapy as noted at Lexington Hospital with young male heroin addicts, over half of whom are black. Fort notes especially the addicts' lack of self-esteem and high degree of potential anxiety, against which they build a complex system of defenses. He finds that addicts need to be in a group with other addicts to explore their problems and to discover their similarities and then differences without group rejection. Fort outlines some of the problems which addicts must face after preliminary work in a group, such as anxiety about homosexuality, aggressive response, and emergence of tolerant group standards. "The key to the value of the group seems to be . . . the possibility of group support diminishing the anxiety and making it possible thereby to bring the defenses into awareness. The difficulty seems to lie in the new dependence on the group" (p. 155).

Gasser, Edith S., John Langrod, Katherine Valdes and Joyce Lowinson. "The Eysenck Personality Inventory with Methadone Maintenance Patients," British Journal of Addiction 69, no. 1 (March 1974): 85-88.

The Eysenck Personality Inventory (designed to measure extroversion-introversion and neuroticism-stability), which includes a Lie Scale, was administered to three small groups: group one, 20 new admissions to methadone maintenance (six black, three Hispanic, and eleven white): group two, 19 long-term methadone maintenance patients employed as counselors (ethnic distribution similar to group one): and group three, 34 college psychology students (mainly white).

There were no significant differences correlated with ethnic background, age, sex, previous treatment, or other medical problems between and within groups. Short-term heroin users showed a stronger tendency to neuroticism features than long-term users. The student group showed a higher Lie Score, indicating less frankness in admitting feeling and behavior than the other two. The authors conclude by this measurement that former heroin patients on methadone maintenance are no more anxious or incapable of coping with stress than so-called "normals."

Gearing, Frances Rowe. Reports to Methadone Maintenance Evaluation Unit, Columbia University School of Public Health and Administrative Medicine, New York City. "Successes and Failure in Methadone Maintenance Treatment of Heroin Addiction in New York City," November 10, 1970; "Methadone Maintenance Treatment Programs in New York City and Westchester County, Progress Report for 1971: The Year of Expansion," April 28, 1972; "Methadone Maintenance Treatment: A Six Year Evaluation," August 21, 1972; "Methadone Maintenance Treatment: Five Years Later, Where Are They Now?" November 8, 1972; "Arrest Histories Before and After Admission to a Methadone Maintenance Treatment Program," No date, about 1970; "Methadone Maintenance Treatment Programs Progress Report for 1972: Developing Trends and A Look to the Future," June 1, 1973.

With the initiation in the early 1960s of an experimental methadone maintenance treatment program in New York City by Dole and Nyswander, Gearing was appointed to head an independent evaluation unit of that program. Some of the results of her ongoing evaluative research from 1970-73 are in the above reports.

In summary, the findings for the situation from 1965-73 are: Methadone maintenance in New York during this period has increased dramatically (under 3,000 admitted in 1970: 33,000 in 1973). Treatment units, originally inpatient, have become predominantly ambulatory. Privately run units have proliferated in recent years. (These are not under Gearing's surveillance or evaluation.) The racial pattern among admissions has been relatively constant except for an increase in Hispanic patients in the later years (1969-70 admissions: 40 percent white, 40 percent black, 18 percent Hispanic, and 2 percent other; 1972: 32 percent white, 40 percent black, 24 percent of Spanish origin, and 1 percent other). Males predominate, but in recent years the proportion of females has increased. The median age has

declined. The one year retention rate was 73 percent for the
total period for inpatient programs and 78 percent for ambulatory
programs. The Westchester County (suburban) group showed a
lower retention rate (61 percent). There were no observable
ethnic differences in retention rates.

The reasons for discharge from the programs show some
ethnic differences (for example, most blacks, both male and
female, are discharged for alcohol abuse; most whites and
Hispanics, male and female, for drug abuse).

Those who remain in the methadone maintenance programs
show substantial change based on the four criteria on which
success is measured: marked reduction in heroin use, decrease
in arrests, increase in employment or education, and greater
willingness to accept help for other problems, such as alcohol
abuse or psychiatric problems. These improvements cut across
ethnic lines.

Gearing, Frances Rowe, Methadone Maintenance Treatment Program—
Progress Report for 1973—The Year of Change, New York:
New York State Drug Abuse Control Commission, July 1974.

By mid-1972, waiting lists for admission to public treatments
had disappeared. Admission to public treatment units decreased
between 1972 (N = 16,020) and 1973 (N = 10,950), but admissions
to privately-run units increased. More than half of all 1973 admissions were in private units as compared to only 28 percent
in 1970 and 1971.

The changes in demographic characteristics of the more
recent admissions are seen to be an increase in younger addicts,
in females, and in proportion of Hispanics.

Admissions in the last couple of years are less likely to be
employed: they have a higher incidence of serious medical problems, poly drug use (including alcohol) is greater, and they
have more arrest records and a higher degree of "behavior
problems." These trends are particularly observable among
female admittees. There is a higher rate of deaths in the recent
cohorts. Death, especially among males, is more likely to be
of a violent nature.

Of those admitted over the period 1964-73, black patients
have a lower retention rate (staying in the program) than other
ethnic groups.

Observation of ongoing treatment reveals that there has been
an increase in persons selecting long-term detoxification (N =
445, or 4 percent) and in those who have become completely
methadone free (N = 355, or 3 percent). However, 270 patients (2

percent) have tried detoxification but have gone back to high
dosage methadone maintenance.

Gearing, Frances Rowe, Methadone Maintenance Treatment for Heroin
   Addiction in New York City—An Eight-Year Prospective Over-
   view, New York: Columbia University School of Public Health,
   July 1974.

   The methadone maintenance program in the New York City
   areas has grown from a one unit facility serving six persons in
   1964 to one in which, by 1973, 40, 600 patients were being treated
   in 168 separate treatment units. This evaluative report gives
   information on the age, sex, and ethnic characteristics of the
   patients over that time period. Changes in social productivity
   (as measured by employment and/or schooling), problems (such
   as alcohol and health) that hamper rehabilitation, changes in
   patterns of arrest, and changes in mortality rates are related
   especially to date of admission and to sex.
   The ethnic breakdown of the entire patient population (1964-
   73) is 32 percent white, 42 percent black, 25 percent Spanish,
   and 1 percent other (N = 44, 220). This pattern remained
   the same for blacks over the various time periods, but among
   Hispanics the rate showed a steady increase, from 19 percent
   in 1968 to 27 percent in 1973.

Gearing, Frances Rowe and Dina D'Amico. The Hispanics and Asiatic
   Populations on Methadone Maintenance in New York City, A
   Study in Contrast. Mimeographed. Report to Methadone Main-
   tenance Evaluation Unit, Columbia University School of Public
   Health and Administrative Medicine, New York City, October
   15, 1974.

   See annotation in Section 5: "Drug Use and Abuse Among
   Puerto Ricans."

Gearing, Frances Rowe and Morton G. Schweitzer. "An Epidemiologic Evaluation of Long-Term Methadone Maintenance Treatment for Heroin Addiction," American Journal of Epidemiology,
   100, no. 2 (August 1974): 101-12.

   An epidemiological evaluation of long-term methadone maintenance treatment of heroin addicts. Four cohorts selected by
   date of their admission to the maintenance program were studied
   for demographic characteristics, death rates, increase in social
   productivity (as measured by employment, schooling, vocational
   training, or homemaker activities), and decrease in anti-social
   behavior, especially as measured by number of arrests.

The four cohorts differed in that the first group entered the program when almost all patients were involved in an inpatient program; later, most cases were ambulatory. All were voluntary treatment seekers. Ethnically, about 40 percent of each cohort were black, but the percentage of persons of Spanish origin among total numbers increased in the later admissions—from 19 percent of the total in first cohort (1964-68) to 26 percent of the 1971 cohort. Orientals numbered about 1 percent of each group and had a considerably higher average age (52 years). In the first group (which covered a span of five years) the total number was 1,330; in 1971 alone there were 12,080 admissions, reflecting the marked acceleration in opening of treatment units.

Socially productive behavior of the patients increased with length of time in the maintenance program, their arrest records decreased, and their death rate leveled out to resemble the death rate for the general New York population.

About 25 percent of the treatment patients do not seem to become socially rehabilitated: alcohol and other drugs (such as barbiturates and amphetamine) are found to be used by this group. Alcohol is the major problem for patients over 30 and for blacks; multiple drug abuse is more commonly the problem of the white and/or younger addicts.

Gerard, Donald L. and Conan H. Kornetsky. "Adolescent Opiate Addiction: A Study of Control and Addict Subjects," Psychiatric Quarterly 29, no. 3 (July 1955): 457-86.

An evaluation of the significance of personality malfunction and familial socioeconomic status as factors in drug addiction among 32 adolescent males 16-21 years of age admitted to Lexington Hospital and compared with a control group of 23 subjects matched by factors such as sex, age, and ethnic background. Sixty-eight percent of the addicts are black, 15 percent Puerto Rican, and 15 percent white. The authors find that "the addicts exceeded the controls in personality malfunction to a statistically significant and clinically impressive extent" (p. 484). The data support their hypothesis that psychiatric pathology is an important factor in addiction and that addiction is therefore "a highly individualized process" (p. 484). Their data on the familial socioeconomic status of the addicts suggest that the attitudes and expectations of the parents, rather than just socioeconomic status, are a key factor in addiction. They conclude that other more subtle emotional factors in family background are also important, such as "denial of limitations, wish-fulfilling distortions of reality, and an orientation toward status goals rather than toward goals of satisfactions and security" (p. 485).

Gerard, Donald L. and Conan Kornetsky. "A Social and Psychiatric Study of Adolescent Opiate Addicts," Psychiatric Quarterly 2, no. 1 (January 1954): 113-25.

A report of the social and psychiatric characteristics of 32 adolescent male opiate addicts admitted to Lexington Hospital. The majority are black and Puerto Rican youth living in low status segregated communities, but their families are usually comfortable economically, with middle class status, education and values. Therefore, the authors conclude that "there is no essential relationship between drug addiction and membership in particular socioeconomic groups" (p. 115). Their families are, however, characteristically "productive of serious difficulties in adjustment" (p. 117). All of the subjects show marked disturbances in their adjustment patterns: they exhibit schizophrenia, delinquency-dominated character disorders, or inadequate personalities. Several common adaptive functions of opiate addiction are described: the difficulties of functioning as a drug addict make easier the avoidance of the patient's problems; opiate use helps to treat some of the overt psychiatric symptomology; and drugs help to relieve and control the stress and anxiety which are felt in interpersonal relationships. "Opiate drug use gave, to these patients, regressive and oral satisfactions which were accompanied by a feeling of comfortable separateness from, and a lack of involvement in, their current difficulties in living" (p. 125).

Glaser, Daniel, James T. Inciardi and Dean V. Babst. "Later Heroin Use by Adolescent Marihuana-Using, Heroin-Using, and Non-Drug-Using Adolescent Offenders in New York City," International Journal of the Addictions 4, no. 2 (June 1969), 145-55.

A study of the extent to which marijuana use leads to heroin use, based on a five and ten year follow-up of New York City teenage males, including blacks and Puerto Ricans who were referred to the New York City Youth Counsel Bureau from 1957-68 and not brought before court. It is found that approximately 50 percent of those referred as adolescent heroin users have adult records of heroin use; 40 percent of the adolescent marijuana users become adult heroin users; and 15 percent of the non-drug using delinquents become heroin using adults. Higher rates of subsequent heroin use are revealed for those non-drug using adolescents who are black or Puerto Rican, have two or more co-defendants, have dropped out of school, or have prior referrals to court. The authors caution that these results are obtained from slum delinquents, and are therefore probably not so applicable to suburban marijuana using youth.

Glaser, Daniel, Bernard Lander and William Abbott. "Opiate Addicted and Non-Addicted Siblings in a Slum Area," Social Problems 18, no. 4 (Spring 1971), 510-21.

A comparison of 37 addicted and 37 non-addicted siblings of families residing in a slum area in New York City made in order to seek explanations for addiction to opiates. They interpret the data as supporting the "relative deprivation-differential antici-pation theory" which explains contemporary drug usage "primarily by the fact that this usage gives addicts a sense of belonging and achievement, even many periods of hope, in sharp contrast to the 'atonie' or tonelessness' for them of the square scene" (p. 512). The typical male addict differs from his non-addict sibling in his early involvement in delinquency, use of marijuana, arrest, incarceration, and limited schooling and employment. They also found a significant difference in early reference group orienta-tion in these sibling pairs. The addicts are involved at an early age in the illegal institutions of the street, while the non-addicted seek conventional employment.

Glaser, Daniel and Mary Snow. Public Knowledge and Attitudes on Drug Abuse in New York State. New York: New York State Narcotic Addiction Control Commission, 1969.

A market research firm was hired to pick a representative sample from among New York State residents to survey their responses to questions about drug use in their neighborhood, how much they knew about narcotics, what they knew and felt about treatment facilities, and information on the most effective educational media regarding drug abuse. The sample was of 6,106 persons; those 13 years old and over were surveyed.

When asked which of a list of 12 social problems existed in their neighborhoods, blacks and Puerto Ricans mentioned more problems than whites. Burglary was the most cited problem for all groups, but drug abuse was second for blacks and Puerto Ricans and only fifth for whites. In the suburbs, drug use was ranked third by whites and fifth for blacks. City residents in general and blacks in particular mentioned more problems ex-isting in their neighborhoods than did the other people questioned in the survey. Asked if they personally knew people who used drugs, 20 percent of the whites residing in New York City, 17

percent of the blacks, and 17 percent of the Puerto Ricans said
they knew someone who used marijuana. Asked the same question
regarding heroin, the percentages respectively were 7 percent, 12 percent, and 12 percent. However, among 17-19 year
olds, the figures were 52 percent, 42 percent, and 46 percent
for marijuana, and 16 percent, 26 percent, and 24 percent for
heroin. Acquaintance with amphetamine and barbiturate users
was more frequent among whites than among either blacks or
Puerto Ricans. About 25 percent of the Puerto Rican respondents in New York City said they didn't know what they would do
if a member of their family were a drug user, with both older
and very young subjects responding in this way. Puerto Ricans
were also inclined to say they favored locating treatment facilities in the neighborhood where drug problems exist. Generally,
however, persons who know drug users are more willing for
treatment facilities to exist in the local neighborhoods.

Gottlieb, David. "Alienation and Rebellion Among the Disadvantaged."
    Drug Dependence: A Guide for Physicians. Chicago: American
    Medical Association, 1969, pp. 53-61.

    An interpretation of the characteristics and goals of black
    male addicts in the ghetto, based on interviews with and records
    of black male Job Corps enrollees. It is found that they have
    middle class aspirations, seeking acceptance and material pros-
    perity, in contrast to rebelling middle class white youth. Gott-
    lieb finds that the black youth have suffered discrimination due
    to their race in education, employment, medical attention, and
    from instability in the home. He describes some of their gene-
    ral characteristics, focusing on the failure of black fathers to
    participate actively in the socialization of their children and on
    the reliance of black adolescent males on their mothers. Black
    children turn to drugs to escape from an unpleasant reality, as
    an adaptation to maladjustment. Since Gottlieb sees addiction
    in the slums as "intimately linked with poverty and other social
    abuse," the only way to eliminate drug addiction in the long run
    is "to admit the deprived to equal participation" (p. 60) in the
    affluent society.

Greene, Mark H. and Robert Dupont. "Heroin Addiction Trends,"
    American Journal of Psychiatry 131, no. 5 (May 1974): 545-50.

    Data collected from various sources indicate that heroin use
    in Washington, D.C. peaked in 1969 and has declined steadily
    since that date. Two general explanations are given: availability
    of various treatment facilities, and a major law enforcement

effort toward the reduction of a supply of heroin in the city.
New drug abuse problems were observed: illicit or street methadone and an increase in amphetamines. The authors comment
that "there still exists a demand for opiates and a better understanding of the etiology of drug-abusing behavior" continues to
be a critical need.

Grupp, Stanley E. "A Note on the Use of Lexington Subjects to Investigate Addict Mobility," International Journal of the Addictions 2,
no. 2 (Fall 1967): 339-43.

A critique of Ball and Bates' "Migration and Residential Mobility of Narcotic Drug Addicts" regarding the desirability of
using Lexington Hospital subjects as the basis for generalizing
about the mobility of all addicts. Using questionnaires distributed
to 215 addict patients in Nalline areas in Oakland, California
and Chicago, Illinois and to 88 patients from Lexington Hospital
and statistics from New Jersey, the author found the Lexington
subjects to be less mobile than either the Nalline or New Jersey
subjects. Grupp suggests that "Lexington subjects may not be
an adequate population for making generalizations about the mobility of all addicts" (p. 343). He compares Lexington with the
Nalline areas in terms of white and nonwhite mobility and finds
that the Lexington subjects, both white and nonwhite, are more
stable residentially than the Nalline area subjects.

Hamburgher, Ernest. "Contrasting the Hippie and the Junkie," International Journal of the Addictions 4, no. 1 (March 1969): 121-35.

A description of the differences between hippies and junkies
(heroin addicts) with regard to age, sex, race, location, socioeconomic origins, patterns of drug abuse, employment, appearance, and art and music. The author mainly summarizes previous studies, although he also gives a random sample verbal
questionnaire to people who have "the appearance of hippies"
in San Francisco and Detroit, two days in each city. He concludes that hippies are white, middle class, and located in clearly
demarcated areas of certain cities, and are usually between 18
and 21 years of age. They flaunt middle class appearances by
their rebellious styles of dress and use marijuana, LSD, and
the amphetamines. In contrast, the junkies are nonwhite, poor,
living in all deprived areas of the cities, and between 19 and 35
years of age. They imitate middle class appearances and do not
use hallucinogens but concentrate on heroin.

Helmer, John and Thomas Vietorisz. Drug Use, The Labor Market, and Class Conflict. Washington, D.C.: The Drug Abuse Council, 1974.

In their introduction, the authors state that it is their hypothesis "that narcotics use is one of several interrelated social responses to labor market failure. What exactly has constituted this 'failure' has varied from episode to episode in the growth of widespread narcotic use in American society." Using historical survey as their primary method, they trace various periods of public attention to narcotics: Chinese and opium, 1875-80; blacks and cocaine and opium, 1905-20; white working class and opium, 1910-20; Mexican Americans and marijuana, 1930-37; and black working class and heroin, 1950-70. Drug policies, the authors say, have not only given legitimacy to anti-working class politics, they have "provided at the same time a method of putting the class against itself and identifying ehtnic or racial minorities as scapegoats for larger or more fundamental social ills." "Once we realize . . . the problem of widespread addiction is a recurrent and cyclical one, we are forced to examine the social constraints which have operated in each case or episode in the cycle."

Helpern, Milton and Yong-Myun Rho. "Deaths from Narcotism in New York City," International Journal of the Addictions 2, no. 1 (Spring 1967): 53-84.

A detailed account of the increasing number of deaths due to narcotic addiction in the city of New York from 1950 through 1964, utilizing statistics from the Chief Medical Examiner's Office, pathologic and illustrative data. The pattern of narcotic addiction in New York City is briefly presented. Statistical information is provided regarding the yearly incidence of deaths, monthly incidence, racial and sex incidence, age distribution, marital status, occupation, geographic distribution, and place of death. Black deaths due to heroin are 12 times greater than for whites; there are 612.9 deaths per 10,000 black inhabitants compared to 14.4 per 10,000 whites. Black male deaths due to heroin are ten times greater than for white males, while black female deaths are in a ratio of 15:1 for whites. The average age of death for both sexes over 12 years old is 29. Puerto Ricans are considered to be whites in this study. There is also a detailed, illustrated description of the gross and microscopic findings of the autopsies in the cases examined, emphasizing the external evidences of narcotics use and the characteristic appearance of the lungs which suggests the acute, rapid death caused by an intravenous overdose. The authors conclude that "the increasing incidence and total number of deaths due to addiction are of great significance and provide an important indicator of the extent of the problem" (p. 84).

Hill, Harris E., Charles A. Haertzen and Robert Glaser. "Personality Characteristics of Narcotic Addicts as Indicated by the MMPI," Journal of General Psychology 62, first half (January 1960): 127-39.

An examination of the most frequent personality deviations revealed by MMPI test scores of three groups of addicts: teenage, white, and black. Using the responses of 270 hospitalized addicts, including 70 blacks and 88 whites, the authors find three subgroups in the combined black and white sample of adult addicts: psychopathic, neurotic, and schizoid. Except for a small number of individuals, all of the groups produce abnormal composite profiles on the psychopathic deviate scale. The adolescents produce as deviant a pattern of profiles as the adult addicts. Blacks differ from the white group mainly in their greater resemblance to the classic psychopath. The authors conclude that "personality characteristics of narcotic addicts are either associated with psychopathy or are predominantly psychopathic in nature, although they may include many of the classical psychoneurotic and psychotic features" (p. 138). In addition, the similarity of the personality characteristics among adolescent addicts, adult addicts, and non-addict delinquents "suggests that psychopathology has considerable significance in the etiology of addiction" (p. 138).

Hughes, Patrick H., Noel W. Barker, Gail A. Crawford and Jerome H. Jaffe. "The Natural History of a Heroin Epidemic," American Journal of Public Health 62, no. 7 (July 1972): 995-1001.

An evaluation of the reasons for the rise and decline of an epidemic of heroin addiction among black youth in Chicago and the effects of societal control measures on that epidemic. The authors interviewed 91 black active street addicts, 123 black methadone patients, and 302 black narcotic addicts entering treatment in the Illinois Drug Abuse Program between May 1969 and September 1970. They also interviewed officials of the Chicago Police Department and examined court and police records, newspaper accounts, and legislative hearings from that period. They find that immediately after World War II, a polydrug epidemic among non-delinquent, teenage blacks developed, associated with a hip youth culture including jazz musicians and well known entertainers. This epidemic peaked in 1949 and declined during the 1950s, leaving in its wake a large number of active addicts. The authors examine the enforcement, legislative, judicial, and mass media responses and detail the cost of maintaining the heroin habit and the quality of heroin. They find that the decline of the epidemic is closely correlated with the increasing cost and decreasing quality of heroin available. The community did not respond to the epidemic until it had already been on the decline for at least a year; it then "mobilized to control it through punitive legislation, a special narcotics court, and expansion of narcotics enforcement personnel" (p. 1000). The authors explore some of the implications of this history for research and treatment programs and suggest the need for stressing quick and effective containment of new heroin outbreaks.

Hughes, Patrick H. and Gail A. Crawford. "A Contagious Disease Model for Researching and Interviewing in Heroin Epidemics," Archives of General Psychiatry 27, no. 2 (August 1972): 149-55.

Hughes and various colleagues have worked extensively on developing an epidemiological approach to narcotic addiction. In this report, he and Crawford differentiate between macroepidemics of heroin abuse (neighborhoods producing 50 or more new addicts in a span of only a few years), microepidemics (producing less than 50 but more than a single case), and isolated cases.

Some of the findings are: The largest heroin outbreaks continue to occur in underprivileged neighborhoods—in Chicago between 1967 and 1971, of the eleven macroepidemics identified, seven were in black neighborhoods and two were in Puerto Rican-white neighborhoods. The majority of addicts are produced by macroepidemics; neighborhoods which have undergone rapid population change seem to be especially vulnerable. Many of the isolated cases were initiated to heroin use by a sibling or a spouse and were frequently persons without close friends; in both micro and macroepidemics, the introduction to heroin is through friends and as another drug to already polydrug users. First use (often as a "free taste") occurs most frequently in a small group with newly initiated users rather than in a larger group or at a party. After addiction, the need for a constant source of heroin forces the drug abuser into frequent association with other addicts to assure a stable drug distribution system. Macroepidemic neighborhoods tend to have multiple supplier sources and addiction becomes endemic in the community.

The researchers stress that the new users or newly addicted are the most "contagious," suggesting that to control new out-breaks early identification of users is important. They also found that the same pattern of contagion among friends can be utilized for getting addicts into treatment; in other words, the disease and the possible cure can spread through the same interaction system.

Hughes, Patrick H., Gail A. Crawford, Noel W. Barker, Suzanne Schumann and Jerome H. Haffee. "The Social Structure of a Heroin Copping Community," American Journal of Psychiatry, 128 no. 5 (November 1971): 551-8.

Through the identification and monitoring of dealers and con-sumers at a heroin distribution location on the South Side of Chicago, a cohesive role structure was observed and is des-cribed in this report. Using a field worker, an ex-addict who was trusted among the heroin-copping community members, data were collected for over a year. A highly differentiated system of roles was found among the 127 members of the community under observation: eight big dealers, eight street dealers, 19 part time dealers, three bag followers (attractive women), five touts (older addicts who direct buyers to sellers), 48 hustlers (non-employed addicts) and 36 workers (employed addicts). Only two role members were non-addicted and motivated only by eco-nomic gain. The others, except the hustlers, financed their habits primarily through drug dealing or employment. (Average weekly habit costs were $1,000 for the big dealers, $205 for the part time dealers, $268 for the hustler, and $111 for the workers.) Visits in the homes of 34 of the role members found that none of the copping community lived in luxury as the pre-vailing stereotype holds; some of the hustlers were "carrying the stick" (had no fixed place of residence). Most lived with family or girl friends, with the addict's total income going for drugs.

Rated on a psychosocial subscale, (economic autonomy, severity of addiction, subjective discomfort, employment fit-ness, mental health, quality of interpersonal relationships, degree of criminality, and social attractiveness), the dealers ranked high on mental stability and social attractiveness attri-butes that are "requirements of the dealer role." Part time dealers scored lower and are probably not disciplined enough to carry on big dealer responsibilities. Big dealers, on the other hand, score low on employment fitness and high on crimi-nality. The hustlers showed low soores on all subscales except

subjective discomfort, and workers scored rather high on all
the scales.

The authors' primary interest in developing the model is to
improve the effectiveness of treatment. It is their contention
that persons in the defined distribution roles have different levels
of motivation for treatment, and that community programs must
consider special approaches for involving the various groups.

Hughes, Patrick H., Clinton R. Sanders and Eric Schaps. "The
    Impact of Medical Intervention in Three Heroin Copping Areas,"
    Proceedings of the Fourth National Conference on Methadone,
    San Francisco, January 1972.

Following techniques for identifying, counting, and reaching
addicts on the streets, the authors analyze how successful attempts were to recruit and hold addicts in methadone treatment
programs. Three major copping areas in Chicago, predominantly populated by blacks, Mexican Americans and Puerto Ricans,
served as a basis of recruitment (no white copping areas were
known at the time).

Among the number contacted in the streets and available in
April and May, 1971 (not in jail, in other programs, voluntary
abstentions or other reasons for not being available), 85 percent of blacks, 69 percent of Mexicans, and 79 percent of Puerto
Ricans from copping areas were admitted during six months.
Of those admitted, 76 percent of blacks, 80 percent of Mexicans and 53 percent of Puerto Ricans were in treatment six
months later. Despite attempts to enroll all persons copping
in the Mexican American neighborhood and the fact that two-
thirds of the target subjects enrolled, the weekly census showed
no decline or a slight increase because new addicts emerged
and old addicts returned from jail or other treatment programs.
Addicts recruited for admission to methadone treatment do as
well as those who volunteer.

Hunt, G. Halsey and Maurice E. Odoroff. "Followup Study of Narcotic
    Drug Addicts After Hospitalization," Public Health Reports 67,
    no. 1 (January 1962): 41-54.

A follow-up exploration through interviews and police and
hospital records of 1, 912 addict patients living in New York
City and discharged from Lexington Hospital between July, 1952
and December, 1955. The 1,533 voluntary patients are 42.8 percent white, 43.7 percent black, 10 percent Puerto Rican, and
3 percent Chinese, while the 379 involuntary patients are
73.5 percent black, 17.5 percent white, 8.2 percent Puerto

Rican, and less than 1 percent Chinese or other. Three out
of four of the voluntary group are men; two-thirds are under
30 years of age. The study attempts to ascertain if contact can
be achieved with discharged addict patients, if it is possible to
determine which patients become readdicted and which remain
abstinent, and what factors are related to the relapse rate. The
follow-up team was able to achieve some kind of contact with
98.4 percent of the dischargees and to determine readdiction or
abstinence. They found that over 90 percent of the patients became readdicted and that over 90 percent of the readdicted became readdicted within six months after release from the hospital. The major significant variable in the rate of readdiction
was age: men over the age of 30 generally had lower readdiction
rates than those under 30. Age was not significant for female
patients. Significant readdiction rates are found for the non-
voluntary (as compared to the voluntary) patients over the age
of 30, for the white (as compared to the black) non-voluntary
patients under the age of 30, and for patients under the age of
30 staying in the hospital over 31 days (as compared with those
staying 30 days or less). Ethnic group and sex are not found to
be significant variables for either the voluntary or involuntary
groups. These findings confirm that "hospital treatment can
initiate rehabilitation but it must be completed after the patient
returns to the community" (p. 54). The authors advocate aftercare facilities.

Hunt, Leon Gibson. Heroin Epidemics: A Quantitative Study of Current
Empirical Data, Monograph Series. Washington, D.C.: Drug
Abuse Council, May 1973.

The third report of the Drug Abuse Council's Monograph
Series, this study, using data from other sources, explores the
nature of the spread of heroin use and its implications for policy,
especially for that designed to prevent or control heroin "epidemics."

Hunt points out that it is well established that the spread of
opiate use occurs mostly within friendship or peer groups. This
is especially true among blacks (close to 90 percent). Whites
and Puerto Ricans were found to have more contact through
medical sources although they, too, have high peer group initial
contact. The contagious person is the new user (within first
year of use); established users lose contact with non-drug using
peers as they become integrated into the drug subculture. Policies which stress removal of the established drug abuser from
the community to deter spread of addiction are questionable, because such a person has already lost his contact with non-users.

Hunt further finds that while heroin use in major metropolitan areas may be leveling off or declining, there appears to be an increase in heroin addiction in smaller communities.

Jackson, Anna M. "Drug Abuse Referrals to a Child Diagnostic Center," Rocky Mountain Medical Journal 70, no. 11 (November 1973): 32-38.

A diagnosis of drug abuse cases referred to the Children's Diagnostic Center (CDC) located at the University of Colorado Medical Center in Denver, Colorado. An absence of black referrals in a center located in a relatively heavily populated black community was conspicuous, and led the authors to question the reasons why and to suggest that factors underlying the absence need to be researched. "It could be, for example, that black adolescents are referred directly to detention centers without evaluations more frequently than white adolescents. If different dispositions do exist for black and white adolescents, racial biases on the part of referring persons may be involved."

Johnson, Bruce D. Marijuana Uses and Drug Subcultures. New York: John Wiley, 1973.

Johnson develops his drug subculture theory on previous research findings and data obtained from a study of 3,500 college students and their patterns of drug use and drug selling. He elaborates on the observations of other researchers (for example Goode and Carey) that the illegality of cannabis use is a crucial factor in the pattern of selling and buying of drugs, and that buying and selling are crucial factors in determining depth of involvement in drug subcultures. Heavy subculture involvement includes multiple drug use and experimentation with hard drugs. Johnson extends his subculture theory, based on empirical evidence, into two drug subcultures structured along racial lines, black and white. In the white drug subculture, marijuana users progress to hallucinogens, amphetamines, sedatives, and methedrine; those in the black subculture take up heroin and cocaine. His data, even among college students, support this hypothesis. Johnson maintains, as others have, that present drug laws play a crucial part in maintaining drug subcultures and their noncomitant social behavior, including hard drug usage.

Johnson, Weldon T. and Robert Bogomolny. "Selective Justice: Drug Law Enforcement in Six American Cities," National Commission on Marihuana and Drug Abuse, Drug Use in America: Problem in Perspective, vol. 3: The Legal System and Drug Control.

Washington, D.C.: U.S. Government Printing Office, 1973: 498-650.

An examination of the operation of the criminal justice system in the last half of 1971 in six cities. Of about 500,000 drug arrests in the United States, 225,000 involved marijuana and were excluded from this analysis. Using various sampling selection ratios, the fate of approximately 16,500 non-marijuana drug arrestees was analyzed. The detailed data included careful examination of the court processing of whites and minorities. In the remainder of this abstract, the numbers in parentheses are percentages for various variables among each racial group, respectively white, black, Spanish-speaking, and other (probably Oriental and Indian).

The total sample reflects the overrepresentation (white (W) = 30 percent, black (B) = 53 percent, Spanish-speaking (S) = 16 percent, other (O) = 0.1 percent) of blacks and Spanish-speaking peoples among non-marijuana drug arrestees. For each city, minorities are usually overrepresented in comparison with their proportions in the population from 1970 census data: Chicago (arrestees: W = 30, B = 58, S = 11, O = 1; population: W = 66, B = 33, S = 7, O = 1), Dallas (arrestees: W = 70, B = 26, S = 4, O = 0; population: W = 74, B = 25, S = 8, O = 1), Los Angeles (arrestees: W = 40, B = 40, S = 19, O = 1; population: W = 77, B = 18, S = 18, O = 5), Manhattan (arrestees: W = 24, B = 56, S = 20, O = 0; population: W = 71, B = 25, S = 12, O = 4), Miami (arrestees: W = 51, B = 38, S = 10, O = 0; population: W = 76.5, B = 23, S = 45, O = .5), Washington, D.C. (arrestees: W = 6, B = 93, S = 0, O = 0; population: W = 28, B = 71, S = 2, O = 1).

Further, minorities are usually overrepresented among "opiate only" arrests (W = 19, B = 62, S = 19, O = 0), multiple drugs with an opiate arrest (W = 29, B = 61, S = 8, O = 1) and ancillary (instruments, etc.) arrests (W = 25, B = 58, S = 15, O = 1) and underrepresented among stimulants only (W = 67, B = 21, S = 9, O = 2) and hallucinogens only (W = 88, B = 6, S = 5, O = 1) arrestees. Although 60 percent have no previous record, minorities are somewhat more likely to have a history of more than one year of heroin/cocaine use (W = 11, B = 23, S = 30, O = 13) and extensive previous contact with the law (W = 16, B = 21, S = 24, O = 37). On the other hand, race was not systematically associated with detection and apprehension variables, previous investigation (W = 24, B = 26, S = 20, O = 25), police buys (W = 5, B = 6, S = 6, O = 0), small drug seizures (W = 51, B = 47, S = 40, O = 36), large seizures (W = 18, B = 20, S = 24, O = 27), multiple arrest charges (W = 53, B = 53,

S = 49, O = 83), arrests in public places (W = 42, B = 45, S = 51, O = 62), and the use of arrest or search warrants (W = 11, B = 11, S = 9, O = 3).

There are also no important racial differences in disposition: among adult arrestees, about a third are convicted (W = 32, B = 29, S = 34, O = 24), and about half of the drug charges are dismissed (W = 47, B = 49, S = 44, O = 42), while the rest skip bail or have cases pending. There are few racial differences in the stage at which the case is dismissed: charge phase (W = 14, B = 3, S = 4, O = 13), complaint phase (W = 32, B = 31, S = 36, O = 24), preliminary hearing stage (W = 27, B = 29, S = 30, O = 42), or pretrial phase (W = 22, B = 32, S = 26, O = 0). Among those convicted, almost all plead guilty (W = 91, B = 86, S = 92, O = 100). However, judges somewhat more frequently sentence minorities to spend some time in jail (W = 38, B = 48, S = 51, O = 95) and are less likely to give them a fine or probation (W = 43, B = 33, S = 29, O = 5).

Thus, with the possible exception of sentencing, all races progress through the criminal justice system with about the same outcome; systematic racial discrimination does not appear. Likewise, detailed data presented in the article indicate that sex, age, and occupation are not systematically related to disposition or sentence within the court. Strangely enough, the type of drug, the amount seized, the presence of a warrant or previous investigation, the number of multiple charges, type of counsel, and previous contact with the courts seem to be either weakly or not related to conviction and sentence imposed. Only an arrest for buying or selling (relatively uncommon) leads to a significantly increased probability of conviction and a prison sentence.

The major variable influencing conviction and sentence is the city. Thus, 13 percent in Chicago, 27 percent in Manhattan, and 58 percent in Miami are convicted. Among those convicted, 26 percent in Chicago, 30 percent in Washington, 43 percent in Miami, 49 percent in Manhattan, and 55 percent in Dallas must spend some time in jail.

Johnston, W. Cecil. "A Descriptive Study of 100 Convicted Female Narcotic Residents," Corrective Psychiatry and Journal of Social Therapy 14, no. 4 (Winter 1968): 230-6.

A portrait through interviews of 100 female narcotic addicts admitted to the Narcotic Rehabilitation Center in New York. There are 58 black women, 25 Puerto Ricans and 17 white women from the ages of 17-59. Their average age is 30.18 years. The overwhelming majority uses heroin. Thirty-six live with a legal

spouse and also usually with a child, while 28 live alone and 18
live with children or relatives. Most of them lack adequate parental figures. Their responses to interviewers' questions on neurotic traits, home life, self-evaluation, neighborhood, employment, and sexual history are included. The group is found to
be insecure, anxious, and frightened, with feelings that men
are inadequate and that they themselves have difficulty in assuming proper sex roles. They begin using heroin out of curiosity:
friends initiate them into addiction, and the addict community
functions as a protective shield to help the women avoid coping
with their problems. In comparison to men, women are found
to begin addiction later and to avoid arrest more. The author
concludes that through the Narcotic Rehabilitation Center the
residents will achieve a better self-image and learn how to form
new interpersonal relationships and new work habits.

Joseph, Herman. "A Probation Department Treats Heroin Addicts,"
Federal Probation 37, no. 1 (March 1973): 35-39.

Discussion of a voluntary methadone maintenance program
created by the New York City Criminal Courts Office of Probation in 1970 for eligible probationers. Joseph outlines the criteria for admission, the physiological effects of methadone, the
administration of probation clinics, authority and treatment,
and administrative problems. He finds that 82 percent of the 900
patients admitted to the clinics between 1970 and 1972 have remained in the program, while half of the patients who completed
probation continue methadone treatment in other clinics. Around
ten percent of the total admitted during this period have been re-
arrested. The patients are 45 percent black, 28 percent Hispanic,
and 27 percent white. They are overwhelmingly male, between
18 and 25 years old, with 16 years the mean age of onset of addiction. Over 90 percent are high school drop-outs with an estimated fifth grade level of reading and arithmetic comprehension.
"Educational retardation is not due to low intellectual endowment.
Most of our patients are bright in a street-wise sense" (p. 38).
Joseph warns of the limitations of probation and parole methadone maintenance but recommends it as a validated medical treatment.

Jurgensen, Warren P. "New Developments at the Lexington Hospital,"
Rehabilitating the Narcotic Addict. By the Vocational Rehabilitation Administration. Washington, D.C.: U.S. Government Printing Office, 1967, pp. 83-86.

Summary of the patients, hospital climate, clinical research, and developments in treatment at the Lexington Public Service Hospital. The addict as characterized by this study is younger than before, more likely to be black or of Spanish origin, since Chinese addicts have virtually disappeared, and likely to stop treatment against medical advice. The black addict in particular feels more anger and futility than revealed in earlier studies.

Kaplan, John. "Marijuana and Heroin Addiction," Marijuana—The New Prohibition. New York: World Publishing, 1970, pp. 232-62.

A review of studies on the relationship between marijuana use and heroin addiction. The data show no strong causal connection among most of society except among poor urban blacks, Mexican Americans, and Puerto Ricans, who comprise the majority of heroin addicts. Kaplan points out that no studies explain why only the lower class ethnic minorities move from marijuana to heroin use, and why only marijuana is associated with heroin use. He argues that there is no causal relationship between marijuana and heroin use and that therefore the theory of marijuana as a stepping stone to heroin does not justify criminalization of marijuana.

Kittrie, Nicholas, Juanita Weaver, William Trencher, Joan Wolfgang, Arnold Dahlke and Joseph Tro. "The Juvenile Drug Offender and the Justice System," National Commission on Marihuana and Drug Abuse, Drug Use in America: Problems in Perspective, vol. 3. Washington, D.C.: U.S. Government Printing Office, 1973.

The authors comment in their Introduction that within the realm of adult drug abuse the social response is an ambivalent conflict between punishment and treatment. For juveniles, however, the justice system's approach at least is that the handling of delinquent youths should attempt to be therapeutic and reforming instead of penal; this allows greater discretion in handling of drug delinquents and the possibility of innovative approaches toward the youthful offender.

Their research was defined as primarily factfinding, and emphasized a comparative look at data and program alternatives used within several jurisdictions within the Washington, D.C. metropolitan area.

Using juvenile case records and interviews with individuals within the judicial system (July 1971–December 1971), they compared jurisdictional patterns such as arrest data, demographic characteristics, types of drugs involved, and previous conviction patterns.

There were frequently marked and expected differences between the inner city Washington, D.C. area and the outlying, suburban counties. Although juvenile arrests in all areas were predominantly male and between 17 and 18 years old, the arrestees in Washington, D.C. were 70 percent nonwhite, while in the other areas they ranged from only 18 percent to 19 percent. There were more unemployed among the D.C. group and there was a high ratio of public arrests and cases involving opiates (46 percent). (Other areas had an opiate involvement of 15 percent or less). Among the total sample, 54 percent had had previous contact with the police; in the D.C. area 74 percent had had previous contact.

Much of the report deals with the judicial procedures regarding juveniles in the sample jurisdictions and the treatment programs available in each. The Washington, D.C. treatment programs reflect a wide array of philosophic and program arrangements. The issue that evokes the greatest concern in that area is the use of methadone in treatment: the authors claim that members of the black community are disturbed by this treatment for juveniles whom, they believe, are not yet hard core addicts.

Kleber, Herbert D. "Narcotic Addiction—The Current Problem and Treatment Approaches," Connecticut Medicine 32, no. 2 (February 1969): 113-16.

A short outline of the heroin addiction pattern in New Haven, Connecticut (based on police records) with suggestions for treatment. Kleber reports that in New Haven the problem is concentrated among blacks, although nationally black addiction is decreasing and white and Puerto Rican addiction are increasing. He finds the heroin users to be young, maturing by about the age of 40, often pushers as well as users, and with a wide range of personality traits centering around passivity and dependency. Half of them lost their fathers by the age of 16.

Kleinman, Paula and Irving F. Lukoff. "Generational Status, Ethnic Group, and Friendship Networks: Antecedents of Drug Use in a Ghetto Community," mimeographed. New York: Center for Socio-Cultural Studies on Drug Use, Columbia University School of Social Work, July 1975.

This paper is a replication of an earlier study (Lukoff and Brook 1974) conducted in the Bedford-Stuyvesant/Fort Greene ghetto of Brooklyn, the area of Brooklyn having the highest rate of known addiction. Quota sampling, with an oversampling of British West Indian blacks, provided a weighted sample size of

883. Callbacks were not made when respondents were not at home. Interviews with Puerto Ricans were conducted in English. The findings: American blacks and whites had the same level of heroin experimentation (three percent had tried it), and whites were more likely to have tried marijuana, psychedelics, amphetamines, and barbiturates. Use of all drugs increased with social class: four percent of the lower class (blue collar job and no high school graduation) and ten percent of the middle class (white collar job and high school graduate) had used marijuana and other drugs. Class differences did not explain racial differences in drug experimentation. British West Indian blacks were much less likely than either whites or American blacks to use drugs. Males were more likely than females to use drugs, younger persons more likely than middle-aged or older persons. Among the middle-aged (30-49 years old), whites were more likely than blacks (27 percent versus 14 percent) to use marijuana and hard drugs; similar differences (30 percent versus 16 percent) were found among the young (18-29 years old). Migrants to the city were less likely than those born in the city to try drugs and use hard drugs. In fact almost all hard drug use occurred among natives, regardless of ethnic group or social class. The drug use of friends (as perceived by the respondent) was by far the most influential factor in drug use, and this relationship was not greatly affected by aged, ethnicity, migrant status, or social class.

Koval, Mary. "Opiate Use in New York City," mimeographed. New York: Summary of Report of New York State Narcotic Addiction Control Commission, November 1969.

A report on rates of opiate use in New York City and its five boroughs and in 30 Health Center Districts by sex, ethnicity, and age. Indices of social, economic, and health problems, such as financial dependency, juvenile delinquency, out of wedlock births, health, infant mortality rates, unemployment, poverty, and schooling, are presented to give a complete demographic picture of each neighborhood. The study shows that two out of every 100 persons 15-44 years of age in New York City are opiate users. The majority, around 53 percent, live in Manhattan, and over one-third of the opiate users live in Central Harlem. Areas of high incidence of opiate use are also areas of high rates of problems, although the reverse does not always apply. Half of the addicts in the city are black, over one-fourth are Puerto Rican, and less than one-fourth white; one out of ten is under 20 years of age; and four out of five are male. Koval concludes that "although it is evident that opiate use is concentrated among

the nonwhite population, in general, there is no consistent relationship between high drug use areas and areas with high proportions of nonwhites or Puerto Ricans. An area of a high proportion of addicts is often an area with larger proportions of
nonwhites or Puerto Ricans but not all areas with large proportions of these ethnic groups have high addiction rates" (p. v).

Lander, Bernard and Nathan Lander. "A Cross-Cultural Study of
Narcotic Addiction in New York," Rehabilitating the Narcotic
Addict. Vocational Rehabilitation Administration. Washington,
D.C.: U.S. Government Printing Office, 1967, pp. 359-69.

Preliminary findings of a study of a New York City block
known to be high in the incidence of narcotics use, based on
in-depth interviews with 30 subjects, participant-observations,
and census data. Thirty-three out of 49 resident addicts are
Puerto Rican; ten are black, and six are white. The authors
briefly describe the hierarchy for the distribution and marketing
of heroin, the dilution of heroin and consequent use of other
drugs in conjunction with heroin, and the amount of violence
used by drug addicts to obtain money to support their habit.
The authors point to the lack of substantiation for the theory
of a low sex drive among heroin users, the lack of a typical
family pattern distinguishing addicts from non-addicts, and
the lack of an addict society, since the addict usually has only
one partner. They argue that there is no clear personality type
for the addict and that there is no clear correlation between addiction and slums, whereas they see a close correlation between
education, vocation, and addiction. The article is followed by
discussion.

Langrod, John. "Secondary Drug Use Among Heroin Users," International Journal of the Addictions 5, no. 4 (December 1970):
611-35.

A delineation of the overall secondary drug use patterns
among 422 male heroin users interviewed prior to their institutionalization in treatment facilities in New York City. Ethnic
composition of the group is 45 percent black, 30 percent Puerto
Rican, and 25 percent white. The study shows that almost all
heroin addicts use marijuana, while over one-third report using
such drugs as cocaine, amphetamines, and barbiturates, with
3.4 the mean number of secondary drugs used. Secondary drug
abuse is thus characteristic of heroin users and tends to increase
more with length of heroin use rather than with age or cost of
the drug habit. Ethnicity is found to be closely related to the

amount and kind of secondary drugs being used. Whites are more
than six times as likely as blacks or Puerto Ricans to abuse a
larger number of secondary drugs, more likely to have used all
secondary drugs other than cocaine more than six times, and
more likely to initiate drug use with all drugs other than marijuana before using heroin and to have access to legal medical
and pharmaceutical sources to obtain drugs. One of the important
ethnic differences is found to be in the area of family cooperation and affection. Whites are better educated than the other
races, more likely to come from an intact home, to have a higher
income and not to have addicted or alcoholic relatives. Yet they
are less likely to get along well with their families before, during, and after addiction. "It is possible that whites, despite
their more favorable social circumstances, may be using heroin
and secondary drugs because of greater emotional problems
compared to blacks and Puerto Ricans, for whom heroin use
may be more of a social phenomenon, given its greater availability. Drugs for the ghetto addict may serve more as an escape from an oppressive socioeconomic situation than is the
case for the white addict" (p. 633).

Larner, Jeremy (ed.). The Addict in the Street. New York: Grove
Press 1964.

    See the annotation in Section 5: "Drug Use and Abuse Among
Puerto Ricans."

Larrier, D., M. Cline, F. Brophy and A. Pischera. "Deaths Among
Narcotic Abusers in New York City, January–June, 1970,"
Contemporary Drug Problems 1, no. 4 (Fall 1972): 711-25.

    A goal of the study was to help evaluate the reliability of the
Narcotics Register of New York City (collected from routine
reports of medical, legal and social service agencies) as a
source of information on narcotic users. Comparison by number and characteristics of narcotic abusers who died in New
York City during the first six months of 1970 was made with
narcotics users as known through the register up to 1969.
    Compared by age, sex, and ethnicity, the two groups held
no significant differences: of the 574 deaths, 56 percent were
black, 29 percent white, and 15 percent Puerto Rican. Eighty-
two percent were male. Twenty-one percent were under 19
years; 26 percent, 20-24 years; 20 percent, 25-29 years; and
33 percent, 30 years and over.
    The leading cause of death (67 percent) was acute and chronic
intravenous narcotism (overdose); other causes were homicide,

accidents, drug-related and non drug-related disease. Among the overdose cases, whites were more likely (79 percent), Puerto Ricans (69 percent), and blacks (62 percent) to die from drug overdose. Analysis of the death cases not listed in the register found more young people, suggesting that the register may understate drug abuse among the young.

Laskowitz, David and Stanley Einstein. "Personality Characteristics of Adolescent Addicts: Manifest Rigidity," Corrective Psychiatry and Journal of Social Therapy 9, no. 4 (Fourth Quarter 1963): 215-18.

An investigation of manifest rigidity as a personality characteristic of adolescent addicts in terms of sex, race, and length of addiction. The Metcalf Manifest Rigidity Scale was administered to 126 newly admitted New York City hospital patients between the ages of 17 and 21, and the results are compared to 45 male, non-addict delinquents from Rikers Island. The study includes 59 Puerto Ricans, 75 blacks, and 61 whites. Although addict subgroups are not found to differ significantly with regard to sex, significant differences are found in ethnicity and length of drug use. The Puerto Rican addicts are the most rigid; blacks are intermediate, and white addicts are the least rigid. Patients involved in drug use for a longer period of time are found to be less rigid than relatively early users. No significant differences in rigidity are found between the male addicts and the male non-addict delinquents.

Lawson, Clarence, Spelman Young and John N. Chappel, "The Generation Gap Observed Among Black Heroin Addicts in Chicago." Paper presented at Fifth Methadone Conference, Washington, D.C. (March 1973).

Based on their observations in several treatment centers on the South Side of Chicago, the authors differentiated between two groups of heroin addicts in the Chicago urban ghetto. The first is the older criminal-addict who became "strung out" in the late forties and fifties when "syndicate" policy restricted heroin sales to black communities and the police paid little attention as long as the drug stayed in its "proper" place. These addicts were criminals who happened to be addicted, according to Lawson and his colleagues. They had a style of life deeply involved in crime, with a certain status in the community for their ability to hustle. The second group of addicts, who came out of a new epidemic of heroin use in the late sixties and seventies, the authors describe as addict-criminal; addiction comes before the criminal activity. This group, composed of younger black youths, is more hostile, and is likely to respond to threatening or different situations with violence. Several brief case histories are given.

Lemert, Edwin M. and Judy Rosberg. "The Administration of Justice to Minority Groups in Los Angeles County," University of California Publications in Culture and Society 2, no. 1 (April 15, 1948): 1-28.

An exploration of data on treatment of whites, blacks, Asian Americans, and Mexican Americans in the administration of justice on felony charges in Los Angeles County. The authors conclude that blacks are treated by the courts as more deviant than Mexican Americans, although both minorities are discriminated against in terms of arrests, convictions, and sentences. They cite interesting statistics on felony charges for Narcotics Act violations: 8.3 percent of blacks charged with felonies are charged with violating the Narcotics Act, compared to 5.3 percent of Mexican Americans, 6.0 percent of Jews, 0 percent of Japanese, 44.4 percent of Chinese, 1.7 percent of whites, and 0 percent of Filipinos and American Indians. However, there is no explanation for these figures, particularly the extremely high rate for Chinese, and no follow-up on these figures for Narcotics Act violations, except for sentencing for whites, blacks and Mexican Americans.

Lerner, A. Martin and Frederick J. Oerther. "Recent Trends in Substance Abuse: Characteristics and Sequelae of Paregoric Abuse," International Journal of the Addictions 2, no. 2 (Fall 1967): 312-27.

A review of paregoric addiction patterns from 1956-65 in Detroit, Michigan, using statistics from the Narcotics Bureau and the Detroit General Receiving Hospital. A brief background sketch of the medical use of paregoric and the legal, narcotic, and socioeconomic conditions in Detroit are provided. The authors then discuss statistics on the occurrence of paregoric abuse and characteristics of paregoric abusers. Nine hundred and seventy are black, 90 white, 18 Mexican American, and only one Asian male. There are five blacks to one of all the other races. There are nine men to every woman. In this study there are 85 black women, 52 whites, and no others. The intravenous injection of paregoric and some of its complications, such as narcotic addiction, infections, bacteremia, pulmonary abnormalities, and occlusive venous sclerosis, are described. The pattern of rising incidence of paregoric addiction was abruptly halted in Detroit in 1964, due to legislation limiting access to paregoric. The author recommends that paregoric "be made a universal nonexempt narcotic" (p. 327).

Levi, Mario and Margaret Seborg. "The Study of I.Q. Scores on Verbal vs. Nonverbal Tests and vs. Academic Achievement Among Women Drug Addicts from Different Racial and Ethnic Groups," International Journal of the Addictions 7, no. 3 (Fall 1972): 581-84.

An analysis of the validity of I.Q. scores on nonverbal as well as verbal tests and of I.Q. scores compared with academic achievement among institutionalized women drug addicts. The subjects are 335 literate women inmates, 200 white, 67 Mexican American, and 68 black at the California Rehabilitation Center Women's Unit at Patton during the summer of 1969, and 79 "illiterate" women at the same institution, 14 white, 28 black, and 37 Mexican American. It is found that the verbal tests do not reliably measure the I.Q. of black women and Mexican Americans who both perform much better on non-verbal intelligence tests. Even on these tests, however, the Mexican Americans and blacks score lower than whites. The authors hypothesize that this may be due to the fact that these nonverbal tests are still culturally slanted, and recommend that new tests be devised "to take these facts into consideration" (p. 584). They conclude that "the findings indicate very clearly that the results of the usual group verbal I.Q. tests administered to members of minority groups are very misleading, i.e., they do not reflect the real intellectual capacity of the testees" (p. 584).

Levy, Stephen J. "Drug Abuse in Business: Telling It Like It is," Personnel 4, no. 5 (September-October 1972): 8-14.

A study of 95 volunteer subjects drawn from resident population of four drug free voluntary residential therapeutic communities in New York City regarding their use of drugs when they were employed. They were asked not to falsify answers and told that a possible outcome of the study might be that business firms would adopt programs to help addicts. The sample was 74 percent male, 87 percent using heroin as their major drug; 48 percent black, 20 percent white, 25 percent Puerto Rican, 1 percent Dominican, and 1 percent Oriental.

One of the striking aspects of the data, the author says, was the variety and range of jobs held by the former addicts. Ninety-one of the 95 said they used drugs during working hours while

employed (40 using the lavatory for shooting up); 48 said they
sold drugs to other employees; 37 said they stole goods or
materials from their places of employment; 28 said they had
stolen cash or checks from others. No crimes against persons
were reported. None had been discharged for drug use.

The interviewees said they could mask their drug use because
of their skill in covering up and the lack of awareness of employers. Levy comments that the data reflect that managerial personnel are either unaware of or unwilling to face up to the drug
problems within their firms.

Lipscomb, Wendell R. "Drug Use in a Black Ghetto," American Journal
of Psychiatry 127, no. 9 (March 1971): 1166-69.

Interviews of 92 ghetto black and Mexican American youths in
a work training program in northern California, focusing on the
use of marijuana. The results verify that ghetto youth do try
and sometimes regularly use a variety of drugs, but that these
drugs do not affect their performance in the training program.
The most popular drugs used are alcohol and marijuana, in that
order. Lipscomb found that there is a significant discrepancy
between the amount of drug use admitted by the youths and their
estimate of the amount of drug use in the community. He suggests
that "drug use and drug experimentation in the ghetto is such an
accepted cultural phenomenon that attempts to change it by laws
and institutions outside the ghetto will meet with failure until the
nature of the ghetto itself is changed" (p. 1169).

Louisiana Commission on Law Enforcement and Administration of
Criminal Justice. "Narcotics in Louisiana," Louisiana Narcotics Crime Control. Baton Rouge, Louisiana; Louisiana Commission on Law Enforcement and Administration of Criminal
Justice, 1969, pp. 7-17.

A summary of a study by William Bloom and Ron Lewis on
the incidence of heroin addiction in New Orleans, where over 90
percent of the narcotic law offenders in Louisiana are based.
They studied arrest records of 609 hard narcotic addicts in New
Orleans from 1961-66 and interviews of 200 illegal drug users
contacted by the Narcotics Squad over a six month period ending
October 1967. The 609 arrestees are 17.4 percent women and
82.5 percent men and are 26 percent white and 74 percent black.
Their ages range from 17-62 years, with a median age of 28;
all persons under the age of 17 years are referred to the Juvenile
Bureau. Over 90 percent prefer heroin, but all use narcotics
interchangeably when unable to obtain their favorites. Among the
200 interviewed addicts, 42 percent begin their drug careers

with marijuana before the age of 20, and only 13.6 percent begin with heroin. In contrast to the males, most of the few women interviewed list heroin as the first drug used. In order to raise enough money to support their habit of $24-$30 a day, addicts must usually resort to stealing a staggering amount of property. The women addicts are usually prostitutes supporting both their own and their pimps' habits. A small number of addicts are able to keep steady jobs and legally maintain their habits by limiting their addiction to what they can afford. The study finds that there is no longer a narcotics syndicate in New Orleans. The Mafia left in the early 1950s, and since then several blacks have taken over the heroin industry, working independently and in competition with each other. The structure, supply routes, profits, and dilution of heroin in New Orleans is described. The typical New Orleans narcotic addict is a 26-year-old black male who prefers heroin to other drugs, first began drug abuse with marijuana in his midteens, lives in the central city ghetto, re-sorts to illegal means to support his habit, and has been arrest-ed before for non-drug offense. The Commission concludes by warning that drug abuse of all types, especially marijuana and narcotics, is spreading to younger age groups with middle class status throughout the state.

Lucas, Warren C., Stanley E. Grupp and Raymond L. Schmitt. "Single and Multiple Drug Opiate Users: Addicts or Nonaddicts?" HSMHA Health Reports 137, no. 2 (February 1972): 185-92.

Examination of data from 213 opiate users in Chicago, Oak-land, Santa Rita Rehabilitation Center (California) and Lexing-ton Hospital to determine the extent of addiction to multiple drugs and to identify the characteristics of single and multiple drug opiate users. They differ in their marital status, formal edu-cation, and race, but are similar in terms of age, sex, and kind of drugs used. Most of the single drug users have never married, while those using three or more drugs are usually separated or divorced. As the number of drugs used increases, the amount of formal education increases. Blacks are predominant in the single and two drug use patterns, whereas whites outnumber blacks in the three and four drug use pattern and clearly dom-inate blacks in the five or more drugs pattern. All of the drug users are around 30 years old. Most multiple drug users abuse opiates and amphetamines. Males dominate all drug use pat-terns, but as the number of drugs used increases, the propor-tion of women increases. Using two methods of measurement, the authors demonstrate that a majority of all categories of

drug users are addicts. They conclude, however, that their
data suggest non-addicts in the multiple drug use categories.
Since people tend to conform to the images that others have
of them, "caution and restraint should be used in placing all
opiate users in treatment programs which in fact define them
as addicts. Such a procedure might well have a self-fulfilling
effect" (p. 191).

Lukoff, Irving F. and Judith S. Brook. A Socio-Cultural Exploration
of Reported Heroin Use. Mimeographed. Columbia University,
April 1974.

   Although it is not contested that drug addiction is heavily
concentrated in areas where poverty is pervasive and among
ethnic groups which are economically most deprived, Lukoff
and Brook summarize studies which suggest that addicts are
not drawn from the least resourceful or depressed part of that
disadvantaged population. Following this review, they hypothesize that greater contact with drug users occurs among natives,
not migrants, regardless of ethnic or social class status. They
believe that migration introduces particular strains that increase
disparity between generations, and that peer group processes,
frequently found to be important in drug abuse, are an attendant
rather than dominant part of the process.
   A quota sample (N = 568) in the Bedford-Stuyvesant area of
Brooklyn, New York was selected: 53 percent female, 47 percent male; 244 blacks, 145 British West Indians, 99 Puerto
Ricans, and 80 whites. British West Indians, though they share
a common racial identity with American blacks, were held separate because of their different socio-cultural history, which
provided a measure of control in the identification of socio-
cultural processes on drug use as distinct from the accommo-
dation blacks make to racism.
   Findings: Within a community where poverty prevails, addicts are disproportionately drawn from among the better educated, occupationally white collar, and higher income segment.
Ethnic group membership is also related to having contact with
drug users within the family: Puerto Ricans had the highest reported contiguity (22 percent), followed by blacks (15 percent),
then British West Indians (9 percent), and then whites (8 percent)—a pattern that persisted when social class was controlled.
Heroin use is concentrated among young native-born individuals,
and most heavily among the first generation natives. Controlling
for the fact that native-born are also of higher socioeconomic
status than immigrants, support for the original hypothesis—that

migrant-native differences are more salient than social class—
was found. The acquisition of middle class child-rearing values
correlates positively with greater drug association, according
to an imperative-cognitive attitude index used to differentiate
generational differences.

These findings raise questions about many prevailing notions
of the etiology of drug addiction and the interpretation of available data.

Lukoff, Irving F., Debra Quatrone and Alice Sardell. Some Aspects
of the Epidemiology of Heroin Use in a Ghetto Community: A
Preliminary Report. United States Department of Justice, July
1972.

The first of a series of reports on a five year evaluation project of the effects of inner-city methadone maintenance clinics
on drug users, crime, and the community as a whole.

Six hundred community residents of the Bedford-Stuyvesant
section of Brooklyn, New York, were interviewed to determine
attitudes toward drug use in the community. Social and economic
data were used to supplement the interviews. The ethnic breakdown used in analysis was: black British West Indians, other
blacks, Puerto Ricans (regardless of race) and all others (mainly
whites).

As the authors state, the data produced some surprising results. Within the study community, reported heroin use is highest among the higher socioeconomic status persons of each ethnic group. Other study reports which suggest that social deprivation is the independent variable base their claims on a comparison of the ghetto community with the general community rather
than between groups within the ghetto community itself. Recency
of migration did not correlate positively with drug use; it was
the "native" population with higher incidences. Reported use
was not found to be higher among "incomplete" families, and
households with female heads (except the Puerto Rican) showed
a lower rate of drug abuse.

Puerto Ricans had the highest rate of reported use among
family members of relatives (21 percent), blacks next (14 percent), with British West Indians (9 percent) and whites (8
percent) proportionately lower. British West Indian families seem
to have an insulation that reduces their use of and exposure to
drug use.

Since the findings tend to contradict the commonly held view
that addicts tend to be the most deprived members of their community and are, on the contrary, the higher status persons within
an overall deprived area, the author suggests that explanations

other than social deprivation alone are necessary in understanding the patterns of heroin use. Contiguity and perception of environmental factors are contributing to addiction and whether residents feel that their family members are susceptible to addiction are also discussed.

Maddux, James F. and Linda Kay McDonald. "Status of 100 San Antonio Addicts One Year After Admission to Methadone Maintenance," Drug Forum 2, no. 3 (Spring 1973): 239-52.

See the annotation in Section 3: "Drug Use and Abuse Among Mexican Americans."

Malzberg, Benjamin. "A Statistical Study of Psychoses Due to Drugs or Other Exogenous Poisons," American Journal of Psychiatry 106, no. 2 (August 1949): 99-106.

A discussion of the characteristics of 166 first admissions with psychoses due to drugs or other exogenous poisons to all mental hospitals in New York State from 1944-47. Psychoses due to drugs or other exogenous poisons represent only .2 percent of all first admissions, occurring more frequently among females than males. "The largest single category is probably that arising from the use of opium or its derivatives" (p. 106). About 60 percent of all these first admissions with psychoses due to drugs are between the ages of 35 and 54; the average age is 46, with the women about one year older than the men. These first admissions include a high percentage of intemperate alcohol users and a higher proportion of separated and divorced than general first admissions, and are more frequently urban than rural dwellers. There is no significant difference on degree of education, although the psychoses due to drugs include a higher percentage with high school or college education than general first admissions. Blacks have a higher rate of first admissions with drug psychoses, with a great excess among black males and substantially less among black females. Foreign-born whites are fewer than their proportion to the population, while native-born whites are in excess of their proportion.

McCord, William. "The Defeated," from Life Styles in the Black Ghetto by William McCord, John Howard, Bernard Friedberg and Edwin Harwood. New York: W. W. Norton 1969, pp. 138-63.

A description of alcoholism, drug addiction, and psychotic delusions as various responses of the defeated urban black based on extensive interviews. McCord clears up what he considers to be misconceptions about drug addiction. He sees drug

addiction as decreasing rather than increasing, except in the
ghetto-ized black community. Drug addiction does not cause
crime but may in fact prevent it, especially violent crimes.
Drug addiction does not, in and of itself, cause serious damage
to the mind or body and can be cured. McCord delineates some
of the characteristics of the drug addict, citing studies by Chein
and Fort to substantiate his contention that one of the main reasons why some blacks turn to heroin is to avoid heterosexual
entanglements, since addicts are ambivalent about heterosexual
expression.

McFarland, Robert L. and William A. Hall. "A Survey of One Hundred
   Suspected Drug Addicts," Journal of Criminal Law, Criminology
   and Police Science 44, no. 3 (September-October 1953): 308-19.

   A study of 100 suspected drug addicts, 82 black and 18 white,
referred to the psychiatric staff of the House of Correction unit
of the Psychiatric Institute of the Chicago Municipal Courts between April 1951 and July 1951. Characteristically, this group
is male, black, with an average age of 23.8 years, below average
intelligence, an unstable vocational history, unstable home background, and an arrest record prior to initial use of narcotics.
The majority admit past heroin addiction but deny current usage.
They are diagnosed in general as having "behavior disorders"
characterized chiefly by pyschological immaturity. Due to their
lack of motivation, absence of anxiety, low intelligence, low
self-esteem, and hostility to authoritarian figures, they are
deemed to have poor potential for therapeutic treatment. The
relationship between the court and the psychiatric unit and the
effectiveness of the clinic are discussed in depth.

Miller, Gail. "Narcotics: A Study in Black and White," City 3, no.
   3 (June 1969): 2-9.

   A contrast between heroin use in the black community, which
receives little attention, and heroin, marijuana, and hallucinogen
use in the white suburbs, which receive a great deal of attention
from law enforcement authorities. The history of drug use in
the United States is described, followed by contrasting drug use
on the East Coast (mainly heroin) and on the West Coast (mainly
marijuana and barbiturates). The author cites federal statistics
and describes various programs treating drug abuse. Miller
calls for changing the classification of marijuana from a narcotic
to an hallucinogen and therefore freeing federal and local authorities to turn their attention to heroin use in the black community.
She also feels that the black community's suspicions of the drug

trade as a means for whites to keep blacks down and to make
profits seem to be justified.

Miller, Jerome S., John Sensenig, Robert B. Stocker and Richard
Campbell. "Value Patterns of Drug Addicts as a Function of
Race and Sex," International Journal of the Addictions 8, no.
4 (August 1973): 589-98.

A value-ranking research instrument (Rokeach) in which subjects rank two sets of values (terminal values such as happiness)
and instrumental values (such as responsibility) was administered
to 284 patients admitted to the National Institute of Mental Health
(NIMH) Clinical Research Center at Lexington, Kentucky, (136
black males, 76 white males, 34 black females, and 28 white
females).

The black addicts were considered by the authors to be less
alienated from traditional middle class achievement-oriented
values than the white addicts; they ranked values related to
opportunity and a reasonable level of affluence higher. Whites,
on the other hand, were more concerned with interpersonal and
intrapersonal relations.

The most significant sex differences were on the items of
cleanliness and self-respect. Females scored higher than males,
leading the authors to suggest a concern among female addicts
for the lives they lead as addicts, frequently involving prostitution. They state that the lifestyle accompanying addiction may
have a less negative effect on male than on female addicts.

The authors warn that intervention procedures that assume
that addicts are a homogeneous group are simplistic, and that
further exploration in this area is needed.

Milton, E. Ohmer, Jr. "A Study of 363 Cases of Institutional Behavior
Problems in a Drug Addict Population," The Journal of General
Psychology 31, first half (July 1944): 15-22.

A comparison of 363 male drug addicts who are behavior
problems in the Lexington Hospital with the general population
of patients and a comparison of 64 male drug addicts reported
for adverse behavior with a matched group with no adverse behavior reported. Milton finds that 38.5 percent of the patients
violated rules more than once. Although blacks are only 8.9
percent of the general hospital population, they compose 28.3
percent of the adverse behavior group and are "the most maladjusted group within the institution" (p. 17). "This might be
expected; it is felt by many that the colored man is more primitive in his behavior and is not as mature emotionally as is the

white man. However, since the entire staff of the hospital is
composed of white men, it is possible that certain infractions
of rules are tolerated for white patients and are not for colored
ones" (p. 17). Young patients between the ages of 20 and 35 tend
to comprise the majority of the adverse behavior group, although
there is no difference between the mean mental ages and I.Q.s
of the adverse behavior group and general patients. Adverse behavior occurs most frequently during the first five months of
incarceration, and those who are repeated rule-breakers tend
to commit more serious offenses the first time.

Musto, David F. The American Disease: Origins of Narcotic Control.
New Haven, Connecticut: Yale University Press, 1973.

A psychiatrist-historian's account of narcotic addiction control in the United States from the post-Civil War period to the
present. A major theme is that American concern with narcotics
is a political problem beyond medical or legal considerations.
Musto presents some documentation that public pressure for
control of particular drugs is closely related to anxiety about
the status of minority populations: for example, cocaine and
blacks at the height of the lynchings at the turn of the century,
opium and Chinese at the time of the anti-Asian campaign, and
marijuana and Mexican Americans in the Southwest following
the Depression.

Nail, Richard C., Eric Gunderson and Ransom J. Arthur. "Black-
White Differences in Social Background and Military Drug Abuse
Patterns," American Journal of Psychiatry 131, no. 10 (October
1974): 1097-1102.

The authors gathered data on the drug abuse patterns and
social backgrounds of 833 navy enlisted men (764 white and 69
black) admitted to a drug rehabilitation center. Black subjects
reported better school adjustment, less delinquency, and fewer
difficulties in their home lives than did whites. They had used
heroin more frequently than whites but were less involved with
hallucinogenic drugs. The authors suggest that different cultural
patterns may underlie the drug abuse behaviors of the two groups.
White users seem to be expressing new varieties of delinquent
or antisocial behavior, while blacks are following long established subcultural patterns of drug use.

Nash, George. The Impact of Drug Abuse Treatment Upon Criminality: A Look at 19 Programs. Trenton, New Jersey: New Jersey
Division of Narcotic and Drug Abuse Control, December 1973.

A study of 19 representative drug abuse treatment programs
in New Jersey between July 1, 1972 and June 30, 1973. The
special thrust of the study was to assess the impact of treatment
on criminality as indicated by arrest records. Ethnic distribution for the total sample was 52 percent white, 43 percent black,
and 5 percent Hispanic. In methadone maintenance, it was 54
percent white, 39 percent black, and 7 percent Hispanic;
in drug free treatment, 49 percent white, 46 percent black, and
5 percent Hispanic; in detoxification, 50 percent white, 48 percent black, and 2 percent Hispanic. Ninety-three percent of
all clients were heroin addicted.

A high arrest record prior to treatment was in evidence:
83 percent of the methadone clients (numerically the largest
group) and 57 percent of the drug free clinic clients. The great
majority of arrests were for crimes to support a drug habit, for
example, breaking and entering and robbery. Four-fifths of the
arrests occurred after the subjects had started using heroin.
The number of arrests declined after treatment and in relation
to length of time in treatment. Drug free program clients showed
lower arrest rates during and after treatment than methadone
maintenance. But background characteristics, especially employment history, seemed to be crucial correlators.

The proportion of clients who were in treatment at the beginning of a quarter and were still in treatment at the end of the
quarter showed sizeable variations between programs: in methadone maintenance, 10 percent "left" and 1 percent "graduated."
In the detoxification programs, 89 percent "left" and none "graduated." The remaining percentage represents the "still in treatment" population. The numbers of new entrants during the quarter
under study indicated a decline in drug free programs; methadone
maintenance programs were filled to capacity, so any trend
there was not discernible.

Costs per client also showed great variance. The average
cost per client in methadone maintenance was $1,200; the average
cost in drug-free programs was $3,900.

Newman, Robert G., Sylvia Bashkow and Margot Cates. "Applications
Received by the New York City Methadone Maintenance Treat-
ment Program During Its First Two Years of Operation," Drug
Forum 3, no. 2 (Winter 1974): 183-91.

The New York City Methadone Maintenance Treatment Program, operated by the Health Services Administration, began
accepting applications for treatment in November 1970. In 25
months 37,428 applications were received and 11,915 persons

admitted to the 43 clinics. The criteria for admission were:
being no more than 18 years of age, New York City resident,
and at least a two year history of mainlining heroin. Demand
rose steadily from inception of program through the summer
of 1972; during the last three months of 1972 (the end of the
survey period) the number of applications dropped markedly.
Ethnic distribution over the survey period showed a constant
proportion of Puerto Rican applicants (approximately 25-30
percent) and a dramatic increase in black applicants in the
later months. Up to March 1971, blacks comprised 38 percent
and whites 36 percent; in December 1972 blacks were 54 percent
and whites 20 percent. The authors give no explanation for this
change but express hope that the later figures more closely reflect that the programs are reaching the addict population in an
equitable way.

Newmeyer, John A. and George R. Gay. "The Traditional Junkie,
The Aquarian Age Junkie, and the Nixon Era Junkie," Drug
Forum 2, no. 1 (Fall 1972): 17-30.

A study whose purpose is to update and extend findings given
in an earlier report confirming a changing of the demography of
heroin abuse. The previous grouping was by "year of first use
of heroin": OSJ (Old Style Junkie, first use prior to 1964), TJ
(Transition Junkie, first use between 1964 and 1967), NJ (New
Junkie, use after 1967) was changed to "year hooked" and extended to include a new category: VNJ (Very New Junkie, hooked
after January 1969).

Earlier trends found to continue were a downward trend in
the proportion of blacks and an upward trend in Caucasians, females, and persons of Catholic background. There was a reverse of the earlier finding that heroin use was spreading to
younger age groups. A sharp rise in the proportion of veterans
of the Vietnam War was found, leading the authors to include
a lengthy footnote on the tendency of government sources to down-
grade estimates of the incidence of addiction among returning
GI's.

The authors caution the reader to be aware that the Haight-
Ashbury Clinic population from which they obtained their data
is not fully representative of heroin abuse as a whole. They
specifically say that "many black, Chicano, and Oriental addicts
do not feel comfortable in a predominantly white, hippie environment and hence may be isolated from any care." However, the
clinic sees more heroin users than any other single similar
clinic in the nation, and probably no type of user is unrepresent-
ed in its population.

The most striking trend, as stated by the authors, is the decreasing number of nonwhites among the addict population. The
heightening of revolutionary consciousness among young, lower
income black males and its concomitant view of heroin as counter-
revolutionary, they state, may be part of the explanation. They
see a change in the heroin subculture from a more traditional
quasi-criminal character to one infused with quasi-hippie over-
tones.

New York State Drug Abuse Commission (Anthony Cagliostro, Chair-
man). The New York State Drug Abuse Program - Current
Activities and Plans. Albany, New York: New York State Drug
Abuse Commission 1973-74.

An overview of the New York State Drug Abuse Control Commission program and orientation. It includes tables of projected
drug use in New York State based on the 1970 random sample
survey of the Narcotic Addiction Control Commission (NACC)
which was renamed the Drug Abuse Control Commission (DACC)
in 1973. As given in other reports of this survey, two-thirds
of New York heroin users are nonwhites. Eighty-four percent
were rated as being of lower or lower middle socioeconomic
status.

"New York Tries to Kick the Habit," Ebony 24, no. 11 (September
1969): 29-37.

A short article with many photographs giving statistics on
drug addiction and describing the New York State Narcotic Commission's program for rehabilitation. The New York program
combines all of the major treatments available. The author
agrees with their early findings: "there are no panaceas, easy
answers or instant cures for drug addiction; there is no single
type of treatment which is effective with all addicts; yet, addiction is nevertheless treatable, controllable and curable" (p. 37).

O'Donnell, John A. and Judith P. Jones. "Diffusion of the Intravenous
Technique Among Narcotic Addicts," Journal of Health and Social Behavior 9, no. 2 (June 1968): 120-30.

The history of intravenous injection of heroin, based on a
sample of 700 men and 311 women admitted to Lexington Hospital
in 1935, 1940, 1945, 1950, 1955, 1960, and 1965. About half
of them are black, the rest white. Intravenous injection (IV)
appears to have started between 1925 and 1930, possibly origin-
ating with white addicts in the South, and then spreading very
rapidly between 1930 and 1940. The diffusion after 1935 was

more rapid among blacks than whites; it did not differ much between women and men. This diffusion has been found to be associated with heroin use, use at an early age, and use for kicks
and pleasure. The authors interpret the data as supporting the
hypothesis that involvement in a drug subculture has facilitated
the spread of intravenous injection. "It is suggested that IV
use is preferred by addicts both because they find drug effects
more pleasurable when so administered and also because it may
be needed to make perceptible the effects of today's highly diluted
heroin" (p. 129).

Nurco, David. Occupational Skills of Narcotic Addicts. 1229 West
Mount Royal Road, Baltimore, Maryland. United States Department of Health, Education, and Welfare and the Maryland Psychiatric Research Center Drug Abuse Study, 1972.

An investigation into the vocational histories of 99 male Baltimore addicts: one-third from a prison group, one-third from
a mandatory treatment group, and one-third from a voluntary
treatment group. The ratio of blacks to whites, three to one,
reflects the total population ratio.

Nurco found that while everyone surveyed (addicts, ex-addicts,
employers, and treatment personnel) believed rehabilitative programs should include improvement of employment possibilities,
in practice, vocational training and job placement do not have
high priority. Furthermore, the different lifestyle of the addict
and how this affects employability have not been considered in
the full picture.

Some characteristics of the study subjects were: 18 percent
of the prison group had finished high school compared to 21 percent of the mandatory group and 39 percent of the voluntary
group. A majority (54 percent) had no juvenile court record.
The average age of first illegal drug use was 16 years; age at
time of study, 27 years. Twenty-two percent were unemployed
(for the prison group this refers to the months prior to incarceration); 25 percent worked in construction or "structural" jobs.
Few came from families with welfare assistance. Some race
differences were: less movement of residence during childhood
among blacks than whites; 70 percent of the blacks employed
full time compared to 84 percent of the whites; 48 percent of the
blacks confined as a result of the first offense tried in court
compared to 20 percent of the whites.

Some employment findings were: After addiction, unemployment decreased. The voluntary group showed the widest range
of employment but also the highest rate of unemployment (nearly

one-fourth). The length of continuous employment (job stability) increased after addiction.

In pre-addiction, the reasons for leaving a job were 50 percent negative, 35 positive, and 15 percent employer-initiated. After addiction, 58 percent quit for negative reasons of their own, 21 percent for positive reasons, and 20 percent for employer-initiated reasons. Structural work was the most common among the subjects and the type of job in which they remained the longest. It was also the major occupational category of their fathers and the type of work in which formally learned skills were used. Nurco postulates that the prevalence and stability of structural work among these persons may be related to the fact that such jobs are more available and/or less in conflict with the life style of an addict.

He concludes by commenting that if providing viable occupational alternatives to an addict's drug "career" is to be successful, a higher priority must be given to that goal than at present.

Nurco, David N. Narcotics Addiction-Utilization of Services. Pamphlet report. Baltimore, Maryland: The Maryland Psychiatric Research Center and the Maryland Drug Abuse Administration, 1972.

This study "investigates the use of community services by narcotic addicts for the purpose of determining their experience with, and their attitudes toward, helping agencies." Thirty-three addicts each from a prison group, a mandatory supervision group (an abstinence program for paroled addicts), and a voluntary treatment group were studied.

Although each group was racially the same (three-fourths black and one-fourth white) in order to represent the racial composition of the known total Baltimore addict population, the groups differed somewhat among each other: the voluntary group was more heterogeneous, better educated, and less likely to have had a mother working outside the home. Although all addicts had had periods of abstinence, those in the voluntary group attributed this more often to the drug treatment program than those in the other groups, where incarceration was the given reason.

Compared racially, the black study subjects were more likely to have moved less during childhood, were less likely to be employed full-time (70 percent black as compared to 84 percent white), somewhat older at time of first illegal drug use (16.9 years as compared to 14.9 for whites), and more likely to be confined as a result of their first offense tried in court. Most respondents (90 percent), black or white, rated their family backgrounds as stable.

Although use of voluntary services for social, economic, and emotional difficulties prior to addiction was not common, blacks were more likely to have requested such services. After addiction, however, whites were more likely to seek help. They were also more likely to receive services. Whites were more likely specifically to seek drug abuse treatment and/or psychiatric services than blacks; blacks requested unemployment and housing services far more frequently. Regarding involuntary correctional services prior to addiction, blacks were far more likely to have criminal court services and whites more likely to have received juvenile court service. Although about two-thirds of all services received were perceived as helpful, 60 percent of the drug treatment and 50 percent of the psychiatric services were so viewed. Over 80 percent of public welfare services were seen as helpful. Blacks generally had more positive views.

Nurco, David and Mitchell Balter. Drug Abuse Study. Maryland Commission to Study Problems of Drug Addiction, Baltimore: Maryland State Department of Mental Hygiene, 1969.

A study whose major purpose is to determine the usefulness of various agencies (health, social, educational, and correctional) in identifying drug abusers not known to the police or to such public facilities as the U.S. Mental Health Hospital in Lexington, Kentucky.

Data on 833 addicts drawn from the Baltimore City Police Narcotics Unit files for a two year period, 1966-68, showed the predominant addict population in Baltimore to be unemployed black males, under 30 years old, who were high school dropouts, who had been convicted of non-violent crime, and whose chosen drug was heroin. Police lists outside of Baltimore were more likely to carry names of younger white males (frequently students) who used marijuana as their chosen drug.

A comparison of drug abusers listed in the Maryland Psychiatric Case Register (November 1966-June 1967) yielded 551 cases; 57 percent were not known to the police department. Those who were known were more likely to be urban, older black males who were heroin or cocaine users. The younger, female, and/or white drug users were far less likely to come to the attention of the police. A higher percentage of females was found to abuse barbiturates, hypnotics and tranquilizers, while males tended to abuse opiates, synthetics, and narcotics.

The general conclusion is that a sizeable number of persons who abuse drugs are not known to the police department; it is the black, inner-city heroin user who is most known to such authorities. The health, educational, social, and correctional agencies surveyed varied in providing additional information; their input was related to their involvement in the total drug abuse scene or in the selective utilization of services and programs by drug abusers. No agency or police department alone provides a complete picture of drug abuse.

Nurco, David, Eugene V. Farrell and Zili Amsel. The Extent of Indigency Among Narcotic Abusers. Baltimore: Maryland State Department of Health and Mental Hygiene, Maryland Psychiatric Research Center, and Drug Abuse Administration, September 1972.

It is the contention of the authors that a provision exists for financing service to narcotic abusers through Title IV funds, the social security programs which include the states' official social service activities. The purpose of the study is to determine whether known narcotic abusers are usually indigent, and therefore eligible for treatment through such programs.

In the first part of the study, three samples selected from the Maryland Narcotics Addict Register in 1971 were checked against indexes of indigency: inclusion on Medicaid or social service services lists, residence in public housing and/or residence in low income areas.

Part two of the study was a brief analysis of cases active in the Baltimore City Juvenile Court on one day in 1972. Of the total 2,882 cases, 635 (or 22 percent) were drug abusers. Of these 635, 57 percent were black and 42 percent white. Of the narcotic abusers, 87 percent were black and 14 percent white. Over three-quarters of all the drug abusers were receiving no help specifically related to their drug problems. The indigence indices indicated that 38 percent of all the drug abuse cases were from families receiving public assistance and 37 percent were receiving Medicaid. A racial breakdown was not given.

Patterson, John T. and Leyland R. Hazlewood. "Crime: Its Impact on Business and the Economy of Central Harlem." Mimeographed. The Small Business Chamber of Commerce of New York, 1970.

A survey documenting the impact of crime on the economic life of Harlem, based on interviews, questionnaires, statistical methods, and general research. Black and white business operators in 15 areas of Central Harlem (representing three percent of all business operators in Central Harlem) were interviewed. The study shows that about 90 percent of the economic loss due to crime is caused by thefts to support the narcotic habit which cost Central Harlem around $1.8 billion in 1970.

Furthermore, most of the total estimated thefts in New York City
due to drugs, about $2.3 billion in 1970, are committed in Cen-
tral Harlem; only $500 million is estimated to be stolen in the
rest of the city. The authors estimate that in 1970 the 40,000
addicts living in Central Harlem paid $600 million to pushers,
thus making addiction more costly to Harlem than all other forms
of criminal activity combined. Nine out of ten businesses in Central Harlem have been robbed, half of them in 1970. Most of the
businesses recover nothing and most find insurance difficult or
impossible to obtain. The police estimate that 90 percent of the
crime in Harlem is committed by addicts; this survey shows that
businessmen estimate that addicts are responsible for at least
70 percent of the crime in Harlem. Therefore, the authors conclude, "it is meaningless to attempt to fight crime and its consequences in Central Harlem without effectively attacking or controlling the narcotics industry" (p. 37). They urge a series of
steps, centered around law enforcement and publicity, to imple-
ment a war against crime in Harlem.

Perlis, Leo. "Drug Abuse Among Union Members," Drug Abuse in
   Industry. Edited by W. Wayne Stewart. Miami, Florida: Halosand Associates, 1970, pp. 75-80.

   An account of data compiled by the AFL-CIO Department of
   Community Services in 20 cities on the extent of drug abuse in
   unionized industry. Preliminary reports indicate that there is
   no major problem with drug abuse in most cities. Where the
   problem exists, it is minimal but spreading. Drug abuse is concentrated on the East and West Coasts, mainly in the personal
   service trades, stores and offices (it has always existed to a
   degree in the entertainment world). There is a minor problem
   in other industries such as the meatpacking, automobile, and
   garment industries. Users are predominately black, Mexican
   American, and Puerto Rican, although drug abuse is spreading
   to all groups. Most users are young (under 20 years old), and
   are just entering the labor market and bringing their drug habits
   with them from school, the street, or home. Perlis recommends
   a program "to develop and promote educational and informational
   campaigns" (p. 76) by both the unions and employers. He calls
   for a "just approach" based on detection, referral, treatment,
   and rehabilitation, including employment and possible retraining.

Powers, Robert J. "The Vocational Maturity of Inner-city Narcotic
   Addicts," Rehabilitation Counseling Bulletin 4, no. 17 (June
   1974): 210-14.

A study to determine whether addicts have career attitudes
as mature as those of their peers and whether addicts and their
peers have career attitudes as mature as those of a normative
sampling of students. The subjects were 103 clients of a civil
commitment narcotic rehabilitation program (group I) and 46
members of a YMCA vocational training program (group II).
Demographically the two peer groups were similar: both were
from "disadvantaged" areas of the inner-city, predominantly
black or Puerto Rican (group I: 60 percent black, 25 percent
Puerto Rican, 15 percent white; group II: 67 percent black, 18
percent Puerto Rican, 15 percent white), with a mean age in the
twenties and a mean level of school completed 10 years in group
I and 11 years in group II. Evaluation of career maturity was
by Crite Matural Inventory (CMI-A).

The results showed that the addict group had less career
maturity than either group II or the 7th grade students on which
the test had been standardized. Group II did not differ significantly from student groups until the student subjects were at the 9th
grade level or above.

The author states that addicts, in manifesting less mature
vocational attitudes, can be expected to have greater difficulty
than their peers both in choosing an occupation and in adjusting
to it, and that faciliative efforts, such as counseling and work
stimulation projects are needed for employment success.

Preble, Edward J. and John J. Casey. "Taking Care of Business—
The Heroin User's Life on the Street," International Journal
of the Addictions 4, no. 1 (March 1969): 1-24.

An analysis of the lifestyle and activities of lower class, predominantly black and Puerto Rican heroin users in New York
City, based on participant-observation and on interviews with
over 150 patients at the Manhattan State Hospital Drug Addiction
Unit. The authors describe the history of heroin use in New York
City. Between World War I and World War II, heroin use was
limited to the entertainment and gangster world. Heroin use
was interrupted during World War II. From 1947 to 1951, heroin
use expanded to lower class black and Puerto Rican people who
could work and yet support their habit, since heroin was cheap;
an entire set of social relationships, cohesion, and identity developed. From 1951-57, heroin began to be popular among teenagers, leading to increased prices commensurate with the increased risk of selling to youth. From 1957-61, there were new
opportunities for independent operators: the syndicate withdrew
somewhat from the market because the risks had become too
great and their other sources of revenue had become endangered.

From 1961–69 the price for heroin increased further. The panic
of November 1961, caused by a shortage of heroin, led to the
realization that heroin could be further adulterated and the price
increased and people would still pay for it. The price increase
led to a breakdown in social cohesion among addicts, who began
to prey on each other, on their own families, and on strangers
in order to raise enough money to support their habits.

The authors also outline the process of heroin distribution
in New York City and the economic careers of heroin users.
Their economic careers revolve around supporting heroin use,
mainly through crimes against property and the person. Preble
and Casey show that addicts no longer avoid crimes of violence
or direct confrontation; instead they avoid crimes not involving
financial gain. The economic institutions that have developed
due to this lifestyle of the addict are described. The authors
argue that heroin use today by lower class minority groups is
based not on the need for a euphoric escape from the ghetto, but
rather on the pursuit of a meaningful life which heroin use provides. Heroin users are not passive; they are extremely active,
aggressive, alert, flexible, and resourceful. "If they can be
said to be addicted, it is not so much to heroin as to the entire
career of a heroin user" (p. 21). The authors suggest that "the
career of a heroin user serves a dual purpose for the slum in-
habitant; it enables him to escape, not from purposeful activity,
but from the monotony of an existence severely limited by social
constraints, and at the same time it provides a way for him to
gain revenge on society for the injustices and deprivation he has
experienced [through outwitting the Man, stealing from the richer,
etc.]" (p. 22).

Preble, Edward and Gabriel V. Laury. "Plastic Cement: The Ten
Cent Hallucinogen," International Journal of the Addictions 2,
no. 2 (Fall 1967): 271–81.

A report on the hallucinatory effects of glue sniffing, based
on tape-recorded interviews with 40 teenage subjects. Half of
the sample, of whom 14 are Puerto Rican and 6 black, come
from a slum area and half are patients in a children's unit of
a large mental institution, consisting of 12 Puerto Ricans, 6
blacks, and 2 whites. After a short description of the rituals
and effects of glue sniffing, the authors give excerpts from interviews with both groups, showing how glue sniffing produces
an altered state of mind. The authors attribute the sudden interest in glue sniffing which began in the early 1960s to the widespread sociocultural movement interested in chemically induced
altered states of mind.

Press, Edward and Alan K. Done. "Solvent Sniffing: Physiologic
     Effects and Community Control Measures for Intoxication from
     the Intentional Inhalation of Organic Solvents," Pediatrics 39, no.
     3 (March 1967): 451-61.

   A review of published reports on solvent sniffing, correspon-
dence with medical and law enforcement personnel in many areas
of the U.S., and a direct study of 16 boys in Salt Lake City, Utah
who were interviewed and retested frequently. The prevalence
and incidence of solvent sniffing and the substances involved are
briefly summarized. The characteristics of sniffers that emerge
from these studies focusing on glue sniffers are detailed. Most
sniffers are between 10 and 15 years of age, although significant
numbers are under 10 years old. There has been a large preponderance of boys over girls, which may be related to the fact
that girls are less apt to commit crimes bringing them to the
attention of authorities. A greater proportion of Mexican Americans are involved in sniffing, while blacks are underrepresented
in terms of their distribution in the general population. Although
I.Q. is not a significant variable, poor school adjustment and
scholastic performance are found to be common to all sniffers.
The families of sniffers are broken, either physically or psychologically, with the father having no effective relationship with
the boy and with one or both parents commonly abusing alcohol.
Although the relationship between criminality, narcotic and/or
alcoholic addiction, and sniffing is unclear, the authors feel that
it is probable that a causal relationship exists. The authors also
cite instances of accidents, antisocial activities, and homicide
resulting from sniffing.

Ramer, Barry S. "Screening Patients for a Successful Methadon
     [sic] Maintenance Treatment Program," Methadon [sic] Work-
     shop Proceedings. Edited by P. H. Blachly. Portland, Oregon:
     University of Oregon, March 1971. Pp. 19-22.

   A delineation of the characteristics of 400 individuals seeking
methadone treatment in San Francisco, California and the program and background characteristics leading to success in the
methadone maintenance program. Most of the patients are 20-
35 years old, unemployed, have a daily habit of $40-80, have
been using narcotics daily for over three years, and are addicted
by the time they are 19 years old. They are 80 percent male
and 20 percent female; 30 percent are married, 44 percent
single, and 26 percent separated, widowed or divorced. The
patient racial composition is consistent with the racial proportions of the San Francisco population: 70 percent white, 12 percent black, and 12 percent Mexican American. There are only

6 percent Asians in the program, whereas Asians are 13 percent of the population. The program, staffing, and utilization
of services of the San Francisco Center for Special Problems
Methadone Maintenance Treatment Program are described. The
profile of the successful patient is that he or she is over 29
years old, from a minority group, is not actively psychotic or
with complicated medical problems, has tried detoxification
many times, has been addicted for over three years, completed
high school, and has been regularly employed at some time.
Ramer feels that this addict does not fit the typical description
of "the addict personality," and therefore seriously calls into
question the traditional conception of the "addict personality."
Program characteristics leading to success are briefly enumer-
ated.

Reasons, Charles. "The Politics of Drugs: An Inquiry in the Sociology
of Social Problems," Sociological Quarterly 15, no. 3 (Summer
1974): 381-404.

In this primarily theoretical discussion, Reasons traces the
development of the drug problem in America. Using a subjective
approach he emphasizes societal reaction as the basis for a
social phenomenon, such as drug use being labelled a "social
problem."
He traces the development of the earliest anti-drug sentiment
in this country and relates it to moral and spiritual zealots who
were opposed to tobacco and alcohol as to other drugs. Racist
and nativistic sentiments were played upon and exploited in moral
crusades. The "opium-dazed Oriental" in the West and the
"cocaine-crazed Negro" in the South were frequently alluded to
in the literature. It was thought that drug use wasn't really
American: "narcotic use, like alcohol use, led to the lack of
rationality and self control which were the cornerstones of
proper 'WASP' behavior."
The drug user was referred to as a "dope fiend" and portrayed
as a moral degenerate. Thus early laws which were passed were
directed to the user: importation of drugs was not controlled.
The statutes, especially those directed to the Chinese, were,
says Reasons, "a symbolic gesture to indicate the superiority
of whites over Orientals," and "the passing of such statutes
legitimized one culture over another."
As public demand increased for federal laws to control importation, drug trade interests influenced the wording of the
bills to allow a flow of drugs into the country for medicinal and
commercial interests. A growing view of the addict as a criminal—dangerous, alien, nonwhite, and disrespectful of laws—

shifted the focus of control to judicial decision and punitive solutions. The total effect of such policies and the "harms produced by illegal use of drugs in our society—i. e., crime, disease, death—are almost entirely a consequence of our drug
policy rather than the pharmacological effect of such drugs."

Reed, Thomas, Jerome S. Miller, John Sensenig and John V. Haley.
"A Comparison of College Students and Narcotic Addicts on a
Risk-Cautious Dimension," International Journal of the Addic-
tions 7, no. 3 (Fall 1972): 493-510.

A comparison of 40 white college students (23 males and 17
females) enrolled in an undergraduate course at the University
of Kentucky with 68 narcotic addict patients at the Clinical Research Center in Lexington, Kentucky, in order to determine
differences on risky or cautious solutions to problem situations.
There are 53 male and 15 female addict patients, including 38
black males and 5 black females. A modified form of the Stoner
choice dilemmas, with six risky and six cautious problems, was
administered to both groups. It is found that students see themselves as more risky or cautious than others, depending on the
situation, and admire the most extreme values employed. They
predict responses for addicts in terms of stereotype-directed
response patterns, conjecturing that addicts will choose riskier
solutions for all situations, without differentiating between risky
and cautious values. Actually the addicts, although differentially
responsive to underlying values, are found to be less risky on
risky items and less cautious on cautious items than the students,
suggesting that the addicts are less sensitive and responsive to
the values employed than the students. Some of the reasons for
this are discussed. The authors conclude that the results suggest
that "addicts are not as alienated from or as unaware of social
values as may be commonly assumed" (p. 508).

Richman, Alex, Marvin E. Perkins, Bernard Bihari and J. J. Fishman. "Entry into Methadone Maintenance Programs: A Follow-
up Study of New York City Heroin Users Detoxified in 1961-1963,"
American Journal of Public Health 62, no. 7 (July 1972):
1002-7.

A follow-up study of 100 addicts who had been detoxified 8
to 10 years previously in Beth Israel Medical Center, New York
City. Twenty-three percent had entered a methadone maintenance
program by the end of 1971, 15 percent had died, 13 percent
were "alleged abstinent," 9 percent were in prison, 8 percent were in other treatment, 19 percent were known to be

addicted and living in the community, and 14 percent were not
located. There were ethnic differences in admissions into methadone maintenance treatment: 35 percent of the white males had
been admitted compared to 30 percent of the Hispanics and 17
percent of the blacks. Among females, 6 percent of the whites
had been admitted, 12 percent of the Hispanics, and 17 percent
of the blacks.

Richardson, Henry, Jeffrey Brooks, Mark Cohen and Joseph Kern.
"A Three Year Follow-up Study of 43 Heroin Addicts in a Suburban Community," Journal of Drug Education 4, no. 4 (Winter
1974): 339-398.

A follow-up study of 43 clients (95 percent black, 86 percent
male) in a heroin detoxification program in Freeport, Nassau
County, New York three years after initial contact. At the end
of the follow-up period only one client was "drug free." Heroin
use was reduced: 6 clients were still addicted, with 4 using
it on weekends; 2 using various drugs, 12 using street methadone, and 2 multi-drug users. Eight were in jail, 6 were on
methadone maintenance, and 4 had died of overdose.

The authors point out that this study differs from other recidivism studies in that its setting is surburban; the result, a
high incidence of relapse, is the same, however. The authors
conclude that a problem "whose major components are psychological and social cannot be solved medically." They also suggest
a reconsideration of the advisability of devoting a substantial
portion of treatment funds and manpower to detoxification.

Richter, Ralph W. and Roger N. Rosenberg. "Transverse Myelitis
Associated with Heroin Addiction," Journal of the American
Medical Association 106, no. 6 (November 4, 1968): 1255-7.

Detailed medical case histories of four black men who, after
abstaining from heroin from one to six months due to hospitalization or imprisonment, were admitted to Harlem Hospital shortly
after taking heroin again intravenously. They suffered from acute
myelitis (paralysis in the legs) and sensory loss. One patient
died five weeks after taking heroin again, another died later.
One man still suffers from mild paralysis with sensory loss
and another from severe paralysis and sensory loss. "These
factors suggest an allergic or hypersensitive reaction" (p. 1257)
with heroin, quinine, or other adulterants.

Robins, Lee N. and George E. Murphy. "Drug Use in a Normal Population of Young Negro Men," American Journal of Public Health
57, no. 9 (September 1967): 1580-96.

An investigation of the patterns of drug use in a normal, un-
selected group of young black men between 30-35 years old in
St. Louis. Through record research and interviews, the authors
find that ten percent of the sample of 235 black youths have been
addicted to heroin, four percent of whom have been treated for
addiction in a U.S. Public Health Hospital. No regular heroin
user in the sample avoided official detection; 86 percent of them
are reported as addicts to the Federal Bureau of Narcotics. Few
men who deny drug use are arrested for violating narcotics laws.
"Our findings indicate that fairly reliable lifetime prevalence
figures for heroin addiction can be obtained from an unduplicated
cumulative list of men arrested for drug law violations" (p. 1595).
They find that heroin addicts, past and present, are using a variety of drugs, suggesting that addiction is not simply physical
dependence, but also the readiness of the addict to use drugs to
alter the level of consciousness. Half of the sample uses some
drug illegally; all of them use marijuana. Half of the marijuana
users have never used any other drug; one-third of them have
used marijuana for less than a year. Those marijuana users
who never become heroin users rarely become known to the
police. The younger a person is when he begins to use marijuana, the more likely he is to become addicted to heroin. The
authors are surprised at the lack of correlation they find between
drug use and occupational status of the guardian and between drug
use and any school problems before the age of 15. Black male
youth are found to be most vulnerable when their fathers are absent from the home, when they possess a record of juvenile delinquency, and when they drop out of high school.

Robins, Lee N. A Follow-up of Vietnam Drug Users. Interim Final
    Report Special Action Office Monograph Series A, #1, Wash-
    ington, D.C.: U.S. Government Printing Office, April 1973.

    A study designed to measure the extent and nature of drug
use among returning Vietnam veterans. The Special Action
Office for Drug Abuse Addiction which sponsored this study was
established by Executive Order in June, 1971. Four principal
government agencies participated: the Department of Defense,
the Department of Labor, the National Institute of Mental Health,
and the Veteran's Administration.
    September 1971 was the period of departure from Vietnam
from which the sample was taken: it consisted of 500 general
returnees and 500 drug positives. All military personnel de-
parting from Vietnam at that time were screened by urinalysis
for drug use at DEROS (Date Expected Return from Overseas),
but only male enlisted personnel were included for study.

Among the approximately 50 percent who used drugs, the most common pattern (18 percent) was to use all types of drugs included in the study: narcotics, barbiturates, and amphetamines. Most used drugs repeatedly and over considerable time. Continued use of drugs after return to the U.S., however, was considerably lower than expected. Although many felt they had been "strung out" (addicted) in Vietnam, only a small proportion seemed to be heavily involved in drugs after returning.

Demographically, the man most likely to be detected at DEROS as a drug positive was young, single, of low rank, of little education, from a broken home, with an arrest record before service, and had used drugs before entering the military service. Race was not correlated with drug use.

None of the above characteristics were of use in forecasting continued narcotic use after return. Patterns of use both before and in Vietnam were the best predictor of narcotic use after return to the states.

Surprisingly, blacks who were drug positive at DEROS were not significantly more likely to be unemployed than blacks in the general sample or than white high school dropouts.

Roebuck, Julian B. "The Negro Drug Addict as an Offender Type," Journal of Criminal Law, Criminology and Police Science 53, no. 1 (March 1962): 36-43.

A comparison of some social and personal characteristics of 50 narcotic drug law offenders with 350 inmates of other offender types, based on institutional records and interviews. Roebuck finds significant differences which clearly distinguish the narcotic drug laws offenders: they are younger (with a median age of 25 compared to a median age of 33 for the others); they are more literate, with an S.A.T. grade median of 8.6 compared to 5.0 for the others; they are of average intelligence, with a median I.Q. of 100 compared to 86 for the others; and they are much more concentrated in urban areas, with 94 percent with urban backgrounds compared to 65 percent for the others. Fewer of them come from disorganized family backgrounds or are involved in serious delinquencies in school, at home, or in the community. The most important factors that Roebuck sees in their background are maternal dominance and paternal passivity and encouragement of passive activity in isolation from others, such as reading, drawing, and listening to music. They are introduced to heroin by older addict companions when they are adolescents and young adults, and usually are not delinquent prior to their addictions. All of them listen to jazz as their main recreation; half are jazz musicians. All of them abhor violence and alcohol,

which is a personality irritant. They become criminals only to
support their habit since legitimate work does not pay enough,
and they therefore become vulnerable to police apprehension.
No one is found to be a gangster or racketeer; they are small-
time street peddlers who sell drugs to earn enough money to
support their own habits.

Rollins, Joan H. and Raymond H. Holden. "Adolescent Drug Use and
the Alienation Syndrome," Journal of Drug Education 2, no. 3
(September 1972): 249-61.

A drug survey of junior and senior high school students in a
large New England city which found higher drug use among males,
eighth graders, children from broken homes, and children who
do not plan to complete high school. It is suggested that these
adolescents are enmeshed in an "alienation syndrome" and need
a variety of services for prevention and rehabilitation. The
sample consisted of 1000 students, 82 percent white, 15 percent
black, and 2 percent other. Twenty-four percent of the black
students said they had tried heroin, compared to 7 percent
of the whites. For other drugs the difference was not as large
but, except for alcohol, black students had experimented with
other drugs to a greater extent that white students.

Rosenberg, Chaim M., Gerald E. Davidson and Vernon D. Patch.
"Patterns of Drop-Outs from a Methadone Program for Narcotic
Addicts," International Journal of the Addictions 7, no. 3 (Fall
1972): 415-25.

An evaluation of the effectiveness of methadone maintenance
of 1400 heroin addicts who voluntarily applied for treatment at
the Boston City Hospital Drug Dependency Clinic from August,
1970 through April, 1971. Over two-thirds of the applicants are
under 26 years old; their mean age is 24. Over 80 percent are
male, and 60 percent are black. The average patient has been
addicted to narcotics for two to four years. Concurrent multiple
drug use is uncommon. The authors describe the kinds of treatment the hospital used, the proportional treatment of total applicants, and the follow-up of 577 narcotic addicts who dropped
out of the methadone maintenance program. Although more white
than black patients tend to remain in treatment, the two groups
do not differ in terms of sex ratio, age, education, or marital
status. The authors discuss the outcome of patients in treatment
and conclude that methadone maintenance "leads to a rapid reduction in heroin use and criminal behavior for most of those who
remain in treatment" (p. 422) and "provides them with a degree

fo stability upon which social and psychological growth can gradually develop" (p. 423).

Royfe, Ephrain H. "An Exploratory Examination of the Social and Psychological Characteristics of 100 Pennsylvania Drug Addicts,"
Pennsylvania Psychiatric Quarterly 5, no. 4 (Winter 1965):
38-47.

An analysis of social and psychological aspects of the Pennsylvania Board of Parole records for 100 male drug addicts who
were released on parole in Philadelphia between September 1,
1959 and January 30, 1962. Ninety percent are black, eight percent white, one percent Puerto Rican, and one percent Chinese.
"The fact that known drug addiction is generally confined, with
the exception of certain professional groupings, almost wholly
to Negro slum areas demonstrates the fact that certain segments
of our population may accept this from [sic] of social behavior"
(p. 39). The migrant black population is underrepresented in
proportion to their numbers in the addict group: 74 percent of
the sample were born in Pennsylvania and 95 percent had lived
in Pennsylvania for 11 years or more prior to their last arrest.
Only 36 percent admit to using marijuana prior to opiate use;
none use marijuana in conjunction with opiates, thus showing
that marijuana use does not necessarily lead to opiate use. The
reasons why they use drugs are focused mainly around the need
for an identity within a group (67 percent) and relief of tension
(27 percent); only 30 percent began use due to curiosity or kicks
(subjects could choose more than one answer, so the percentages
add up to more than 100). On intelligence tests, 39 percent of the
blacks score as dull normal or below, but psychiatrists who have
interviewed the parolees consider these I.Q. scores to indicate
socio-cultural deprivation rather than a basic lack of intelligence
Nearly half of the addicts have failed the Armed Forces test,
and 35 percent have received less than honorable, dishonorable,
or medical discharges. The number of divorced or separated
addicts is double that of the black males in the area, which indicates the instability and disturbing influence of drugs on marriage. Most addicts are between 26-35 years old, with a general drop-off after the age of 35; 88 percent were convicted before they were 25 years old. The author recommends intensive
mandatory supervision for the addicts and better coordination
of institutional services and community resources.

Scher, Jordan. "Patterns and Profiles of Addiction and Drug Abuse,"
International Journal of the Addictions 2, no. 2 (Fall 1967):
171-90.

An exploration of various aspects of drug abuse, based on Scher's experiences in the Narcotics Court and as a psychiatric consultant to the Sheriff's Office and the Cook County Jail in Chicago, Illinois. He claims to be the first, before Winick, to postulate the existence of two groups of addicts: the "hard" narcotic addicts, with a controlled or limited habit, and others who sooner or later voluntarily abstain from drugs. In describing adolescence and drug use, he notes that those who turn into serious users are usually too curious to try something new and different. Marijuana use "cuts across all categories of preferential adult drug use" (p. 174). Opiate use before 21 years of age is predominantly white, with only 26.6 percent black, 22.4 percent Puerto Rican, and 3.3 percent Mexican American, whereas blacks constitute a majority of users after 21 years of age: 53.3 percent of all addicts are black, compared to 28.1 percent white, 12.2 percent Puerto Rican and 15.6 percent Mexican American. He details the addict's three-pronged struggle to maintain euphoria, limit tolerance, and avoid withdrawal, and argues that short treatment only reinforces "the addictive process itself by facilitating the recovery of the most ecstatic highs" (p. 176). Maintaining euphoria is the primary motivator of the addict along with reducing tolerance. Avoidance of withdrawal is a less important motivator than these two. Scher backs the hypothesis of the group as the primary inducer. The amphetamine cycle, the psychedelic cycle, theatrogenic abusers, and drugs and the law are described. Scher concludes that although he has no one solution to the problem, there must be many solutions to the many problems posed by drug abuse.

Selby, Earl and Miriam Selby. Odyssey: Journal Through Black America. New York: G. P. Putnam's Sons, 1971.

Interviews conducted by white authors with black people around the United States over a period of two years on such subjects as politics, the civil rights movement, what it means to be a black woman, turmoil on the campus and in the streets of South Carolina, growing up in the ghetto, the black church, and drugs as a way of life. The chapter on drugs includes interviews with black men in the Street Workers Program sponsored by the Addicts Rehabilitation Center in New York City. The main theme concerns the lack of confidence and self-hatred of black youth who want to be white and successful and who turn to drugs in order to imitate the successful hustler. The director for the Addicts Rehabilitation Center emphasizes his faith in God as helping him resist returning to drugs.

Sells, S. B., Lois R. Chatham and George W. Joe. "The Relation
of Selected Epidemiological Factors to Retention in Methadone
Treatment," Proceedings of the Fourth National Conference on
Methadone Treatment. San Francisco: National Association for
the Prevention of Addiction to Narcotics, January 8-10, 1972,
pp. 89-90.

An examination of a sample of 542 male opiate addicts treated
at 13 methadone programs supported by the National Institute of
Mental Health, made in order to determine the characteristics
of those patients who remain in treatment for at least one year.
Blacks, who are 57.6 percent of the sample and are primarily
older males, tend to have a higher retention rate in the program
compared to whites, who are younger. Mexican Americans, who
are 17.5 percent of the sample, tend to have a higher retention
rate. The authors conclude that "age, race-ethnic status, early
daily use of heroin or other opiates [before age 17], and failure
to complete high school, are not significant predicators of early
drop-out, once the patient has completed a minimum of two
months in treatment. On the other hand, those who have a history
of juvenile delinquency may require special attention" (p. 90).

Shepherd, Charles W., David E. Smith and George R. Gay. "The
Changing Face of Heroin Addiction in the Haight-Ashbury,"
International Journal of the Addictions 7, no. 1 (Spring 1972):
109-22.

Identification of the characteristics of heroin addicts, based
on 773 charts of the Haight-Ashbury Medical Clinic in San Francisco. The authors divide heroin addicts into three groups: the
new junkies who are white with middle class background and began
using heroin as a form of escape after January, 1967, with little
previous use of other drugs; the transition junkies who are white
and middle class and began using heroin before 1964, with little
or previous use of any drugs, including alcohol.

Snow, Mary. "Maturing Out of Narcotic Addiction in New York City,"
International Journal of the Addictions 8, no. 6 (December 1973):
921-38.

In this study evidence of maturing out of addiction was dis-
covered for 23 percent of a sample of addicts who were first
reported to the New York City Narcotics Register in 1964 and
were followed through 1968. A comparison of those who had
matured out (the inactive group) with those who had not matured
out (the active group) revealed differences in age distribution.
Members of the inactive group were more likely to be older than

those of the active group. When background characteristics were
considered, only ethnicity and sex were significantly differentiating factors. Whites were somewhat more likely (27 percent)
to become inactive than blacks (22 percent) or Puerto Ricans
(20 percent). Among the inactive cases, whites became inactive
at an earlier age or in areas of lower drug use.

Snow states that "the discovering that the inactive group is
so heterogeneous, with members highly differentiated by age,
ethnicity, sex, and area of residence suggests that very different
life experiences, very different routes into addiction, and very
different circumstances and reasons for becoming active may
be represented within the group." She also raises questions as
to how many of the inactive cases have really matured out as
described by Winick: could it be that many have merely achieved
a state of anonymity that keeps them off official reports?

Sokol, Jacob. "Glue Sniffing in Los Angeles," Drug Addiction in Youth.
    Edited by Ernest Harms. New York: Pergamon Press, 1965,
    pp. 46-48.

A short summary of data collected from 89 juveniles booked
on the charge of glue sniffing in Los Angeles. They range in age
from 8 to 18 years and the racial breakdown is 45 whites,
37 Mexican Americans, and 7 blacks. Sokol describes the
methods used for sniffing glue, the sensations produced by glue
sniffing and the results of physical examinations revealing abnormalities in the blood, urine, and liver of glue sniffers. He
analyzes glue sniffing as a psycho-social phenomenon, caused
by environment, insecurity, frustrations, physical size, and ego
status.

Stephens, Richard and Emily Cottrell. "A Follow-Up Study of 200 Nar-
    cotic Addicts Committed for Treatment under the Narcotic Addict
    Rehabilitation Act (NARA)," British Journal of Addiction 67, no.
    1 (March 1972): 45-53.

An assessment of relapse into heroin addiction in a follow-up
study of 200 male narcotic addicts who completed the NARA program of six months of inpatient treatment followed by three years
of aftercare service. The men were discharged from the Lexington and Fort Worth Hospitals in 1969. Fifty-eight are black, 34
Spanish, and the rest white. This assessment is based on questionnaires sent to the patients and their counselors. The relapse
rate into use of narcotics is 87 percent, which is consistent with
the relapse rate of 80-90 percent found in other studies. This
study supports the findings of other research that older addicts

(over 30 years) slowly relinquish their addictive patterns, although the authors disagree with Winick on the relationship between length of addiction and relapse and on the reasons why the addict matures out of addiction. They find no correlation between length of addiction and relapse. Those who find jobs are less liable to relapse than those unable to find employment. Ethnicity and education are found to be generally unrelated to relapse. Counselors and patients cite three general factors contributing to relapse: the use of narcotics to alleviate interpersonal stress, the craving for or enjoyment of the euphoric effects of narcotics and of the addict subculture, and depression, frustration and inability to cope with problems. The stated reasons for abstinence thus do not support Winick's hypothesis of burning out.

Stephens, Richard C. and Rosalind Ellis. Narcotics Addicts and Crime: Analysis of Recent Trends. New York State Drug Abuse Control Commission, 1974.

Using four cohorts of male addicts ages 24-25 criminally certified to the New York State Narcotic Control Commission from 1969-72, Stephen and Ellis try to establish if there is a changing pattern in arrests over that time period. The total sample of 589 was 47 percent black, 26 percent white, and 27 percent Puerto Rican.

The data showed that drug arrest and property crimes account for over three-quarters of all arrests, but that crimes against persons show a steady increase. The crimes against persons, however, were in combination with a property offense in 85 percent of the cases, which supports the "mugger" concept that the addict is primarily interested in obtaining money but may use violence to attain his goal.

Stephens, Richard C. and Gerald T. Slatin. "The Street Addict Role: Toward the Definition of a Type," Drug Forum 3, no. 4 (Summer 1974): 375-89.

There have been previous efforts to make a typology of narcotics addicts and to document the dual pattern of addiction in American society: one group consisting primarily of nonwhite heroin users in ghetto areas of large urban centers, and the other of middle-aged whites concentrated in southern states. While this pattern may be shifting as regards non-ghetto drug abuse, the street addict has been seen as representing a final stage in the evolutionary process within the urban drug subculture.

Stephens and Slatin studied an addict population to explore the conceptual definition of a street addict as one who used more than one narcotic, preferred heroin, cocaine or a combination of both, used drugs intraveneously, obtained drugs illegally, had sold drugs, had engaged in criminal activity, had been arrested, and had experienced at least one withdrawal previous to Lexington. The sample was 1,096 patients committed to the NIMH Hospital in Lexington, Kentucky prior to May, 1969; of 824 males, 376 were white, 417 black, and 31 of Spanish origin. Of the 262 females, 129 were white, 110 black, and 33 of Spanish origin.

The street addict type was found in greater numbers among minority males (40 percent) than among white males (24 percent); among females this differential is not evident (29 percent for whites and 29 percent for blacks).

The street addict role type was checked against other variables (such as the cost of the daily habit and the age when intravenous use was begun). There was a consistent reinforcement of the typologies of street addict and non-street addict. The separation was more clear cut for whites, however, leading the authors to hypothesize that the cultural milieu in which a black addict grows up may more often and more quickly socialize him into the street addict role.

Stephens, Richard C. and Robert S. Weppner. "Legal and Illegal Use of Methadone: One Year Later," American Journal of Psychiatry 130, no. 12 (December 1973): 1391-4.

This study (which replicated one conducted a year earlier) found that the use of methadone, both legal and illegal, had increased. The role of the pusher as supplier of illicit methadone declined, while other suppliers, particularly addict friends, became more important. The reasons for the use of illicit methadone changed dramatically; methadone's low cost and ease of procurement aided its emergence from a substitute drug to a drug of choice. The study seems to indicate that the black market in methadone was flourishing, and had possibly grown in the short span of one year.

Comparison of total admissions to the Lexington, Kentucky Hospital showed a decrease in the percentage of blacks (60 percent in 1971 versus 49 percent in 1972), but their representation among methadone users remained constant.

Swartz, June and Raymond Jabara. "Short-Term Follow-up of Narcotic Addicts," Rehabilitation Counseling Bulletin 17, no. 4 (March 1974): 604-5.

A follow-up of veterans who left a multimodality (maintenance, detoxification, and abstinence) methadone facility in Baltimore, Maryland between 1971 and 1972. Race, job status, and degree of drug use were variables considered. Information was obtained on 89 subjects, or 62 percent of the veterans who had left the facility.

The findings were that 75 percent of the subjects were still using drugs, of which 38 percent were addicted to either heroin or methadone, and that 49 percent were either in school or working. Although not statistically significant, there was an observed tendency toward lower addiction and higher employment rates among the blacks (who represented 63 percent of the total sample).

Taylor, Susan D., Mary Wilbur and Robert Osnos. "The Wives of Drug Addicts," American Journal of Psychiatry 123, no. 5 (November 1966): 585-91.

Extensive interviews with 16 wives of drug addicts treated at the Greenwich House Counseling Center in New York City made to determine why women marry addicts and why they remain married to them. Although one woman is black and three are Latin, no racial differences are cited. The women identify strongly with their mothers and view their fathers as weak. They are attracted to their husbands by their minimal adult heterosexual demands and by their passive qualities, which enable the women to control and dominate them. The authors explore other reasons why these women marry addicts, such as masochism and rebellion against the woman's family, but do not find them valid.

Treadway, Walter L. "Some Epidemiological Features of Drug Addiction," British Journal of Inebriety 28, no. 2 (October 1930): 50-54.

A description of some of the characteristics of drug addicts in the U.S., based on 1,384 male addicts reported as violators of federal law between July 1 and October 31, 1929, and on a study conducted by the U.S. Public Health Service of 1,660 addicts, of whom 1,384 are male and 276 female. Among the first group, he finds that nearly 30 percent (322) are Asian, while only 172 are black and 880 white. The proportions among the women drop: 201 are white, 71 black, and 4 Asian. Most addicts are in their thirties and forties: the average age for males is 38 years and for females 34.2 years. Some drug addicts hold lawful and gainful jobs, but they keep their doses of drugs small over the years; most addicts increase their doses and are migratory and irregularly employed. There is no way of knowing how many addicts exist. Treadway cites statistics ranging from 110,000 to 200,000, the majority concentrated in the cities. He then details the arrest records, educational status, employment history, and use of alcohol among addicts. Over 60 percent establish their habit between the ages of 20 and 34; the chosen drug is morphine or heroin, administered with a hypodermic, intravenously, or by smoking, in that order of choice. The precipitating causes of addiction are found to be previous use of drugs in medical treatment, self-treatment for relief of pain, influence of other addicts, and curiosity, bravado or thrills.

Vaillant, George E. "A Twelve-Year Follow-Up of New York Narcotic Addicts: I. The Relation of Treatment to Outcome," American Journal of Psychiatry 122, no. 7 (January 1966): 727-37.

An exploration of the relationship between the kind of treatment received by drug addicts and periods of abstinence, as revealed by the life histories of 100 male black and white addicts first admitted to Lexington Hospital between August, 1952 and January, 1953. Relying on medical and prison records and interviews with the patients and their relatives, Vaillant describes the general characteristics of the sample, the relationship of outcome to treatment, and family characteristics of the addicts which might be related to treatment response. He finds that 46 percent are off drugs and living in the community. His most dramatic findings are that 96 percent of all addicts who seek voluntary treatment for their addiction relapse within a year, whereas 67 percent of the addicts who serve at least nine months in jail and a year of parole are abstinent for a year or more. He concludes that "the most significant variable in determining abstinence in the confirmed addict appeared to be the presence or absence of constructive but enforced compulsory supervision" (p. 737).

Vaillant, George E. "Twelve-Year Follow-Up of New York Narcotic Addicts: II. The Natural History of a Chronic Disease," New England Journal of Medicine 275, no. 23 (December 8, 1966): 1282-8.

A report on the occupational and drug histories of 50 urban narcotic addicts (half of whom are black) from New York City who were admitted to Lexington Hospital between 1952 and 1953. The study covers a twelve year period when the sample ranges

from 16-42 years of age. The average addict is found to remain
addicted for ten years or more, despite frequent voluntary and
forced withdrawals. However, Vaillant's findings back up those
of Winick on maturing out: by the age of 42, only 25 percent are
still using narcotics and 40 percent have achieved stable abstinence. The mortality rate of addicts is two to five times that
expected for males of similar age; the excess is due to the addict's own actions (but not suicide), and the death rate from
complications of alcoholism is unusually high. The average
addict remains physically healthy and without psychotic mani-
festations during this twelve-year follow-up. "The possibility
is suggested that marked inability to sustain employment may
precede or even be one cause of addiction" (p. 1288.)

Vaillant, George E. "A Twelve-Year Follow-Up of New York Narcotic
    Addicts: III. Some Social and Psychiatric Considerations,"
    Archives of General Psychiatry 15 (December 1966): 599-609.

    A delineation of the social and personality characteristics
that differentiate addiction from other psychiatric syndromes.
Fifty black and 50 white men first admitted to Lexington Hospital
for addiction between August, 1952 and January, 1953 are followed up by reviews of police and medical records and interviews.
Ethnic differences among blacks, whites, and Puerto Ricans,
who in the rest of this study are considered to be white, do not
seem to lead to different patterns of drug use. Social and personality characteristics are examined. Addicts are characterized by a strong cultural disparity between parent and child,
the sustained dependency of the addict upon relatives, and a high
incidence of broken homes and absent fathers. The overwhelming
majority of the addicts are married, and half have children.
Most addicts, although educationally deprived, have at least
normal (and one-fourth have superior) I.Q. ratings. Vaillant
hypothesizes that "an intelligence above that of his peers or
parents may generate anxiety in the otherwise passive and dependent addict" (p. 603). The addicts' delinquency often precedes drug use. Many commit an unusually large number of
crimes against property, although they give up their delinquent
activity as they get older. Most have a low incidence of psychosis.
The adolescent addict often manifests severe psychopathy sug-
gestive of schizophrenia, but as he gets older the psychopathology appears to have been due to his immaturity and emotionally
unstable character. The severe character disorder from which
he suffers consists of hypomanic defenses, well defended depression, and a strongly anti-social but not schizoid orientation.
Vaillant concludes that "although the ways in which addicts differ

from other delinquent individuals were noted, the study suggests
that the roots of urban addiction may be fruitfully sought in striving to understand the dynamics of repetitive delinquent behavior
in general" (p. 608).

Vaillant, George E. "A Twelve-Year Follow-Up of New York Narcotic
    Addicts: IV. Some Characteristics and Determinants of Absti-
    nence," American Journal of Psychiatry 122, no. 5 (November
    1966): 573-84.

    A study of the 30 best outcomes of 100 young male New York
    City heroin addicts admitted to Lexington Hospital between
    August, 1952 and January, 1953, made to determine why these
    men achieved and maintained stable abstinence from heroin for
    at least three years. Blacks are 47 percent of the ex-addicts
    and 57 percent of the chronic addicts. Comparing them through
    data and interviews with the 30 worst patients who are still
    chronic addicts, Vaillant finds that previous ability to keep a
    job, an intact home until age six, and a relatively late onset
    of addiction are correlated with eventual abstinence. Family
    pathology, the amount of heroin used, and previous criminal
    record are not related to abstinence; compulsory supervision,
    a substitute addiction such as alcoholism, and the establishment
    of meaningful non-parental relationships are found to be impor-
    tant contributors to abstinence. There is no evidence that ad-
    dicts as a group develop other incapacitating mental illnesses
    when they abstain from narcotics. Vaillant sees the addict's
    journey from addiction to abstinence as analogous to the matura-
    tion of the adolescent. Both the addict and the adolescent must
    achieve independence from the family, towards which both feel
    ambivalent. Both must find appropriate channels for their ag-
    gressive and sexual instincts, and both must learn to sustain
    individual responsibility through steady employment. The ad-
    dict's chief obstacle to abstinence is thus seen as his immaturity.

Vaillant, George E. and Robert W. Rasor. "The Role of Compulsory
    Supervision in the Treatment of Addiction," Federal Probation
    30, no. 2 (June 1966): 53-59.

    A critique of treatment methods for addiction: voluntary
    hospitalization, short imprisonment of less than nine months,
    long imprisonment of at least nine months but less than a year
    of parole, imprisonment of at least nine months and parole of
    at least a year, and community follow-up by a social agency.
    The authors examined hospital and prison records of 100 New
    York City addicts (half of whom are black and half white) ad-
    mitted to Lexington Hospital in 1952-1953 and interviewed almost

three-fourths of them. They find that "while 67 percent of treatments defined as imprisonment and parole resulted in community abstinences of a year and more, only four percent of short imprisonments and hospitalizations were followed by abstinences of similar length" (p. 54). They detail the necessity of prolonged hospitalization, the great importance of parole, the factor of maturation in abstinence, parole as only a crutch, alternate explanations for the data, the relationship between addiction and criminality and mandatory sentencing. "In summary, the data in this paper suggest that, in conjunction with other available treatments, as many addicts as is legally feasible should be under the type of constructive but authoritarian control offered by intelligent parole programs" (p. 59).

Voss, Harwin L. and Richard S. Stephens. "Criminal History of Narcotics Addicts," Drug Forum 2, no. 2 (Winter 1973): 191-202.

Using data obtained from 1,096 addicts hospitalized for treatment at Lexington, Kentucky, Voss and Stephens summarize that the relationship between drug use and crime is not a unidirectional one: some addicts were involved in criminal activities before addiction, others apparently turned to criminal activity to finance their drug habit. There was however, a clear increase in criminal activity (including drug selling) after drug use.

Fifty-seven of the 990 had been arrested before their use of narcotic drugs. Negro males were more likely to have been arrested (68 percent). Fifty-two percent of the respondents of Spanish origin said they had been arrested prior to narcotic use. Among female whites in the sample 37 percent had been arrested before narcotic use (N = 94), blacks 43 percent (N = 98), and among females of Spanish origin, 52 percent (N = 25).

Waldorf, Dan. Careers in Dope. Englewood Cliffs, New Jersey: Prentice-Hall, 1973.

A description of the life of the addict and his "career in dope." Waldorf claims, as others do, that legislation which criminalizes the drug user has driven him underground and led to the solidification of a drug subculture. He says that it is society with its laws and behavior toward the addict that has created so many criminals out of addicts: "we delude ourselves if we think that the problem lodges with addicts and not with ourselves and society."

The book is based primarily on the life histories of 422 male heroin users in five treatment facilities of New York State's

Narcotic Addiction Control Commission. These data are sup-
plemented with data from a cohort of female drug users, another
on methadone maintenance, 31 persons off drugs, and 1,000
field reports. The basic male sample was predominantly working
class, native to New York, unmarried, average age 25 years,
54 percent Catholic, 44 percent black, 30 percent Puerto Rican,
and 24 percent white.

Waldorf follows the career of an addict and his actions in
dealing with his environment: how he starts using heroin, how
he becomes addicted, how he raises money to support his needs,
how he often gets arrested and either goes to jail or into mandatory treatment, his health hazards and chance of early death,
and how he sometimes overcomes his heroin use both in the
long and short run.

This is probably the best study of institutionalized addicts
other than at Lexington. However, Waldorf's attempt to make
the book readable to the general public means that many valuable
tables are omitted.

Weppner, Robert S. "Drug Abuse Patterns of Vietnamese War Veterans Hospitalized as Narcotics Addicts," Drug Forum 2, no.
1 (Fall 1972): 43-54.

A sample of 118 former military men hospitalized for narcotics addiction at Lexington, Kentucky, was studied. Vietnamese
veterans did not represent any large increase in that patient
population: two-thirds of all the addicts with military experience
had had experience with drugs before entering service. There
was a larger proportion of black patients without military experience at the Lexington Hospital (67 percent of 406 cases) than
those with military experience in the United States only (57 percent of 46 cases) or in Vietnam (42 percent of 43 cases).

Weppner, Robert S. and Michael H. Agar. "Immediate Precursors to
Heroin Addiction," Journal of Health and Social Behavior 62,
no. 1 (March 1971): 10-18.

An analysis of 1,096 heroin addicts admitted to Lexington
Hospital from July 21, 1967 to May, 1969, made to determine
the immediate drug precursors to heroin addiction and how these
precursors differ among social groupings. The authors compare
292 (39.6 percent) hooked on heroin as their first drug with 446
hooked on heroin after having been hooked on other drugs. The
sample is 50 percent black males, 28 percent white males, 13
percent black females, and 9 percent white females. Their
average education is a 10.1 grade level. Over 90 percent have

been arrested at least once; the average age at which they become hooked on heroin is 21. Although marijuana is the single
most frequently abused drug (35 percent use marijuana before
using heroin), there is a wide variety of other drugs used before
heroin. The authors find consistent significant differences between blacks and whites and between older and younger heroin
addicts. The black and older addicts more frequently begin with
alcohol or marijuana, whereas the whites and younger addicts
begin with a wider spectrum of drugs. To a lesser extent, there
are also differences between males and females and between lower
and higher occupations. The males and patients from the lower
occupations more often begin drug abuse with marijuana, females
begin with alcohol, and the higher occupational category abuses
a wide variety of other drugs first. The authors note that with
the wider range of drugs available and used, the importance of
alcohol and marijuana has diminished. "The results of this study
suggest that generalizations about drugs, whether marijuana or
others, immediately preceding heroin need to be examined in
light of the social context. It is apparent that the role played by
a particular drug as an immediate precursor can vary from one
social group to another" (p. 17).

Wieland, William F. and Carl D. Chambers. "Two Methods of Utilizing Methadone in the Outpatient Treatment of Narcotic Addicts,"
International Journal of the Addictions 5, no. 3 (September 1970):
431-8.

An examination of the characteristics before and after treatment of 128 narcotic addicts in outpatient methadone maintenance
and 162 narcotic addicts in the outpatient detoxification program.
Those addicts in the outpatient methadone maintenance program
have a mean age of 33, are 60 percent white, 39 percent black
and 1 percent other, and are 91 percent male and 9 percent
female. Ninety-seven percent of them are heroin addicts with
15-19 median years of use, 72 percent with previous formal treatment and 92 percent with arrests prior to treatment. After an
average 15 months of treatment, they are 82 percent employed,
with 68 percent having a legal job (mainly manual labor) with
a mean income of $247 per month. Twenty-one percent have
been arrested since beginning treatment. The characteristics
of the outpatient methadone detoxification program patients are
a mean age of 28, 34 percent white and 66 percent black, 80 percent male and 20 percent female, 99 percent heroin addicts with
5.9 mean years of use, 31 percent with previous formal treatment for addiction, and 86 percent arrested prior to treatment.
After six mean months of treatment, 54 percent have legal jobs

(most of them manual labor), and earn a mean income of $251 per month. Eight percent have been arrested since beginning treatment. "The racial difference [between the two programs] is a function of the fact that white patients predominated during the first two years and therefore, began their treatment on the detoxification program [rather than the maintenance program]" (p. 435). After discussing some theoretical and practical implications of the outpatient approach, the authors conclude that "the report confirms the findings of Dole and Nyswander and demonstrates the efficacy of outpatient initiation to methadone maintenance treatment" (p. 437).

Williams, Edward Huntington. "The Drug-Habit Menace in the South," Medical Record 85, no. 6 (February 7, 1914): 247-9.

An argument that although hospital records show an increase in white drug addicts in the South, these records are deceptive. Black "dope fiends" are jamming the jails. The author details the violence, aggressiveness, and immunity to shock that crazed black cocaine addicts experience; he sees a veritable epidemic of cocaine addiction sweeping the South. Williams feels that the cause of this drug epidemic among the lower classes is the enforcement of Prohibition.

Williams, Joyce E. and William M. Bates. "Some Characteristics of Female Narcotic Addicts," International Journal of the Addictions 5, no. 2 (June, 1970): 245-6.

A description of characteristics by race, geographical distribution, age, and source of drugs of 172 female narcotic addicts admitted to Lexington Hospital between June and December, 1965. Two patterns of drug use are found, similar to other studies of male addicts by Bates and Ball. There is a northern urban pattern of younger, primarily black addicts using illegal drugs and there is a rural Southern, primarily white group of addicts about seven to ten years older than the others who use legal or quasi-legal drugs.

Wilner, Daniel M., Eva Rosenfeld, Robert S. Lee, Donald L. Gerard and Isidor Chein. "Heroin Use and Street Gangs," Journal of Criminal Law, Criminology and Police Science 48, no. 4 (November-December 1957): 399-409.

A summary of the chapters in The Road to H dealing with the relationship between heroin use and street gangs, based on a study of 305 young males between the ages of 16 and 20, including seven Puerto Rican and six black gangs. The authors

feel that many of the patterns of gang activities serve to discourage drug use rather than to encourage it. They see two stages
of development in the gangs' relationship to drugs. In the adolescent stage, when they are under 18 years old, the gang par-
ticipates in such activities as fights, rumbles, competitive
sports and general "hell-raising," and serves to give its members shared status, a measure of security, and a sense of belonging. As they grow older, however, the gang members give
up this kind of activity. If they are healthy, they become more
concerned about their individual futures, careers, and a steady
girl, and turn to new activities "more appropriate for their age"
(p. 409). The emotionally disturbed gang members who cannot
face the future as adults turn instead to the ritual of purchase,
sale, and use of drugs in order to maintain a sense of belonging
and to escape personal responsibility.

Wilson, Edward F. and Russell S. Fisher. "Death from Narcotics
    Use: Baltimore City, 1963 through 1968," Maryland State Medi-
    cal Journal 18, no. 10 (October 1969): 49-52.

    A study of the increase in the number of deaths attributed
directly to narcotics in Baltimore from 1963-68, using the
cases documented by the Office of the Chief Medical Examiner.
From 1963-66, there was an average of eight deaths a year due
to narcotics; in 1967 they jumped to 17 and again jumped dramatically to 47 in 1968. This increase is due to the increase in
deaths in the age range of 12-29 years. Black men and women
account for over two-thirds of the increase in total deaths and
three-fourths of the increase in teenage deaths. "It is believed,
probably correctly, that the recent increase in the number of
narcotics deaths reflects directly in the recent increase in the
number of narcotics users" (p. 50), as seen in the increase in
arrests for narcotics violations. After describing the details
of unexpected and sudden death following intravenous injection,
usually heroin, the authors discuss some of the reasons for
these deaths, such as overdose, and describe in detail nine
cases to illustrate their point that the addicts overdose because
of a long absence, usually enforced, from opiates.

Winick, Charles. "Tendency Systems and the Effects of a Movie
    Dealing With a Social Problem," Journal of General Psychology
    68, second half (April 1963): 289-305.

    An analysis of the impact on attitudes towards addiction and
other social problems of the film "Man with a Golden Arm,"
using a questionnaire administered before and after the film's

release to 1,002 young people attending secondary school in New York City. Seventy-one percent are white and 29 percent are black, while 54 percent are male and 46 percent female. One-third of the subjects were interviewed and compared with 50 interviewed narcotic addicts who saw the film. Winick finds that lower class, male, and black viewers are not more likely to change their attitudes about addiction after seeing the film. In fact, middle class and female viewers show a greater tendency to identify with the film's hero, "possibly because the film has no Negroes" (p. 300). Recency of exposure only partially affects attitude change. He also finds that a higher frequency of relatively less adjusted persons see the movie than relatively adjusted persons, that exposure to the film leads to more permissive attitudes toward narcotics, that relatively less adjusted viewers exhibit greater attitude change than relatively adjusted viewers, and that drug addicts see the movie as a justification for their addiction. Winick speculates about the effects of the film in general and concludes that "what society does about a social problem . . . may not be related to what the creators of and audiences for media dealing with the problem may regard as appropriate socially ameliorative action" (p. 304).

Winick, Charles. "The Use of Drugs by Jazz Musicians," Social Problems 7, no. 3 (Winter 1959-60): 240-53.

An investigation into how many jazz musicians use drugs, what the effects are on their performances and fellow players and what the trends in drug use are, based on informal interviews with 409 jazz musicians during 1954-55. Marijuana is used most widely by the sample, with 82 percent trying it at least once, 54 percent occasionally, and 23 percent regularly using it. A smaller degree of use is reported for heroin, with 53 percent using it once, 24 percent occasionally, and 16 percent regularly. Marijuana is believed to make the performance worse than it would be without the drug by 31 percent of all interviewed. There is a much more intolerant attitude towards heroin; 53 percent regard it as dangerous, damaging, and decreasing the quality of the performance. Some of the social factors found to be related to musicians' drug use are the attitude of the band towards drugs, awareness of one's upward or downward mobility, unemployment in the early 1950s, feelings of fatigue after extensive travel, and the need to "unwind." A majority of 67 percent of the heroin users are white in contrast to 33 percent black. Winick speculates that black jazz musicians are not overrepresented among musician drug users because they have high status and income and are highly trained in contrast to the majority of black people in New York City, who have low status and income. Marijuana use is more common among the younger musicians rather than the older ones; heroin use is concentrated among the 25-39 age bracket, after which it abruptly ceases. Winick hypothesizes his maturing out theory that "those who began taking heroin in their late teens or early twenties as a response to the problems of early adulthood, mature out of their addiction by the time they are in their late thirties, for reasons which are not known but possibly because the stresses and strains of life are becoming stabilized for them and because the major challenges of adulthood have passed" (p. 248). He also finds that there appears to be no significant difference between the drug user and the rating of his success by his peers. Winick describes the jazz language, milieu, and deviations other than drug abuse of jazz musicians. He postulates classical musicians rarely use drugs because they are more conformist and respectable than the rebellious and independent jazz musicians. He concludes by describing the intertwined history of jazz music and drug use.

Winick, Charles and Marie Nyswander. "Psychotherapy of Successful Musicians Who Are Drug Addicts," American Journal of Orthopsychiatry 31, no. 3 (July 1961): 622-36.

A comparison of 15 successful, addicted jazz musicians in New York City who voluntarily entered therapeutic treatment with a control group of 15 addict jazz musicians who did not enter treatment. Eleven in each group are black and four are white. The results suggest that treatment leads to non-use of drugs, improvement in work performance, and greater general social adjustment. The five drop-outs differ from the ten patients who stayed in treatment in their lack of interest in drinking, their identification with the "hip" world, and their concern with addiction, rather than various other serious problems, as their major problem. Musician addicts are found to differ from "typical" addicts in their higher I. Q. s, strong and vigorous father figures, relatively late age of onset of heroin use, vocational success and interest, stable marriages, and heterosexuality. The main functions served by drug use seem to be the achievement of some control over rage and hostility and better performance. The authors conclude that the relatively good results of treatment are due to self-selection (voluntary entrance into treatment), thorough briefing of patients, and the patients' familiarity with therapy.

Zimmering, Paul and James Toolan. "Drug Addiction in Adolescents,"
Journal of Nervous and Mental Disease 116, no. 3 (September
1952): 262-5.

A discussion of the development of heroin addiction among
adolescents, using a sample of 301 adolescent males under the
age of 21 admitted to the Psychiatric Division of Bellevue Hospital for narcotic addiction. They are all, except one, black
or Puerto Rican. They are all non-aggressive, verbally adept,
and not typically delinquent. They all have a close and emphatic
relationship with their mothers, and they readily give up object
relationships, which tend to be weak for all of them. They all
experience euphoria, heightened self-esteem, and fantasies of
omnipotence when using drugs, while withdrawing from experiences which would challenge their self-esteem. Discussion
centers around drug addiction as a social rather than a purely
medical problem, and around the cultural milieu where the
mother holds the family together.

Zimmering, Paul, James Toolan, Renate Safrin and S. Bernard
Wortis. "Heroin Addiction in Adolescent Boys," Journal of
Nervous and Mental Diseases 114, no. 1 (July 1951): 19-34.

An analysis of the societal and personality factors leading
to heroin addiction among 22 teenage males (who are, with one
exception, black or Puerto Rican) admitted to Bellevue Hospital
in January-February, 1951. Social characteristics common to
the addicted adolescents are that they suffer from racial discrimination, have easy access to heroin, and show a strong
attachment to their mothers. The authors stress the addicts'
passivity, strong mother attachment, poor object relationships,
omnipotent striving, and tendency to regress. The authors view
heroin addiction as causing drastic personality changes and anti-
social behavior and believe it to be a social-psychological and
police problem.

Zwerin, Michael. The Silent Sound of Needles. Englewood Cliffs,
New Jersey: Prentice-Hall, 1969.

An account through transcribed interviews of the lives of
drug addicts before rehabilitation and of how they became rehabilitated at the Addicts Rehabilitation Center (ARC) in Harlem.
Zwerin presents addicts as alienated from the world in which
they live, with the ARC helping them to "unlearn negative habits
acquired during the period of addiction" and to develop "new
patterns of thought and action so that they can assume more re-
spectful positions within the home environment" (p. 16). He

also stresses the importance of the addicts' environment as a major contributing factor of their addiction. One of the case histories is Rocky, a black man who gradually became an addict after World War II and through group therapy was able to identify his unique problems as a black person which led to his addiction.

DRUG USE AND ABUSE
AMONG ASIAN AMERICANS

Ball, John C., William M. Bates and John A. O'Donnell. "Characteristics of Hospitalized Narcotic Addicts," Health, Education and
Welfare Indicators (March 1966): 17-26.

See the annotation in Section 1: "Drug Use and Abuse Among
Blacks."

Ball, John C. and Man-Pang Lau. "The Chinese Narcotic Addict in
the United States," Social Forces 45, no. 1 (September 1966):
68-72.

A study of 137 male addict patients of Chinese ancestry who
were discharged from the U.S. Public Service Hospital in Lexington, Kentucky between 1957 and 1962. The data are based on
the medical records of the hospital. The authors enumerate
some of the characteristics of the Chinese male addict which
differentiate his life pattern from other addict groups: he is
foreign-born, alienated from American goals and values, lives
in metropolitan areas, is employed in laundries or restaurants,
and is separated from his family. He is 20 years older than the
rest of the addict population in the hospital, with a mean of 53
years of age and a long history of opiate addiction (usually 20
years). Ball and Lau discuss the high incidence of opiate addiction among Chinese American males in terms of the existence
of a cultural pattern of opiate use and of restricted access to alternative modes of behavior. They see the marked decrease
in narcotics use since 1960 as "a reflection of an ongoing process of modernization of the Chinatown communities and the
gradual dissolution of the old type of addict subculture hitherto
fostered by these communities" (p. 72).

Dai, Bingham. Opium Addiction in Chicago. Montclair, New Jersey: Patterson Smith, 1970. (First published in 1937.)

>See the annotation in Section 1: "Drug Use and Abuse Among Blacks."

DeFleur, Lois B. "Biasing Influences on Drug Arrest Records: Implications for Deviance Research," American Sociological Review 40, no. 1 (February 1975): 88-103.

>See the annotation in Section 1: "Drug Use and Abuse Among Blacks."

Drug Abuse Programs: A Directory for Minority Groups. Series 10 #3. Rockville, Maryland: National Clearing-house for Drug Abuse Information, June 1973.

>See the annotation in Section 1: "Drug Use and Abuse Among Blacks."

Eckerman, William C. Drug Usage and Arrest Charges: A Study of Drug Usage and Arrest Charges Among Arrestees in Six Metropolitan Areas of the United States. (Final Report). Washington, D.C.: Drug Control Division, Office of Scientific Support, Bureau of Narcotics and Dangerous Drugs, U.S. Department of of Justice, December 1971.

>See the annotation in Section 1: "Drug Use and Abuse Among Blacks."

Gearing, Frances R. and Dina D'Amico. The Hispanic and Asiatic Populations on Methadone Maintenance in New York City, A Study in Contrast. Mimeographed. Report to Methadone Maintenance Evaluation Unit, Columbia University School of Public Health and Administrative Medicine, New York City, October 15, 1974.

>See the annotation in Section 5: "Drug Use and Abuse Among Puerto Ricans."

Gearing, Frances R. and Morton G. Schweitzer, "An Epidemiologic Evaluation of Long-Term Methadone Maintenance Treatment for Heroin Addiction," American Journal of Epidemiology 100, no. 2 (August 1974): 101-12.

>See the annotation in Section 1: "Drug Use and Abuse Among Blacks."

Helmer, John and Thomas Vietorisz. Drug Use, The Labor Market, and Class Conflict. Washington, D.C.: Drug Abuse Council, 1974.

> See the annotation in Section 1: "Drug Use and Abuse Among Blacks."

Hunt, G. Halsey and Maurice E. Odoroff. "Followup Study of Narcotic Drug Addicts After Hospitalization," Public Health Reports 77, no. 1 (January 1962): 41-54.

> See the annotation in Section 1: "Drug Use and Abuse Among Blacks."

Johnson, Weldon T. and Robert Bogomolny. "Selective Justice: Drug Law Enforcement in Six American Cities," National Commission on Marijuana and Drug Abuse, Drug Use in America: Problem in Perspective, Vol. III: The Legal System and Drug Control. Washington, D.C.: U.S. Government Printing Office, 1973, pp. 498-650.

> See the annotation in Section 1: "Drug Use and Abuse Among Blacks."

Lemert, Edwin M. and Judy Rosberg. "The Administration of Justice to Minority Groups in Los Angeles County," University of California Publications in Culture and Society 2, no. 1 (April 15, 1948): 1-28.

> See the annotation in Section 1: "Drug Use and Abuse Among Blacks."

Lerner, A. Martin and Frederick J. Oerther. "Recent Trends in Substance Abuse: Characteristics and Sequelae of Paragoric Abuse," International Journal of the Addictions 2, no. 2 (Fall 1967): 312-27.

> See the annotation in Section 1: "Drug Use and Abuse Among Blacks."

Levy, Stephen J. "Drug Abuse in Business: Telling It Like It Is," Personnel 49, no. 5 (September-October 1972): 8-14.

> See the annotation in Section 1: "Drug Use and Abuse Among Blacks."

Musto, David F. The American Disease: Origins of Narcotic Control. New Haven, Connecticut: Yale University Press, 1973.

    See the annotation in Section 1: "Drug Use and Abuse Among Blacks."

Namkung, Paul S. "Asian American Drug Addiction—The Quiet Problem." Paper prepared for the National Conference on Drug Abuse, Washington, D.C., December 8, 1972.

    A summary of recent preliminary research and formal and informal statements by Asian Americans about the influence of drugs in their communities. All of the research was done in California, particularly in Los Angeles, which has the highest concentration of Asians in the U.S. It is found that the extent of drug abuse in the Asian community is as serious as in other ethnic communities. Asian deaths from drug overdose in Los Angeles County have risen from 14 in 1969 to 32 in 1971. While the Asian population in California is around three percent, over four percent of the California penal population is Asian; 95 percent of these are there for drug or drug-related causes. The Asian drug pattern is quite unusual; barbiturates are the primary drugs abused in the Asian community. Drug use by female Asians is at least equal to and perhaps as much as twice that of male Asians. Since most Asian youth are not using available drug treatment facilities, there is a pressing need for such facilities in the Asian community. Japanese Americans have initiated most drug abuse treatment and prevention programs in the Asian community, but these programs are culturally designed for Japanese Americans and do not appeal to other Asians. Another complication in the Asian drug problem is that treatment of drug abuse is often handled by the family and close friends rather than by medical or police authorities. Namkung points out some of the stereotypes of Asian Americans which are false and some of the similarities which Asians share with other racial minorities in the U.S., such as racial oppression, alienation, and a negative identity. There is a special section on the unique problems faced by Asian women in terms of drug abuse. Due to sexism, conflicting cultural roles, and family pressures and sanctions, an increasing number of Asian women aged 13-25 are turning to barbiturates in Los Angeles County. Most start using drugs when they are 13, and many end up pushing drugs or stealing to support their habits. The overdose rate for Asian women is three times that for men. Although an increasing number of Asian women are being arrested for drug abuse, most are still sent home to their families without being formally charged. These problems are further aggravated by the recent influx of Asian immigrants, whose social problems make them vulnerable to drug abuse. Namkung summarizes some of the different reasons why various Asian communities suffer from drug addiction and gives recommendations for treating the problem, especially eliminating the restrictive federal guidelines which effectively prevent federal funding of projects aimed at the scattered Asian communities. He concludes by recommending Asian American community control of programs and staffing, training, and research concerning the Asian American drug problem, and calls for the formation of a national multiracial commission so that all minorities can participate in making decisions about federal and state policies concerning drug abuse in their communities.

Ramer, Barry S. "Screening Patients for a Successful Methadon [sic] Maintenance Treatment Program," Methadon [sic] Workshop Proceedings. Edited by P. H. Blachly. Portland, Oregon: University of Oregon, March 1971, pp. 19-22.

　　See the annotation in Section 1: "Drug Use and Abuse Among Blacks."

Reasons, Charles. "The Politics of Drugs: An Inquiry in the Sociology of Social Problems," Sociological Quarterly 15, no. 3 (Summer 1974): 381-404.

　　See the annotation in Section 1: "Drug Use and Abuse Among Blacks."

Royfe, Ephrain H. "An Exploratory Examination of the Social and Psychological Characteristics of 100 Pennsylvania Drug Addicts," Pennsylvania Psychiatric Quarterly 5, no. 4 (Winter 1965): 38-47.

　　See the annotation in Section 1: "Drug Use and Abuse Among Blacks."

Treadway, Walter L. "Some Epidemiological Features of Drug Addiction," British Journal of Inebriety 28, no. 2 (October 1930): 50-54.

　　See the annotation in Section 1: "Drug Use and Abuse Among Blacks."

Abramowitz, Stephen I. and Paul M. Pantleo. "The Effectiveness of
Brief Methadone Withdrawal Among Urban Opiate Addicts,"
International Journal of the Addictions 7, no. 4 (Winter 1972):
629-35.

An inquiry into the effectiveness of brief methadone withdrawal treatment among 16 narcotic addicts, half of whom received
methadone withdrawal intervention at the Denver Community
Mental Health Center's Narcotic Addiction Treatment Program
during the winter of 1970-71. The other eight never returned
after investigating the method of treatment. All of the subjects
are male, predominantly unemployed, Anglo or Spanish American,
about 23 years old, with tenth grade educations, extended drug
abuse patterns, and predominantly clear legal records. Data
were obtained in semi-structured personal interviews. It is
revealed that the methadone withdrawal program has only a
mild impact on the addict's drug use. Persons in the program
report less serious personal consequences and significantly less
serious involvement with legal authorities than the untreated
addicts have. The treated addicts do not differ from the others
in terms of employment status or contact with people who con-
done drug usage.

Aumann, Jon, Mary Hernandez, Manuel Medina, Cheryl Stewart, and
Nancy Wherley. "The Chicano Addict." Mimeographed. Phoenix,
Arizona: Valle del Sol, 1972.

A summary of existing literature on addiction and on Chicanos
in general and an exploration of three major variables influencing
rehabilitation: the characteristics of the Chicano addict; the

characteristic life style of the Chicano addict; and the extent to
which the rehabilitation process is geared to meet the addict's
needs. Information from 232 addict case records from Valle
del Sol Narcotic Prevention Project and interviews with 22 of
these addicts are the basis for the conclusions. The authors
find that the majority of addicts are Chicano, male, Catholic,
23-27 years of age, have eight to eleven years of education,
are married and living with their legal spouses and have one
to three dependent children, were born in Phoenix, Arizona
and live in a barrio (Chicano ghetto), and typically rely on illegal
activities as a source of income. Those with legitimate jobs are
in unskilled labor occupations. Most use heroin, with 67 percent
reporting use six to seven days per week. Most have been arrested three or more times.

Bailey, Pearce. "A Contribution to the Mental Pathology of Races
    in the United States," Mental Hygiene 6, no. 2 (April 1922):
    370-91.

    See the annotation in Section 1: "Drug Use and Abuse Among
    Blacks."

Barker, Gordon H. and W. Thomas Adams. "Glue Sniffers," Soci-
    ology and Social Research 47, no. 3 (April 1963): 298-310.

    A comparison of 28 juvenile male glue sniffers committed
    to the Lookout Mountain School for Boys in Colorado with 28
    other boys, selected at random, committed to the same institu-
    tion for other offenses in 1961. There are certain characteristics
    which differentiate glue sniffers from other delinquents. Although
    family disintegration and lack of paternal involvement were com-
    mon to both, the glue sniffers come from much larger families.
    Glue sniffers are also younger: almost half are 13 or under.
    Glue sniffers are exclusively from urban areas while other de-
    linquents, though mainly from urban areas, also are from rural
    areas. Both are under-achievers in school, but glue sniffers
    have an even poorer record than other delinquents. The vast
    majority of glue sniffers are Mexican Americans, while other
    delinquents include other minority group members. Barker
    and Adams suggest that glue sniffing occurs either to achieve
    status in the counterculture or to escape from family strife,
    failure, boredom, poverty, and loss of dignity.

Blum, Richard. "Mexican-American Families," Horatio Alger's
    Children. By Richard H. Blum and Associates. San Francisco:
    Jossey-Bass, 1972, pp. 155-70.

A comparison of ten Mexican American families who are considered "high risk" in terms of narcotics use and ten "low risk" Mexican American families in California rural areas. All of the families are poor and have similar cultural values. Since the sample is so small, "the families resemble one another more than they differ" (p. 155). Some of the characteristics of the low risk family are a sensitive, affectionate, flexible, confident mother; an active, communicative, and authoritative father; strict standards of conduct, with a certain freedom for the child to make decisions; and life centered around the family. In contrast, the high risk family is characterized by a mother less acculturated to Anglo ways and more ritualistic, with less self-confidence than low risk mothers, a discordant and indirected family life, and a history of child distress and school and police problems. The basic factor influencing low drug use is seen as an ability to accommodate to Anglo ways and to transmit traditional values.

Blumer, Herbert. "The World of Youthful Drug Use." Mimeographed. Berkeley, California: School of Criminology, University of California, January 1967.

   See the annotation in Section 1: "Drug Use and Abuse Among Blacks."

Bullington, Bruce, John G. Munns, Gilbert Geis and James Raner. "Concerning Heroin Use and Official Records," American Journal of Public Health 59, no. 10 (October 1969): 1887-92.

   See the annotation in Section 1: "Drug Use and Abuse Among Blacks."

Callan, John P. and Carroll D. Patterson. "Patterns of Drug Abuse Among Military Inductees," American Journal of Psychiatry 130, no. 3 (March 1973): 260-64.

   See the annotation in Section 1: "Drug Use and Abuse Among Blacks."

Chambers, Carl D., Walter R. Cuskey and Arthur D. Moffett. "Demographic Factors in Opiate Addiction Among Mexican Americans," Public Health Reports 85, no. 6 (June 1970): 523-31.

   An analysis of the hospital records of 106 Mexican American addicts admitted to Lexington and Fort Worth Hospitals in 1961 and 169 admitted in 1967 to determine patterns of Mexican American opiate abuse. Although the total hospital admissions have decreased by nearly 20 percent. Mexican American male addict admissions have doubled. Female Mexican American admissions are less than half those of 1961. There is also a geographical shift, with the percentage of Mexican American addicts residing in California, Texas, and New Mexico changing from 69.6 percent in 1961 to 92.2 percent in 1967. Within these three states, the geographical incidence also shifts from California, which in 1961 had 30 percent of all Mexican American addicts, to Texas, which by 1967 had 60.9 percent of all Mexican American addicts. An overwhelming majority of Mexican American addicts are Catholic and are high school drop-outs. A significantly increasing number of addicts of both sexes attempt marriages which fail, while there is a marked decrease in the number of single addicts. A significant change in the Mexican American addict's primary means of support has also taken place. In general, the number of addicts who maintain legal employment has increased from 50 percent to 69.8 percent, while the number with illegal means of support has decreased from 50 percent to 30.2 percent. The female pattern of illegal employment or unemployed dependency is virtually unchanged. The authors found, on the basis of data collected in 1967, that Mexican American addicts are similar to addicts in general in several ways: first, they are almost all addicted to heroin, which they inject intravenously and purchase illegally from pushers, and they have a history of smoking marijuana before turning to heroin; second, they begin to use heroin while still adolescents and are arrested more than any other racial minority admitted to the hospitals; third, males begin to use drugs earlier than females and are arrested at an earlier age; fourth, the majority of all addicts are arrested at least once before they begin using opiates; and fifth, although recidivism is increasing, the pattern of readmissions is changing from enforced to voluntary. The median age of all Mexican American addicts has remained the same, 25-29 years. However, the mean age for Mexican American males has increased from 26.3 years to 28.2 years.

Chambers, Carl D., Walter R. Cuskey and Arthur D. Moffett. "Mexican-American Opiate Addicts," The Epidemiology of Opiate Addiction in the United States. Edited by John C. Ball and Carl D. Chambers. Springfield, Illinois: Charles C. Thomas, 1970, pp. 202-21.

A description of the social characteristics and admission statistics of Mexican American addicts. See the previous annotation on "Demographic Factors in Opiate Addiction Among Mexican Americans" by the same authors for details of data. These data

are compared to white, black, and Puerto Rican addicts, with
sex as an independent variable. The authors conclude that Mexican Americans are more overrepresented in the addict population than whites or blacks, but not more so than Puerto Ricans.
Although "overrepresentation for whites and Blacks is decreasing,
it is increasing for Chicanos and Puerto Ricans" (p. 221).

Crowther, Betty. "Patterns of Drug Use Among Mexican Americans,"
    International Journal of the Addictions 7, no. 4 (Winter 1972):
    637-47.

An evaluation of the differing patterns of drug use among
Mexican American and Anglo narcotic addicts as revealed by
a sample of 360 male addicts with permanent residence in the
Southwest who entered Fort Worth Hospital between June 1967
and December 1968. The patients—223 of whom were Mexican
American and 137 Anglo—were intereviewed and their hospital
records were examined. The Mexican Americans are 58 percent
of the sample, suggesting an increase in their hospitalization
rate, and most of them come from either San Antonio, Texas
or Albuquerque, New Mexico. Over 80 percent come from
families with four or more children; 76 percent have parents
who did not graduate from high school. None have fathers who
are professionals, and 36 percent have fathers who are not regularly employed. Only 9 percent have completed high school,
while a large percentage have been arrested or institutionalized
or have behaved in a deviant way in addition to drug use. The
Mexican American uses a smaller number of drugs than the Anglo
addict. The most typical pattern is first marijuana and then
heroin use. In contrast to the Anglos, most Mexican Americans
do not use barbiturates, amphetamines, tranquilizers, or psy-
chotogens. Even when medical use, social class, family stability, and prior delinquencies are controlled, these differences
are maintained. There appears to be little difference between
the Anglos and Mexican Americans in terms of delinquent involvement; 82 percent of the Mexican Americans and 77 percent
of the Anglos have been arrested for the first time before the
age of 18. The Mexican Americans do, however, begin drug use
at an earlier age; 42 percent use marijuana before they are 14
years old, compared to 16 percent of the Anglos. The author
suggests that in the Mexican American subculture marijuana
use is as insignificant as tobacco use in the dominant Anglo
culture. She points to the possibility that Mexican Americans
begin narcotic use in order to become addicted and thereby
escape the low status of the Mexican American and do not experiment for "kicks." "It is possible that the lower class Mexican

American sees heroin as a means of escaping responsibility and
the difficult life cycle that envelops him. In contrast, the Anglos'
experimentation with other drugs suggests that the escape function may not be the primary motivating factor in this subculture.
Obviously additional research is needed to examine the attitudinal differences between narcotic users in each culture" (p. 646).

DeFleur, Lois B. "Biasing Influences on Drug Arrest Records: Implications for Deviance Research," American Sociological Review 40, no. 1 (February 1973): 88-103.

   See the annotation in Section 1: "Drug Use and Abuse Among
   Blacks."

Drug Abuse Programs: A Directory for Minority Groups. Series 10
#3. Rockville, Maryland: National Clearing-house for Drug
Abuse Information, June 1973.

   See the annotation in Section 1: "Drug Use and Abuse Among
   Blacks."

Duster, Troy. "The Moral Implications of Psychic Maladjustment in
the Deviant," The Legislation of Morality: Law, Drugs and
Moral Judgment. New York: The Free Press, 1970. Pp. 153-
92.

   See the annotation in Section 1: "Drug Use and Abuse Among
   Blacks."

Eckerman, William C. Drug Usage and Arrest Charges: A Study of
Drug Usage and Arrest Charges Among Arrestees in Six Metro-
politan Areas of the United States (Final Report). Washington,
D.C.: Drug Control Division, Office of Scientific Support, Bur-
eau of Narcotics and Dangerous Drugs, U.S. Department of
Justice, December 1971.

   See the annotation in Section 1: "Drug Use and Abuse Among
   Blacks."

Ellison, Willie S. "Portrait of a Glue-Sniffer," Crime and Delinquency 11, no. 4 (October 1965): 394-9.

   A study of 48 cases of glue sniffing referred to a group counseling program in San Jose, California in 1962. Ellison views
   glue sniffing as a passive retreat from reality and describes
   several typical cases. They are characterized by being from
   13-15 years old, male, Mexican American, from a poor socioeconomic background, of a low intelligence reading, with a weak

personality structure (passive, withdrawn, uncommunicative, unconfident) which tends to break under stress. The author describes and evaluates the program for treatment developed by the Santa Clara Juvenile Probation Department from the point of view that glue sniffing is only a sympton of a larger social problem resulting from fragmented, structurally weak families and a milieu of high delinquency and crime. The program is limited because it offers a temporary substitute of activities and help during times of stress and does not change entire patterns of behavior. He suggests the need to detect and refer glue sniffers to the proper authorities and to develop continuing programs to involve these youth in organized activity as an alternative to glue sniffing.

Gearing, Frances Rowe and Morton G. Schweitzer. "An Epidemiologic Evaluation of Long-Term Methadone Maintenance Treatment for Heroin Addiction," American Journal of Epidemiology 100, no. 2 (August 1974): 101-12.

See the annotation in Section 1: "Drug Use and Abuse Among Blacks."

Gerard, Donald L. and Conan H. Kornetsky. "Adolescent Opiate Addiction: A Study of Control and Addict Subjects," Psychiatric Quarterly 29, no. 3 (July 1955): 457-86.

See the annotation in Section 1: "Drug Use and Abuse Among Blacks."

Gerard, Donald L. and Conan Kornetsky. "A Social and Psychiatric Study of Adolescent Opiate Addicts," Psychiatric Quarterly 28, no. 1 (January 1954): 113-25.

See the annotation in Section 1: "Drug Use and Abuse Among Blacks."

Glaser, Daniel, James T. Inciardi and Dean V. Babst. "Later Heroin Use by Adolescent Marihuana-Using, Heroin-Using, and Non-Drug-Using Adolescent Offenders in New York City," International Journal of the Addictions 4, no. 2 (June 1969): 145-55.

See the annotation in Section 1: "Drug Use and Abuse Among Blacks."

Glaser, Daniel and Mary Snow. Public Knowledge and Attitudes on Drug Abuse in New York State. New York State Narcotic Addiction Control Commission, 1969.

See the annotation in Section 1: "Drug Use and Abuse Among Blacks."

Helmer, John and Thomas Vietorisz. Drug Use, The Labor Market, and Class Conflict. Washington, D.C.: Drug Abuse Council, 1974.

   See the annotation in Section 1: "Drug Use and Abuse Among Blacks."

Johnson, Weldon T. and Robert Bogomolny. "Selective Justice: Drug Law Enforcement in Six American Cities," in National Commission on Marihuana and Drug Abuse, Drug Use in America: Problem in Perspective, Vol. III: The Legal System and Drug Control. Washington, D.C.: U.S. Government Printing Office, 1973. Pp. 498-650.

   See the annotation in Section 1: "Drug Use and Abuse Among Blacks."

Kaplan, John. "Marijuana and Heroin Addiction," Marijuana—The New Prohibition. New York: World Publishing, 1970. Pp. 232-62.

   See the annotation in Section 1: "Drug Use and Abuse Among Blacks."

Lemert, Edwin M. and Judy Rosberg. "The Administration of Justice to Minority Groups in Los Angeles County," University of California Publications in Culture and Society 2, no. 1 (April 15, 1948): 1-28.

   See the annotation in Section 1: "Drug Use and Abuse Among Blacks."

Lerner, A. Martin and Frederick J. Oerther. "Recent Trends in Substance Abuse: Characteristics and Sequelae of Paregoric Abuse," International Journal of the Addictions 2, no. 2 (Fall 1967): 312-27.

   See the annotation in Section 1: "Drug Use and Abuse Among Blacks."

Levi, Mario and Margaret Seborg. "The Study of I.Q. Scores on Verbal vs. Nonverbal Tests and vs. Academic Achievement Among Women Drug Addicts from Different Racial and Ethnic Groups," International Journal of the Addictions 7, no. 3 (Fall 1972): 581-84.

   See the annotation in Section 1: "Drug Use and Abuse Among Blacks."

Lipscomb, Wendell R. "Drug Use in a Black Ghetto," American Journal of Psychiatry 127, no. 9 (March 1971): 1166-9.

See the annotation in Section 1: "Drug Use and Abuse Among Blacks."

Maddux, James F. and Linda Kay McDonald. "Status of 100 San Antonio Addicts One Year After Admission to Methadone Maintenance," Drug Forum 2, no. 3 (Spring 1973): 239-52.

Of 100 chronic heroin users admitted to a methadone maintenance program in San Antonio, Texas in 1970, 78 percent were on methadone maintenance one year later. The employment rate increased from 21 percent at admission to 65 percent one year later. The number of arrests for all subjects dropped only from 129 during the year before admission to 103 during the year after admission, but arrests were primarily for minor offenses: vagrancy, drunkenness, motor vehicle violation and theft under $50.

There was a statistically significant association between "married at some time," "late onset of opioid use," and "employed at time of admission" with employed status one year after admission. This suggests, according to the authors, that subjects who are better adjusted at time of admission have better outcomes. Ethnic distribution of subjects was 88 with Spanish surnames, 9 other white, and 3 blacks.

Musto, David F. The American Disease: Origins of Narcotic Control. New Haven, Connecticut: Yale University Press, 1973.

See the annotation in Section 1: "Drug Use and Abuse Among Blacks."

Perlis, Leo. "Drug Abuse Among Union Members," Drug Abuse in Industry. Edited by W. Wayne Stewart. Miami, Florida: Halosand Associates, 1970, pp. 75-80.

See the annotation in Section 1: "Drug Use and Abuse Among Blacks."

Press, Edward and Alan K. Done. "Solvent Sniffing: Physiologic Effects and Community Control Measures for Intoxication from the Intentional Inhalation of Organic Solvents," Pediatrics 39, no. 3 (March 1967): 451-61.

See the annotation in Section 1: "Drug Use and Abuse Among Blacks."

Press, Edward and Alan K. Done. "Solvent Sniffing: Physiologic Effects and Community Control Measures for Intoxication from the Intentional Inhalation of Organic Solvents [Part Two]," Pediatrics 39, no. 4 (April 1967): 611-22.

  Part Two of a study on solvent sniffing, identifying the physiological effects of solvent sniffing and control measures of forced abstinence, community-wide mental health measures, legislation, and education. The authors conclude that "individual and family treatment aimed at the underlying disorder offers the best hope of affecting a permanent cure of the habitue" (p. 622).

Ramer, Barry S. "Screening Patients for a Successful Methadon [sic] Maintenance Treatment Program," Methadon [sic] Workshop Proceedings. Edited by P. H. Blachly. Portland, Oregon: University of Oregon, March 1971, pp. 19-22.

  See the annotation in Section 1: "Drug Use and Abuse Among Blacks."

Redlinger, Lawrence John and Jerry B. Michel. "Ecological Variations in Heroin Abuse," Sociological Quarterly 11, no. 2 (Spring 1970): 219-29.

  An assessment of the relationship between high rates of addiction, low socioeconomic status, and minority group membership among male addicts in San Antonio, Texas. A sample of 185 addicts listing addresses in San Antonio admitted to the NIMH Clinical Research Center, Fort Worth, Texas between January 1964 and July 1965, is compared with 145 male addicts hospitalized voluntarily in a San Antonio addiction control program between July 1966 and August 1967. The authors find that heroin abuse is "closely and inversely related to social rank, median family income, and median years of school completed" (p. 226) and is directly related to male unemployment and overcrowded housing. Although high addiction rates are strongly correlated with Mexican Americans, they are not associated with blacks, who are also an economically and socially disadvantaged ethnic minority. Redlinger and Michel offer several possible explanations and conclude that "in general, differential accessibility of drugs is the major factor in greater narcotics abuse by Mexican-Americans than Blacks" (p. 227). Mexican Americans control the distribution in San Antonio of drugs which originate in Mexico; they also suspect blacks as potentially dangerous police informers. "In a broader theoretical context these findings support what Cloward and Ohlin (1960) [Delinquency and Opportunity: A Theory of Delinquent Gangs] termed 'opportunity structures,' and their differential distribution through the social structure" (p. 228).

Scher, Jordan. "Patterns and Profiles of Addiction and Drug Abuse," International Journal of the Addictions 2, no. 2 (Fall 1967): 171-90.

   See the annotation in Section 1: "Drug Use and Abuse Among Blacks."

Scott, Neil R., William Orzen, Cynthia Musillo, and Patricia T. Cole. "Methadone in the Southwest: A Three-Year Follow-up of Chicano Heroin Addicts," American Journal of Orthopsychiatry 48, no. 3 (April 1973): 355-61.

   An assessment of a three year follow-up of 61 Mexican American clients of a multimodality drug program in Albuquerque, New Mexico. The data were obtained from admission interviews, medical and urine surveillance records, newspaper clippings, and interviews with current program participants. Upon admission all clients were Mexican Americans, born and raised in New Mexico, and Spanish-speaking; 84 percent were male and 16 percent female. Two-thirds were married or living in common-law relationships, 26 percent were divorced, and 7 percent had never been married. Their median age was 31 years; their median age of beginning heroin use was 17, with 18 percent aged 12-14 years at onset of addiction. These facts point out that there was considerable heroin use in the Albuquerque barrio during the middle and late 1950s. Over half used marijuana as their first drug, but 40 percent began with heroin. There is little evidence of multiple drug use. In the follow-up, 64 percent are found to be still in methadone maintenance, with 26 percent discharged and 10 percent decreased. Their overall health improvement is striking. The most significant ensuing complication is prominent alcoholism, which contrasts with the negative histories of alcoholism at the time of admission. Urine surveillance reveals that approximately 20 percent of the clients in methadone maintenance are using opiates. Nearly half have been arrested during this period; 60 percent are employed, and 21 percent have begun training. Unlike most addicts, the Mexican American addict has abundant family resources available. Virtually all are still close to their intact, extended families; only two of the addicts do not live with their families. Unlike most female addicts, none of the ten Mexican American women are known to be prostitutes; they usually team up with a heroin dealer for a cheap and dependable source of heroin. "Clinically, one is continually impressed with the importance of environmental and social factors associated with heroin use in the barrio. . . . The easy availability of heroin, the widespread experimentation with heroin since the middle 1950s, the high status ascribed to the heroin dealer and to the ex-convict, the excitement of 'cops and robber games' all impress one that the life of the drug addict exists within an exciting well-organized social system that offers a dramatic alternative to the 'straight' and often impoverished life of the barrio. The experience of this program does not confirm the stereotype of the addict as an unhealthy, debauched, fringe member of society, stripped of resources by the endless quest for heroin" (p. 360).

Sells, S. B., Lois R. Chatham and George W. Joe. "The Relation of Selected Epidemiological Factors to Retention in Methadone Treatment," Proceedings of the Fourth National Conference on Methadone Treatment. San Francisco: National Association for the Prevention of Addiction to Narcotics, January 8-10, 1972, pp. 89-90.

See the annotation in Section 1: "Drug Use and Abuse Among Blacks."

Sokol, Jacob. "Glue Sniffing in Los Angeles," Drug Addiction in Youth. Edited by Ernest Harms. New York: Pergamon Press, 1965, pp. 46-8.

See the annotation in Section 1: "Drug Use and Abuse Among Blacks."

Aberle, David F. The Peyote Religion Among the Navaho. ("Viking
   Fund Publications in Anthropology," no. 42.) Chicago: Wenner-
   Green Foundation for Anthropological Research, 1966.

   A brief summary of the physiological effects of peyote and
the ritual and organizations of the peyote cult, followed by general background information on the Navahos from their conquest
by the United States in the 1860s through the 1960s. Aberle
stresses the reduction of livestock, which had been for decades
the main foundation of Navaho economy, as the main factor in the
Navaho acceptance of peyotism in the 1930s, which occurred in
spite of the fact that the Navahos were the least "acculturated"
tribe in the United States, with a fully functioning native religion
and no history of involvement in other nativistic movements like
the Ghost Dance. He takes the position that "nativistic cults
originate in experiences of relative deprivation engendered
by the domination of one group by another which possesses
an alien and more powerful culture" (p. 23). The third
section discusses aspects of the peyote cult as found among
the Navaho: the struggle over peyotism within the tribe,
the ritual of Navaho peyotism and variations, the sym-
bolism of various objects used in the ritual, the beliefs
and values of peyotists, the contrast between the Navaho
and peyote religions, and the bases of Navaho opposition to
peyotism. The fourth section details the course of the author's
research and aspects of the differential appeal of the cult, stressing Aberle's formation of the theory of relative deprivation in
terms of livestock reduction. The last section puts peyotism
in the context of similar religious and redemptive movements
that have arisen among oppressed and deprived groups in other
times and places.

Agar, Michael and Richard C. Stephens. The Methadone Street Scene: The Addict's View. New York State Drug Abuse Control Commission, 1975.

See the annotation in Section 1: "Drug Use and Abuse Among Blacks."

Bailey, Pearce. "A Contribution to the Mental Pathology of Races in the United States," Mental Hygiene 6, no. 2 (April 1922): 370-91.

See the annotation in Section 1: "Drug Use and Abuse Among Blacks."

Barber, Bernard. "A Socio-Cultural Interpretation of the Peyote Cult," American Anthropologist 43, no. 4 (October-December 1941): 673-5.

A brief synopsis of the author's view that both the peyote cult and the Ghost Dance of 1890 are "alternative responses to a similar socio-cultural constellation," the cultural and social disorganization of Native Americans (p. 674). The peyote cult flourished due to its passive, resigned, conciliatory, and compromising acceptance of the existing world, after the Ghost Dance, which threatened white supremacy, was destroyed by the U.S. government.

Bergman, Robert L. "Navaho Peyote Use: Its Apparent Safety," American Journal of Psychiatry 128, no. 6 (December 1971): 695-9.

An investigation of the rate of serious emotional disturbance caused by the use of peyote among 125,000 Navaho Indians, based on the mental health program of the Indian Health Service. Bergman gives the details of five case reports, one case of acute psychosis resulting from the use of peyote, and four others difficult to diagnose. He points out which factors in the peyote experience serve as safeguards against bad reactions. He finds the rate of serious emotional disturbance to be very low, mainly because "feelings made available in meetings are carefully channeled into ego-strengthening directions" (p. 53). He points out that use of peyote in the religion helps the American Indians to cope with identity diffusion.

Blair, Thomas S. "Habit Indulgence in Certain Cactaceus Plants Among Indians," Journal of the American Medical Association 76, no. 15 (April 9, 1921): 1033-4.

A short description of some of the cactaceus and maguey plants which yield intoxicating results to human beings when ingested, whether as drink or food. Blair views peyote as a new menace confronting the nation and creating indolent, immoral, and worthless addicts. He foresees two difficulties in suppressing the use of peyote: the strongly entrenched commercial interests involved in peyote traffic, and the superstition of the Indian, who believes that peyote enables communication with the Great Spirit.

Blumer, Herbert. "The World of Youthful Drug Use." Mimeographed. Berkeley, California: School of Criminology, University of California, January 1967.

See the annotation in Section 1: "Drug Use and Abuse Among Blacks."

Brand, Stewart. "The Native American Church Meeting," Psychedelic Review, no. 9 (1967): 20-35.

A detailed account of the rituals of the Native American Church meeting, which uses peyote to help the participants achieve their goals, such as honoring someone, celebrating a birthday, or bringing good luck to a son in Vietnam.

Brant, Charles S. "Peyotism Among the Kiowa-Apache and Neighboring Tribes," Southwestern Journal of Anthropology 6, no. 2 (Summer 1950): 212-22.

An exploration of the history of the peyote cult among the Kiowa-Apache and a detailed description of the ritual. The author stresses the creative powers of peyote and peyotists' view of peyote as a means to communicate with God, rather than as an object of worship. The danger of legislation bringing peyote under the narcotics laws is detailed, as well as the intensity of activists defending their religion. "The peyote religion functions as an emotional outlet and partial integrating force in a situation which is generally characterized by extreme individualism, economic insecurity, and marked health anxieties. . . . It is safe to predict that the peyote cult will continue under these circumstances, to constitute a major form of emotional outlet" (p. 222).

Bromberg, Walter and Charles L. Tranter. "Peyote Intoxication: Some Psychological Aspects of the Peyote Rite," Journal of Nervous and Mental Disease 97, no. 5 (May 1943): 518-27.

An identification of the physiological effects caused by peyote ingestion; anxiety upon feeling bodily distortion is soon followed by euphoria and visual hallucinations. The authors analyze peyote use as related to basic aspects of survival in two ways: furnishing a tie to nature through its promise of power to the individual user, and easing inferiority feelings and anxieties caused by the pain of conflicting cultures, Indian and white. They conclude that in order to understand peyote intoxication, it is necessary to focus on the "central emotional constellations in the Indian which allow peyote to be invested with such omnipotent force by its adherents" (p. 527).

Callan, John P. and Carroll D. Patterson. "Patterns of Drug Abuse Among Military Inductees," The American Journal of Psychiatry 130, no. 3 (March 1973): 260-64.

See the annotation in Section 1: "Drug Use and Abuse Among Blacks."

DeFleur, Lois B. "Biasing Influences on Drug Arrest Records: Implications for Deviance Research," American Sociological Review 40, no. 1 (February 1975): 88-103.

See the annotation in Section 1: "Drug Use and Abuse Among Blacks."

Dittman, Allen T. and Harvey C. Moore. "Disturbance in Dreams as Related to Peyotism Among the Navaho," American Anthropologist 59, no. 4 (August 1957): 642-49.

An examination of the dreams of 47 Navaho and 12 peyote cultists of Navaho origin for indications of general psychological disturbance. The ratings substantiate the author's hypothesis that the peyote cultists are more disturbed than the other Navahos; the Navaho peyotists have a higher proportion of bad dreams than good dreams. Suggestions of ways to increase the usefulness of dream analysis to judge disturbance in nonliterate groups are made.

Drug Abuse Programs: A Directory for Minority Groups. Series 10 #3. Rockville, Maryland: National Clearing-house for Drug Abuse Information, June 1973.

See the annotation in Section 1: "Drug Use and Abuse Among Blacks."

Johnson, Weldon T. and Robert Bogomolny. "Selective Justice: Drug
Law Enforcement in Six American Cities," National Commission
on Marihuana and Drug Abuse, Drug Use in America: Problem
in Perspective, Vol. III: The Legal System and Drug Control.
Washington, D.C., U.S. Government Printing Office, 1973,
pp. 498-650.

See the annotation in Section 1: "Drug Use and Abuse Among
Blacks."

Kuttner, Robert E. and Albert B. Lorincz. "Alcoholism and Addiction in Urbanized Sioux Indians," Mental Hygiene 56, no. 4
(October 1967): 530-42.

A comparison of the drinking patterns of urbanized Sioux
Indians in Nebraska with those of the reservation Sioux and of
other skid row inhabitants. The sample of urbanized Sioux are
characterized by excessive and social drinking begun in adolescence. Experience with narcotics is nonexistent among the
sample, since "skid row inhabitants and Indians, in particular
cannot support the narcotic habit" (p. 535). Addiction to amphetamines (either inhaled or injected intravenously) and to
glue are common among the alcoholics, however. Adult drinking
habits are described, and the use of alcohol by Sioux is compared
to other tribes. The authors conclude that inadequate family
training is the primary motivation for drinking.

LaBarre, Weston. The Peyote Cult. Hamden, Connecticut: Shoe
String Press, 1964. (First published in 1938.)

The classic, authoritative work on the peyote cult among
the Native Americans. LaBarre describes the botany, ethno-
botany, chemistry and pharmacology of peyote. He then explores
the physiological aspects of peyote intoxication and compares
the rituals of the peyote cult among the Mexicans, Huichol,
Fariahumari, Mescalero Apache, Kiowa-Comanche, and Plains
Indians in general. There is also an examination of the historical
and social context in which the cult takes place: the author points
to the problems of acculturation and cultural diffusion as important factors in the development of the peyote cult. Two append-
ices bring this edition up to date on the increasing political per-
secution of Indians seeking to practice the peyote religious cult
and the recent psychiatric and psychological research on peyote
and mescaline.

Lanternari, Vittorio. "The Peyote Cult," The Religions of the Oppressed: A Study of Modern Messianic Cults. New York: The
  New American Library, 1963, pp. 63-100.

An analysis of the peyote cult as a religion seeking adjustment to new conditions and offering a new program of cultural
emancipation. Lanternari briefly describes the main prophets
of the peyote cult and its morphology, doctrine, rituals, and
myths as a combination of Christian elements linked with the
religion of the past. The Pan-Indian character of the peyote cult
helps to develop unity and solidarity among all of the tribes
forced to deal collectively with the "white man's civilization."
The author analyzes peyotism and the Ghost Dance historically
as reactions to different phases of American governmental policy. The Ghost Dance religion evolved in the period when whites
were pursuing a policy of genocide against the Indians, and this
religion provided motivating force for Indian rebellion and resistance through its promises of redemption and liberation.
Peyotism, on the other hand, developed later as a reaction to
the new American policy of nonviolent but forced acculturation;
it is a "new doctrine incorporating enough of the white man's
ideas to make co-existence feasible while also making it possible for the Indians to free themselves from the religious yoke
of their masters" (p. 97). Lanternari sees the therapeutic use
of peyote as significant but secondary to the cult's solution to
the relationship between Indians and whites. He summarizes the
basic elements from which the peyote cult derives its strength
and significance and puts the cult in the international historical
context of other religious movements by oppressed colonial
people struggling for their liberation.

Lidz, Theodore and Albert Rothenberg. "Psychedelism: Dionysus
  Reborn," Psychiatry 31, no. 2 (May 1968): 116-25.

A comparison of the ritual and characteristics of the worship
of Dionysus of the Archaic Age, the Native American Church,
and psychedelism as exemplified by Timothy Leary's League
for Spiritual Discovery. The authors argue that it is probable
that all three movements have similar social and psychological
functions. All are ecstasy cults, using drugs to achieve freedom from restraint. All developed at a time of crisis and major
cultural change, especially the breakdown of family solidarity,
when it is difficult to develop an individual identity. These movements thus satisfy the impulse to reject individual responsibility
and to get outside of the self in a group setting.

Malouf, Carling. "Gosiute Peyotism," American Anthropologist 44,
    no. 1 (January-March 1942): 93-103.

    A delineation of the differing ceremonies and rituals of the
    Tipi Way peyote cult and the Sioux (or Western Slope) way peyote
    cult among the Gosiute, a Shoshone-speaking people who live on
    two reservations in western Utah, based on interviews and ob-
    servation of the ceremonies. The majority of the Gosiutes belong
    to the peyote cult: they see peyote as a cure for the sick and
    as a supernatural guide in political, economic, and educational
    activities. Malouf views peyotism neither as a variation of abo-
    riginal shamanism with a slight veneer of Christian elements
    nor as primarily a means to produce visions or cure sickness,
    but as a movement in its own right combining all these factors.
    He describes Christian elements and aboriginal practices of
    peyotism, as well as elements which are foreign or contrary to
    previous Gosiute beliefs and practices. "Perhaps the greatest
    value of peyote and the cult evolved around it is that it gives
    the Gosiute society a certain amount of coherence which tends
    to unify the group for the accomplishment of various objectives.
    Tribal unit, in what was aboriginally an atomistic society,
    is something the Gosiute have never yet enjoyed" (p. 103).

Marriott, Alice and Carol K. Rachlin. Peyote. New York: Thomas
    Y. Crowell, 1971.

    A short account of the history of the peyote religion among
    the various tribes of the Plains Indians, the symbolic significance
    of objects used in the rites, the effects of peyote, its legal status,
    and its relationship to witchcraft and the arts. The authors stress
    the attraction of the peyote religion to a people whose civilization
    has been destroyed. They portray the peyote cult as an escape
    from pressing reality for Native Americans.

Opler, M. E. "The Influence of Aboriginal Pattern and White Contact
    on a Recently Introduced Ceremony, the Mescalero Peyote Rite,"
    Journal of American Folklore 49, nos. 191 and 192 (1936): 143-66.

    A study of why the Mescalero Apache first accepted and then
    rejected peyotism. The general pattern of ideology underlying
    Apache ceremonialism before peyote is described. The aborig-
    inal Mescalero religion centered around a strongly individualistic
    shamanism, rivalry and dislike between shamans, cure as es-
    sential to the ritual, and fear of witches. Peyotism incorporates
    many of these older ceremonial patterns and values and intensi-
    fies the virulence of the rivalries. Opler details the rite and
    then explains why the Mescaleros adopted peyote at the time

when they were forced to live on reservations. Small groups
with a heritage of independence and mutual suspicion had to live
together. "Peyote became the intensification and apotheosis of
traditional religious values at a time when frustration and un-
welcome reservation problems turned aggression towards the
nearest and only available victims. . . . The particular emphasis
upon contest and rivalry in Mescalero peyote, then, may be interpreted as a consequence of the interaction of aboriginal patterns and conditions arising from white contact" (p. 166). As
the people adapted to reservation life, the shaman's prestige
declined and the peyote ceremony lost much of its appeal.

Opler, Marvin K. "The Character and History of the Southern Ute
    Peyote Rite," American Anthropologist 42, no. 3 (July–Septem-
    ber 1940): 463–78.

An exploration of the introduction of peyotism to the Southern
Ute, the adoption of the cult at the two agency centers at Ignacio
and Towaoc, and its psychological appeal. The cult was brought
to Ignacio in 1916 by a Sioux, Sam Loganberry. He also brought
it to Towaoc in 1916, but it was not picked up there until a Northern Ute brought it again in 1931. The peyote cult is almost uni-
versally accepted in Towaoc but faces organized opposition from
leading shamans and agency officials at Ignacio. Opler attributes
this difference to the uneven rate of acculturation. The Towaoc
Ute, deprived of their farmland since 1895, have been a wander-
ing people, following their sheep and horses and having little or
no contact with whites. For them, peyotism is a kind of revival-
istic movement, crystallizing ancient Ute conceptions and weld-
ing them into a societal organization hostile to white influence
and Christianity. "At Towaoc . . . peyote ritual serves the function of closing the door on a modern American environment" (p.
476) through its aboriginal mode of curing and its aboriginal view
of life. In contrast, the Ignacio Ute are farmers living on land
adjacent to the whites and are more acculturated than the Towaoc.
Peyote followers have encountered serious difficulties in even
leasing a church. In Ignacio, where the appeal of the old customs
is considerably weakened, the peyote cult "represents a belated
movement in the direction of Christianity" and thereby "encounters the active resistance of shamans who view the breakdown of
old patterns at Ignacio with considerable alarm" (p. 477). Opler
concludes that "peyote will continue to be a potent vitalizing
force at Towaoc until the acculturation process is raised to a
better level" (p. 478).

Opler, Marvin K. "Fact and Fancy in Ute Peyotism," American Anthropologist 44, no. 1 (January–March 1942): 151-9.

An answer to Omer Stewart's criticisms of Opler's article
"The Character and History of the Southern Ute Peyote Rite."
Opler criticizes Stewart's methodology, such as his reaching
of conclusions after only one week of peripheral observation
compared to Opler's eight months of intense observation in 1936
and several months in 1937. Opler points out that, contrary to
Stewart, the former Towaoc chief John Miller did not oppose
peyotism. He welcomed it, but objected, like the other Towaoc
Utes, to the Christian elements incorporated by Sam Loganberry.
Opler refutes Stewart's claim of the "Christian-like" ideology
of the Towaoc rite by reciting the history of peyotism in Towaoc.
"What did happen to the older peyote ceremonial, introduced in
1916, was that it attracted interest for its ability to weld some
of the aboriginal Ute conceptions into societal organization, but
was also, at the same time, repellent because the Christianized
version did not fit the total Towaoc situation. . . . It was not
until 1931, then, that a more acceptable version was presented
which could be taken over without the necessity of vast re-inter-
pretation and pruning in the light of aboriginal ceremonial which
still persists" (p. 159). Opler explains the differences in ceremonies which Stewart details as due to Stewart's observation of
two aberrant minority groups in Towaoc who are atypical of
the aboriginal pattern of Towaoc and who practice a peyote rite
similar to that of Ignacio.

Opler, Morris E. "The Use of Peyote by the Carrizo and Lipan Apache
Tribes," American Anthropologist 40, no. 2 (April–June 1938):
271-85.

An account of the use of peyote by the Carrizo and Lipan
Apache given (after a brief introduction) in his own words by
Antonio Apache, the one remaining Lipan who had lived under
aboriginal conditions. Interviewed in the summer of 1935, he
describes how peyote was obtained by the Lipan from the Carrizo, the gathering of peyote, individual preparation before the
peyote meeting, the rituals of the peyote meeting, the peyote
meeting as a curing ceremony, and individual and medicinal
uses of peyote.

Petrullo, Vincenzo. "Peyotism as an Emergent Indian Culture,"
Indians at Work 8, no. 8 (April 1940): 51-60.

An argument that the peyote cult is "one of the religious
drives, racial and cultural in nature, which permits the Indian

to reestablish some harmony between himself, the world, and God" (p. 58). Petrullo criticizes the focus of most studies on the physiological aspects or ceremonies and instead emphasizes the religious significance of the peyote cult.

Spindler, George Dearborn. "Personality and Peyotism in Menomini Indian Acculturation," Psychiatry 15, no. 2 (May 1952): 151-9.

A discussion of the social and psychological functions of the peyote cult in the processes of Menomini cultural change and the relationship between adaptations in personality structure and adaptations in cultural and social life. This study is based on Rorschach tests and on interviews and participant observation of 15 adult male members of the peyote cult. After summarizing the ritual of the cult, the visions of the participants, and their conversion to the cult, Spindler tests his hypothesis that systematic deviation of the cult group is reflected in a systematic deviation of the individual personality and finds that culture and personality deviations are "practically identical" (p. 158). He sees the cult as a means of integrating the two conflicting cultures of Western values and of the internalized compulsives of the old way of life.

Stewart, Omer C. "The Southern Ute Peyote Cult," American Anthropologist 53, no. 2 (April–June 1941): 303-8.

A critique of Opler's article "Character and History of the Southern Ute Peyote Rite." Stewart cites differences between the ceremony described by Opler and the ceremonies he witnessed in Towaoc. He suggests that these differences are due to two kinds of peyote rites taking place, the Old Sioux Way and the more recent Tipi Way. He points to Christian adaptations in the Towaoc peyote cult, as opposed to Opler's claim that the Towaoc cult is explicitly in conflict with Christianity. Stewart also criticizes the similarities drawn by Opler between aboriginal ceremonies and the peyote ceremony as a reworking of ancient rites. Stewart suggests that a powerful chief, John Miller, may have prevented the Towaoc Ute from adopting the peyote cult in 1916, when they first had contact with it, until 1931, when a large majority adopted it.

Agar, Michael and Richard C. Stephens. The Methadone Street Scene:
The Addict's View. New York State Drug Abuse Control Commission, 1975.

See the annotation in Section 1: "Drug Use and Abuse Among
Blacks."

Amsel, Zili, J. J. Fishman, Leslie Rivkind, Florence Kavaler,
Donald Krug, Mary Cline, Flora Brophy and Donald Conwell.
"The Use of the Narcotics Register for Follow-up of a Cohort
of Adolescent Addicts," International Journal of the Addictions
6, no. 2 (June 1971): 225-39.

See the annotation in Section 1: "Drug Use and Abuse Among
Blacks."

Babst, Dean V., Carl D. Chambers and Alan Warner. "Patient
Characteristics Associated with Retention in a Methadone Main-
tenance Program," British Journal of Addiction 66, no. 3
(November 1971): 195-204.

See the annotation in Section 1: "Drug Use and Abuse Among
Blacks."

Babst, Dean V., Sandra Newman, Norman Gordon and Alan Warner.
"Driving Records of Methadone Maintenance Patients in New
York State," Journal of Drug Issues 3, no. 4 (Fall 1973):
285-92.

See the annotation in Section 1: "Drug Use and Abuse Among
Blacks."

Bailey, Walter C. and Mary Koval. "Differential Patterns of Drug
    Abuse Among White Activists and Nonwhite Militant College
    Students," International Journal of the Addictions 7, no. 2
    (Summer 1972): 191-9.

    See the annotation in Section 1: "Drug Use and Abuse Among
Blacks."

Ball, John C. "Onset of Marijuana and Heroin Use Among Puerto
    Rican Addicts," British Journal of Criminology 7, no. 4
    (October 1967): 408-13.

    A delineation of the situational and personal factors associated
with the onset of heroin use among Puerto Rican addicts, based
on interviews with and medical records of 119 addict patients
discharged from Lexington Hospital between 1935 and 1962.
Heroin use is found to start in an unsupervised street setting
while the subjects are in their teens; usually the adolescent
smokes marijuana with his neighborhood friends before trying
heroin. The adolescent peer group exercises the dominant influence in both marijuana and heroin use; the subjects willingly
ask to join the addict group and are not coerced, seduced, or
misled. The author notes that the situational and personal factors associated with the onset of heroin use have not changed
during these 40 years. "The evidence suggests that the peer-
group behavior leading to the onset of drug addiction has remained unchanged" (p. 413).

Ball, John C. "The Reliability and Validity of Interview Data Obtained
    from 59 Narcotic Drug Addicts," American Journal of Sociology
    72, no. 6 (May 1967), 650-4.

    An examination of the reliability of narcotic addicts' verbal
responses to questions concerning their age, age at onset of
drug use, type and place of first arrest, total number of arrests,
and drug use at the time of the interview. Fifty-nine Puerto
Rican males who had been prisoners admitted to the Lexington
or Fort Worth hospitals between 1935 and 1939 were interviewed.
The results are compared to their arrest records, medical
records and interviews and urinalysis. "Considering the varied
sources of response error, the interview data were quite reliable
and valid" (p. 653). Several factors are cited as contributing
to that validity: previous institutional contact, the interviewer's
familiarity with the addict subculture and the Puerto Rican ghetto,
competency of the interviewer, the project's lack of association
with police authorities, and the use of a structured personal interview focusing upon specific topics.

Ball, John C. and William M. Bates. "Migration and Residential Mobility of Narcotic Drug Addicts," Social Problems 14, no. 1 (Summer 1966): 56-69.

> See the annotation in Section 1: "Drug Use and Abuse Among Blacks."

Ball, John C. and Delia O. Pabon. "Locating and Interviewing Narcotic Addicts in Puerto Rico," Sociology and Social Research 49, no. 4 (July 1965): 401-11.

> A description of the procedures employed and the problems encountered in locating narcotic addicts in Puerto Rico as part of a two year follow-up study of 243 addict patients from Puerto Rico discharged from Lexington Hospital between 1935 and 1962. Some kind of follow-up information was secured for 97 percent of the subjects, and 109 former addicts were located and interviewed in Puerto Rico. It is found that lower class urban slum dwellers still using drugs are more difficult to locate than either middle or upper class families, and that former female addicts are more difficult to locate than former male addicts. Once located, however, most addicts cooperate with the study by providing both a detailed interview and a urine specimen.

Ball, John C. and Richard W. Snarr. "A Test of the Maturation Hypothesis with Respect to Opiate Addiction," Bulletin on Narcotics 21, no. 4 (October-December 1969): 9-13.

> An assessment of the hypothesis that two-thirds of addicts mature out of their addiction as they grow older, based on a study of 108 Puerto Rican addicts admitted to Lexington Hospital between 1935 and 1962. Medical, prison, FBI, Bureau of Narcotics records, and interviews with the subjects and their relatives provide the data. At the time of the study, two-thirds of the subjects were incarcerated or had not given up heroin. The criminality and lack of steady employment for those who continue to use heroin tend to increase with age rather than to decrease. A large minority of addicts, however, do stop using drugs, give up their criminal careers, and tend to have steady employment. "It appears, then, that two major patterns exist with respect to the life course of opiate addiction in the United States. In one instance, the addict becomes increasingly enmeshed in a non-productive or criminal career as his dependence upon opiates progresses into his adult years. In the second case, the addict terminates his drug-centered way of life and assumes, or re-establishes, a legitimate role in society. In this latter sense, it may be said that some one-third of opiate addicts mature out of their dependence upon drugs" (p. 13).

Bayer, Ron. "Repression, Reform and Drug Abuse: An Analysis of the Response to the Rockefeller Drug Law Proposals of 1973," Journal of Psychedelic Drugs 6, no. 3 (July–September 1974): 299–309.

See the annotation in Section 1: "Drug Use and Abuse Among Blacks."

Bernstein, Blanche and Anne N. Shkuda. The Young Drug User: Attitude and Obstacles to Treatment. New York: Center for New York City Affairs, New School for Social Research, June 1974.

See the annotation in Section 1: "Drug Use and Abuse Among Blacks."

Bernstein, Rosalie. "A Profile of Narcotic Addicts on Public Assistance," Narcotic Addicts on Public Assistance. Edited by Patricia M. Pettiford. (New York City Human Resources Administration, Department of Services Study Series 1, no. 1, October 1973): 1–18.

See the annotation in Section 1: "Drug Use and Abuse Among Blacks."

Brozovsky, Morris and Emil G. Winkler. "Glue Sniffing in Children and Adolescents," New York State Journal of Medicine 65, no. 15 (August 1, 1965): 1984–9.

A study of 19 child and adolescent glue sniffers admitted to the psychiatric service of a general hospital in Brooklyn, New York. Over one-half are Puerto Rican; 17 of the 19 are male. The mean age is 13.8 years. Their family backgrounds are largely disorganized, and all of the families are in the lowest income bracket. The subjects manifest severe psychopathogenic symptoms. The study reveals that glue sniffing is practised in groups in order to induce euphoria to replace feelings of depression and helplessness. The experience of visual hallucination induced by glue and the results of electroencephalographic examinations are described. "The imbibing of alcohol by approximately half of these children and the presence of chronic alcoholism in their immediate families point to a potential for later habituation to ethanol and possibly to drugs" (p. 1989). The authors also summarize the limitations of this type of investigative approach.

Brummit, Houston. "Observations on Drug Addicts in a House of Detention for Women," <u>Corrective Psychiatry and Journal of Social Therapy</u> 9, no. 2 (second quarter 1963): 62-70.

    See the annotation in Section 1: "Drug Use and Abuse Among Blacks."

Callan, John P. and Carroll D. Patterson. "Patterns of Drug Abuse Among Military Inductees," <u>American Journal of Psychiatry</u> 80, no. 3 (March 1973): 260-4.

    See the annotation in Section 1: "Drug Use and Abuse Among Blacks."

Chambers, Carl D. <u>An Assessment of Drug Use in the General Population.</u> Special Report No. 1, <u>Drug Use in New York State.</u> New York: New York State Narcotic Addiction Control Commission, May 1971.

    See the annotation in Section 1: "Drug Use and Abuse Among Blacks."

Chambers, Carl D., Walter R. Cuskey and Arthur D. Moffett. "Mexican-American Opiate Addicts," <u>The Epidemiology of Opiate Addiction in the United States.</u> Edited by John C. Ball and Carl D. Chambers. Springfield, Illinois: Charles C. Thomas, Publisher, 1970, pp. 202-21.

    See the annotation in Section 3: "Drug Use and Abuse Among Mexican Americans."

Chambers, Carl D. and James A. Inciardi. "Some Aspects of the Criminal Careers of Female Narcotic Addicts." Mimeographed. Paper presented to the Southern Sociological Society, Miami Beach, Florida, May 1971.

    See the annotation in Section 1: "Drug Use and Abuse Among Blacks."

Chappel, John N., Vickie M. Hayes and Edward C. Senay. <u>Death and the Treatment of Drug Addiction: A Five-Year Study of Deaths Occurring to Members of the Illinois Drug Abuse Program.</u> Illinois Drug Abuse Program and the University of Chicago Department of Psychiatry, 1973.

    See the annotation in Section 1: "Drug Use and Abuse Among Blacks."

Chein, Isidor. "Narcotics Use Among Juveniles," Social Work 1, no.
2 (April 1956): 50-60.

See the annotation in Section 1: "Drug Use and Abuse Among
Blacks."

Chein, Isidor, Donald L. Gerard, Robert S. Lee and Eva Rosenfeld.
The Road to H: Narcotics, Juvenile Delinquency, and Social
Policy. New York: Basic Books, Inc., 1964.

See the annotation in Section 1: "Drug Use and Abuse Among
Blacks."

Cherubin, Charles E. "Investigations of Tetanus in Narcotic Addicts
in New York City," International Journal of the Addictions 2,
no. 2 (Fall 1967): 253-8.

See the annotation in Section 1: "Drug Use and Abuse Among
Blacks."

Cherubin, Charles E. "Urban Tetanus: The Epidemiological Aspects
of Tetanus in Narcotic Addicts in New York City," Archives of
Environmental Health 14, no. 6 (June 1967): 802-8.

See the annotation in Section 1: "Drug Use and Abuse Among
Blacks."

Cherubin, Charles E., Elaine Palusci and Mario Fortunato. "The
Epidemiology of 'Skin Popping' in New York City," International
Journal of the Addictions 3, no. 1 (Spring 1968): 107-12.

See the annotation in Section 1: "Drug Use and Abuse Among
Blacks."

Cole, K. E., Gary Fisher and Shirley S. Cole. "Women Who Kill,
A Sociopsychological Study," Archives of General Psychiatry
19 (July 1968): 1-8.

See the annotation in Section 1: "Drug Use and Abuse Among
Blacks."

Coles, Robert. "Drugs: Flying High or Low [Drug Addiction on Two
Scenes: The Middle Class Youth and the Negro and Puerto Rican
Poor]," Yale Review 51, no. 1 (Autumn 1967): 38-46.

See the annotation in Section 1: "Drug Use and Abuse Among
Blacks."

Dale, Robert and Farley Ross Dale. "The Use of Methadone in a
Representative Group of Heroin Addicts," International Journal
of the Addictions 8, no. 2 (April 1973): 293-308.

See the annotation in Section 1: "Drug Use and Abuse Among
Blacks."

DeFleur, Lois B. "Biasing Influences on Drug Arrest Records: Implications for Deviance Research," American Sociological Review 40, no. 1 (February 1973): 88-103.

See the annotation in Section 1: "Drug Use and Abuse Among
Blacks."

DeFleur, Lois B., John C. Ball and Richard W. Snarr. "The Long-
Term Social Correlates of Opiate Addiction," Social Problems
17, no. 2 (Fall 1969): 225-34.

Report on social characteristics of long-term opiate addicts,
based on 53 former heroin addicts from Puerto Rico incarcerated
between 1935 and 1962. Drug use, arrests, and career patterns
of the subjects are revealed through a field interview, a urinalysis
to check on addiction status, medical reports, FBI reports, and
interviews with friends and relatives. It is found that over three-
fourths of the addicts remain almost continuously addicted over
the average 16-year period from the time they begin to use drugs.
The majority of them are following a criminal career. Those in
the group more actively pursuing a criminal career have been
arrested at a much younger age and often begin their addiction
only after arrest, in contrast to members of the steadily employed group, who are older when they become addicted and whose
first arrest is related to their addiction. Early involvement
with deviant subgroups is thus suggested. Also, "the post-addiction adjustment to conventional society may be substantially
easier for those with higher educational attainment and previous
employment histories" (pp. 232-3).

DeLeon, George, Sherry Holland and Mitchell S. Rosenthal. The
Phoenix Therapeutic Community: Changes in Criminal Activity
of Resident Drug Addicts. Phoenix House Research Unit,
Phoenix House: Studies in a Therapeutic Community (1968-73)
New York: MSS Publications Information Corporation. A short-
ened version of this paper appears as "Phoenix House—Criminal
Activity of Dropouts," Journal of the American Medical Assoc-
iation 222, no. 6 (November 1973): 686-9.

See the annotation in Section 1: "Drug Use and Abuse Among Blacks."

DeLeon, George and Harry K. Wexler. "Heroin Addiction: Its Relation to Sexual Behavior and Sexual Experience," Journal of Abnormal Psychology 81, no. 1 (February 1973): 36-8.

See the annotation in Section 1: "Drug Use and Abuse Among Blacks."

Drug Abuse Council. Survey of City/County Drug Abuse Activities, 1972, MS-8. Washington, D.C.: Drug Abuse Council, September 1973.

See the annotation in Section 1: "Drug Use and Abuse Among Blacks."

Drug Abuse Programs: A Directory for Minority Groups. Report Series 10 #3. Rockville, Maryland: National Clearing-house for Drug Abuse Information (June 1973).

See the annotation in Section 1: "Drug Use and Abuse Among Blacks."

Duvall, Henrietta J., Ben Z. Locke and Leon Brill. "Followup Study of Narcotic Drug Addicts Five Years After Hospitalization," Public Health Reports 78, no. 3 (March 1963): 185-93.

See the annotation in Section 1: "Drug Use and Abuse Among Blacks."

Eckerman, William C. Drug Usage and Arrest Charges: A Study of Drug Usage and Arrest Charges Among Arrestees in Six Metropolitan Areas of the United States (Final Report). Washington, D.C.: Drug Control Division, Office of Scientific Support, Bureau of Narcotics and Dangerous Drugs, U.S. Department of Justice, December 1971.

See the annotation in Section 1: "Drug Use and Abuse Among Blacks."

Einstein, Stanley. "The Future Time Perspective of the Adolescent Narcotic Addict," Drug Addiction in Youth. Edited by Ernest Harms. Oxford: Pergamon Press, 1965, pp. 90-8.

See the annotation in Section 1: "Drug Use and Abuse Among Blacks."

Einstein, Stanley and David Laskowitz. "Attitudes Toward Authority
Among Adolescent Drug Addicts as a Function of Ethnicity, Sex
and Length of Drug Use," Drug Addiction in Youth. Edited by
Ernest Harms. Oxford: Pergamon Press, 1965, pp. 86-9.

See the annotation in Section 1: "Drug Use and Abuse Among
Blacks."

Fiddle, Seymour. Portraits from a Shooting Gallery: Life Styles from
the Drug Addict World. New York: Harper and Row, 1967.

See the annotation in Section 1: "Drug Use and Abuse Among
Blacks."

Fort, John P., Jr. "Heroin Addiction Among Young Men," Psychiatry
17, no. 3 (August 1954): 251-9.

See the annotation in Section 1: "Drug Use and Abuse Among
Blacks."

Gasser, Edith S., John Langrod, Katherine Valdes and Joyce Lowinson.
"The Eysenck Personality Inventory with Methadone Maintenance
Patients," British Journal of Addiction 69, no. 1 (March 1973):
85-8.

See the annotation in Section 1: "Drug Use and Abuse Among
Blacks."

Gearing, Frances Rowe. Reports to Methadone Maintenance Evaluation
Unit, Columbia University School of Public Health and Administrative Medicine, New York City. Mimeographed. "Successes and
Failures in Methadone Maintenance Treatment of Heroin Addiction in New York City," November 10, 1970; "Methadone Main-
tenance Treatment Programs for 1971: The Year of Expansion,"
April 28, 1972; "Methadone Maintenance Treatment: A Six Year
Evaluation," August 21, 1972; "Methadone Maintenance Treat-
ment: Five Years Later, Where are They Now?" November
8, 1972; "Arrest Histories Before and After Admission to a
Methadone Maintenance Treatment Program," No date, about
1970; "Methadone Maintenance Treatment Programs Progress
Report for 1972: Developing Trends and A Look to the Future,"
June 1, 1973.

See the annotation in Section 1: "Drug Use and Abuse Among
Blacks."

Gearing, Frances Rowe. Methadone Maintenance Treatment Program—
Progress Report for 1973—The Year of Change, mimeographed.

New York: New York State Drug Abuse Control Commission,
July 1974.

See the annotation in Section 1: "Drug Use and Abuse Among
Blacks."

Gearing, Frances Rowe. Methadone Maintenance Treatment for Heroin
Addiction in New York City—An Eight-Year Prospective Overview. Mimeographed. New York: Columbia University School
of Public Health, July, 1974.

See the annotation in Section 1: "Drug Use and Abuse Among
Blacks."

Gearing, Frances Rowe and Dina D'Amico. "The Hispanic and Asiatic
Populations on Methadone Maintenance in New York City: A
Study in Contrast." Mimeographed. Report to Methadone Main-
tenance Evaluation Unit, Columbia University School of Public
Health and Administrative Medicine, New York City, October
15, 1974.

A report whose purpose is to uncover demographic differences
among methadone maintenance patients which might help explain
different rates of rehabilitation. The two cohorts—Hispanic and
Asiatic—comprise 25 percent (N = 10,000) and 1 percent (N = 400)
respectively of the total number of patients since 1964. The
Hispanic population is young (50 percent under 30) and 25 percent female. The Asiatic group is older (average over 50) and
predominantly male (90 percent). The majority of the Asiatics
entered treatment with medical problems such as cancer or
gastric hemorrhaging.

Whites and Hispanics are least likely to drop out of the program (60-70 percent are still in the program over a four year
period), Asiatics somewhat more (about 60 percent still in after
four years), and blacks most likely to terminate (about 50 percent).

Observed changes in social productivity as measured by employment and schooling showed Hispanic men closely following
the pattern of the total male population; Asiatic men had a lower
rate. Hispanic women, on the other hand, showed less movement toward social productivity in these terms than whites or
black female patients.

Problems which interfere with rehabilitation were found to
vary between the two groups. Asiatic men have considerable
chronic health and drug abuse problems: alcohol, drugs, and
arrests present problems among Hispanics. Both groups have
a higher death rate than the total patient population. Among

both Hispanic and Asiatic women alcohol is a problem, but poly-drug use, found among Hispanic females, is not prevalent among Asiatic women. Death from violence is more frequent among Hispanic females than among the total female patient population.

Hughes, Patrick H. and Gail A. Crawford, "A Contagious Disease Model for Researching and Interviewing in Heroin Epidemics," Archives of General Psychiatry 27, no. 2 (August 1972): 149-55.

See the annotation in Section 1: "Drug Use and Abuse Among Blacks."

Hughes, Patrick H., Clinton R. Sanders and Eric Schaps. "The Impact of Medical Intervention in Three Heroin Copping Areas," Proceedings of the Fourth National Conference on Methadone, San Francisco, January 1972.

See the annotation in Section 1: "Drug Use and Abuse Among Blacks."

Hunt, G. Halsey and Maurice E. Odoroff. "Followup Study of Narcotic Drug Addicts After Hospitalization," Public Health Reports 77, no. 1 (January 1962): 41-54.

See the annotation in Section 1: "Drug Use and Abuse Among Blacks."

Hunt, Leon Gibson. Heroin Epidemics: A Qualitative Study of Current Empirical Data. Washington, D.C.: Drug Abuse Council, May 1973.

See the annotation in Section 1: "Drug Use and Abuse Among Blacks."

Johnson, Weldon T. and Robert Bogomolny. "Selective Justice: Drug Law Enforcement in Six American Cities," National Commission on Marihuana and Drug Abuse, Drug Use in America: Problem in Perspective, Vol. III: The Legal System and Drug Control. Washington, D.C.: U.S. Government Printing Office, 1973, pp. 498-650.

See the annotation in Section 1: "Drug Use and Abuse Among Blacks."

Johnston, W. Cecil. "A Descriptive Study of 100 Convicted Female Narcotic Residents," Corrective Psychiatry and Journal of Social Therapy 14, no. 4 (Winter 1968): 230-6.

See the annotation in Section 1: "Drug Use and Abuse Among Blacks."

Joseph, Herman. "A Probation Department Treats Heroin Addicts,"
    Federal Probation 37, no. 1 (March 1973): 35-9.

    See the annotation in Section 1: "Drug Use and Abuse Among
    Blacks."

Jurgensen, Warren P. "New Developments at the Lexington Hospital,"
    Rehabilitating the Narcotic Addict. By the Vocational Rehabilita-
    tion Administration. Washington, D.C.: U.S. Government Print-
    ing Office, 1967, pp. 83-6.

    See the annotation in Section 1: "Drug Use and Abuse Among
    Blacks."

Kaplan, John. "Marijuana and Heroin Addiction," Marijuana—The New
    Prohibition. New York: World Publishing, 1970, pp. 232-62.

    See the annotation in Section 1: "Drug Use and Abuse Among
    Blacks."

Kleber, Herbert D. "Narcotic Addiction—The Current Problem and
    Treatment Approaches," Connecticut Medicine 33, no. 2 (Feb-
    ruary 1969): 113-6.

    See the annotation in Section 1: "Drug Use and Abuse Among
    Blacks."

Koval, Mary. "Opiate Use In New York City." Mimeographed. Sum-
    mary of Report of the New York State Narcotic Addiction Control
    Commission, November 1969.

    See the annotation in Section 1: "Drug Use and Abuse Among.
    Blacks."

Lander, Bernard and Nathan Lander. "A Cross-Cultural Study of Nar-
    cotic Addiction in New York," Rehabilitating the Narcotic Ad-
    dict. Vocational Rehabilitation Administration, Washington,
    D.C.: U.S. Government Printing Office, 1967, pp. 359-69.

    See the annotation in Section 1: "Drug Use and Abuse Among
    Blacks."

Langrod, John. "Secondary Drug Use Among Heroin Users," Inter-
    national Journal of the Addictions 5, no. 4 (December 1970):
    611-35.

    See the annotation in Section 1: "Drug Use and Abuse Among
    Blacks."

Larner, Jeremy (ed.). The Addict in the Street. New York: Grove
    Press, 1964.

First person chronicles of heroin addicts in New York City,
edited from tape-recorded interviews. These accounts reveal
their broken homes, lack of a father figure and ethnic, poor
backgrounds. Nine of those interviewed are male, and two out
of the three women interviewed are mothers of addicts, not
addicts themselves. Three interviewees are Puerto Rican; one
seems to be black, and the rest are white. The main similarity
which Larner notes among all the addicts is the "vast chasm . . .
between his self-portrait and his actual needs and desires as
expressed through the life he leads" (p. 16). Larner suggests
an analogy between addicts and psychotics: both are fleeing
reality and want to live by a style and values completely different
from that reality. Larner sees the addict life style as dangerous
and exciting, providing a kind of "Wild West" escape, and urges
either medical treatment or heroin maintenance for addicts.

Larrier, D., M. Cline, F. Brophy and A. Pischera. "Deaths Among
Narcotic Abusers in New York City, January-June, 1970,"
Contemporary Drug Problems 1, no. 4 (Fall 1972): 711-25.

See the annotation in Section 1: "Drug Use and Abuse Among
Blacks."

Laskowitz, David. "The Adolescent Drug Addict: An Adlerian View,"
Journal of Individual Psychology 17, no. 1 (May 1961): 68-71.

An investigation of the characteristics of the male adolescent
drug addict, based on four years of experience at Riverside
Hospital in New York City. Although many of the addicts described appear to be Puerto Rican, the author never mentions
their racial composition, focusing instead on psychological
characteristics of addicts. He finds that addicts feel inadequate
and desire to be shielded and pampered by their mothers. In
terms of the three major life problems defined by Adler, the
addict: first, limits his social relationships to a reaction to
other addicts rather than relating to them; second, overvalues
the masculine role, exemplifying the masculine protest; and third,
is apathetic in trying to obtain employment, fearing failure and
being unable to postpone immediate gratification. Laskowitz
then enumerates various ways of treating the addict through explaining the patient to himself, disarming the patient, and developing the therapeutic relationship.

Laskowitz, David and Stanley Einstein. "Personality Characteristics
of Adolescent Addicts: Manifest Rigidity," Corrective Psychiatry

and Journal of Social Therapy 9, no. 4 (Fourth Quarter 1963): 215-18.

See the annotation in Section 1: "Drug Use and Abuse Among Blacks."

Levy, Stephen J. "Drug Abuse in Business: Telling It Like It Is," Personnel 49, no. 5 (September-October 1972): 8-14.

See the annotation in Section 1: "Drug Use and Abuse Among Blacks."

Lukoff, Irving F. and Judith S. Brook. A Socio-Cultural Exploration of Reported Heroin Use. Mimeographed. Columbia University, April 1974.

See the annotation in Section 1: "Drug Use and Abuse Among Blacks."

Lukoff, Irving F., Debra Quatrone and Alice Sardell. Some Aspects of the Epidemiology of Heroin Use in a Ghetto Community: A Preliminary Report. United States Department of Justice, July 1972.

See the annotation in Section 1: "Drug Use and Abuse Among Blacks."

Nash, George. The Impact of Drug Abuse Treatment Upon Criminality: A Look at 19 Programs. Trenton, New Jersey: New Jersey Division of Narcotic and Drug Abuse Control, December 1973.

See the annotation in Section 1: "Drug Use and Abuse Among Blacks."

Newman, Robert G., Sylvia Bashkow and Margot Cates. "Applications Received by the New York City Methadone Maintenance Treatment Program During Its First Two Years of Operation," Drug Forum 3, no. 2 (Winter 1974): 183-91.

See the annotation in Section 1: "Drug Use and Abuse Among Blacks."

Perlis, Leo. "Drug Abuse Among Union Members," Drug Abuse in Industry. Edited by W. Wayne Stewart. Miami, Florida: Halosand Associates, 1970, pp. 75-80.

See the annotation in Section 1: "Drug Use and Abuse Among Blacks."

Powers, Robert J. "The Vocational Maturity of Inner-city Narcotics
Addicts," Rehabilitation Counseling Bulletin 4, no. 17 (June
1974): 210-14.

See the annotation in Section 1: "Drug Use and Abuse Among
Blacks."

Preble, Edward. "Social and Cultural Factors Related to Narcotic
Use Among Puerto Ricans in New York City," International
Journal of the Addictions 2, no. 1 (January 1966): 30-41.

An analysis of social and cultural factors related to use of
narcotics by Puerto Ricans in New York City, based on research
informants in a half-mile square area which is poor, mainly
Puerto Rican, and 20 percent black. Preble outlines the historical and socioeconomic conditions of Puerto Ricans, and the
challenge to the traditional Puerto Rican patriarchy posed by
women working in the U.S. The delinquency pattern changes from
gang warfare between Puerto Ricans and blacks, Irish, and Italians from 1950-56 to heroin addiction and the cessation of rival
gangs after 1956. Some social and cultural factors which Puerto
Ricans encounter in New York are cited, such as racism and de-
fensive reactions. The most significant factor to Preble is the
disruption of traditional family life and the downgrading of the
Puerto Rican male, with complete destruction of the traditional
respect for authority. "Narcotic use . . . is one solution to the
social and psychological problems of Puerto Ricans which result,
in part, from the social burdens imposed on a recent immigrant
group" (p. 40).

Preble, Edward J. and John J. Casey. "Taking Care of Business—The
Heroin User's Life on the Street," International Journal of the Addictions 4, no. 1 (March 1969): 1-24.

See the annotation in Section 1: "Drug Use and Abuse Among
Blacks."

Preble, Edward and Gabriel V. Laury. "Plastic Cement: The Ten
Cent Hallucinogen," International Journal of the Addictions 2,
no. 2 (Fall 1967): 271-81.

See the annotation in Section 1: "Drug Use and Abuse Among
Blacks."

Richman, Alex, Marvin E. Perkins, Bernard Bihari and J. J. Fishman. "Entry into Methadone Maintenance Programs: A Follow-
up Study of New York City Heroin Users Detoxified in 1961-1963,"
American Journal of Public Health 62, no. 7 (July 1972): 1002-7.

See the annotation in Section 1: "Drug Use and Abuse Among Blacks."

Royfe, Ephrain H. "An Exploratory Examination of the Social and Psychological Characteristics of 100 Pennsylvania Drug Addicts," Pennsylvania Psychiatric Quarterly 5, no. 4 (Winter 1965): 38-47.

See the annotation in Section 1: "Drug Use and Abuse Among Blacks."

Scher, Jordan. "Patterns and Profiles of Addiction and Drug Abuse," International Journal of the Addictions 2, no. 2 (Fall 1967): 171-90.

See the annotation in Section 1: "Drug Use and Abuse Among Blacks."

Snarr, Richard W. and John C. Ball. "Involvement in a Drug Subculture and Abstinence Following Treatment Among Puerto Rican and Narcotic Addicts," British Journal of Addictions 119, no. 3 (September 1974): 233-48.

A study whose aim is to investigate the relationship between drug subculture involvement and subsequent drug use and/or abstinence following treatment. The sample consists of 108 male native Puerto Rican addicts released from Public Health Hospitals in Lexington, Kentucky. The degree of subculture involvement before treatment is based on index of five items: amount spent daily on drugs, history of drug pushing, former treatment, opiate use begun in a group setting, and former marijuana use. The index of involvement was correlated with being cured (being off drugs for at least three years).

The data support the hypothesis that the greater the subculture involvement, the less likelihood of abstinence. With social class controlled the same pattern was found, although a higher percentage of cures was found among middle and upper class subjects. The subculture/abstinence relationship was less clear cut among addicts who started heroin use at an early age, but among addicts who started after 21 years the relationship was stronger, that is, cure was almost non-existent. The authors suggest that late onset of drug abuse may indicate a failure in more legitimate, socially-approved pursuits.

Snow, Mary. "Maturing Out of Narcotic Addiction in New York City," International Journal of Addictions 8, no. 6 (December 1973): 921-38.

See the annotation in Section 1: "Drug Use and Abuse Among Blacks."

Stephens, Richard and Emily Cottrell. "A Follow-Up Study of 200 Narcotic Addicts Committed for Treatment Under the Narcotic Addict Rehabilitation Act (NARA)," British Journal of Addiction 67, no. 1 (March 1972): 45-53.

See the annotation in Section 1: "Drug Use and Abuse Among Blacks."

Stephens, Richard C. and Rosalind Ellis. Narcotics Addicts and Crime: Analysis of Recent Trends. New York State Drug Abuse Control Commission, 1974.
See the annotation in Section 1: "Drug Use and Abuse Among Blacks."

Stephens, Richard C. and Gerald T. Slatin. "The Street Addict Role: Toward the Definition of a Type," Drug Forum 3, no. 4 (Summer 1974): 375-89.
See the annotation in Section 1: "Drug Use and Abuse Among Blacks."

Taylor, Susan D., Mary Wilbur and Robert Osnos. "The Wives of Drug Addicts," American Journal of Psychiatry 123, no. 5 (November 1966): 585-91.

See the annotation in Section 1: "Drug Use and Abuse Among Blacks."

Vaillant, George E. "A Twelve-Year Follow-Up of New York Narcotic Addicts: III. Some Social and Psychiatric Considerations," Archives of General Psychiatry 15 (December 1966): 599-609.
See the annotation in Section 1: "Drug Use and Abuse Among Blacks."

Voss, Harwin L. and Richard S. Stephens. "Criminal History of Narcotics Addicts," Drug Forum 2, no. 2 (Winter 1973): 191-202.
See the annotation in Section 1: "Drug Use and Abuse Among Blacks."

Waldorf, Dan. Careers in Dope. Englewood Cliffs, New Jersey: Prentice-Hall, 1973.
See the annotation in Section 1: "Drug Use and Abuse Among Blacks."

Wilner, Daniel M., Eva Rosenfeld, Robert S. Lee, Donald L. Gerard, and Isidor Chein. "Heroin Use and Street Gangs," Journal of Criminal Law, Criminology and Police Science 48, no. 4 (November-December 1957): 399-409.

> See the annotation in Section 1: "Drug Use and Abuse Among Blacks."

Zahn, Margaret and John C. Ball. "Factors Related to Cure of Opiate Addiction Among Puerto Rican Addicts," International Journal of the Addictions 7, no. 2 (Summer 1972): 237-45.

> An identification of the characteristics of cured opiate addicts, who comprise 20 percent of the 108 Puerto Rican males treated for opiate addiction at Lexington Hospital. The cured subjects have the following social and background characteristics: they are married, living with their spouses rather than with parents or relatives, steadily employed, older than uncured, arrest-free or with fewer arrests than uncured (especially for violating narcotics laws including the sale of drugs), less likely to be heroin addicts, and began using drugs at a later age, with a short length of time between the onset of opiate use and subsequent treatment.

Zimmering, Paul and James Toolan. "Drug Addiction in Adolescents," Journal of Nervous and Mental Disease 116, no. 3 (September 1952): 262-5.

> See the annotation in Section 1: "Drug Use and Abuse Among Blacks."

Zimmering, Paul, James Toolan, Renate Safrin and S. Bernard Wortis. "Heroin Addiction in Adolescent Boys," Journal of Nervous and Mental Disease 114, no. 1 (July 1951): 19-34.

> See the annotation in Section 1: "Drug Use and Abuse Among Blacks."

mobility, in residence of addicts, 77, 124, 168, 174, 202, 216, 228 (see also, nativity); in status of addicts, 37, 114, 169, 183, 194, 202-3; (see also, income, socio-economic status, subculture)
morphine, 77, 103, 175
mortality (see, death)
multiple drug abuse, 39, 71, 91, 94, 112, 126, 138-9, 144-5, 165, 166, 167, 170, 179-80, 196, 202

Nalline areas, 124
Narcotic Addict Rehabilitation Act (NARA), 171-2
Narcotic Rehabilitation Center (New York), 133
Narcotics Bureau (Detroit), 141
Narcotics Treatment Administration (NTA), 85-6, 108
National Commission on Marijuana and Drug Abuse (NCMDA), 26, 29
National Institute of Mental Health (NIMH), 170, 201
Native American addicts, 76, 84, 87, 141, 204-13
Native American Church, 206, 209
nativity of addicts, 77, 82, 85, 137, 145-6, 146, 147, 168, 187, 193, 202, 228 (see also, family, mobility, in residence)
Navaho, peyote cult and, 204, 205
Nebraska, addicts in, 208
Negro addicts (see, black addicts)
Neighborhood Youth Corps, 84
New Haven (Conn.), addicts in, 136
New Jersey, addicts in, 124
New Mexico, addicts in, 195, 202
New Orleans, addicts in, 143-4
New York City, addict crime in, 157-8, 159-60; addicts in, 39, 71, 78, 82, 85, 86, 95-7, 99, 106-7, 110, 113, 114, 115, 121-2, 125, 129, 133, 137-8, 140, 159-60, 169, 174, 175-6, 177, 182-3, 183-4, 185, 217, 220, 226, 228; Central Narcotics Registry, Department of Social Services, 6, 73, 82, 98, 139, 170

New York Medical College, Division of Community Mental Health, 85
New York State, addicts in, 29, 38, 49, 78, 92, 93, 147, 153
New York State Drug Abuse Control Commission (DACC), 50, 92, 153, 172, 178-9
New York State Narcotic Addiction Control Commission (see, New York State Drug Abuse Control Commission)
New York Urban League, 169
nonwhite addicts (see, listings for specific groups, e.g., Asian American, black, Chicano)
Northern Ute, peyote cult and, 211
number of addicts, in United States, 3, 4, 54, 175

Oakland (Calif.), addicts in, 84-5, 124, 144
occupation of addicts, 80, 82, 87, 90, 109, 110, 124, 125, 126-7, 134, 144, 148, 154-5, 158, 159, 161, 168, 172, 174, 177, 180-1, 183, 184, 187, 192-3, 195, 216, 220, 231; age at entering labor force, 158; illegal, 91, 93, 94, 110, 122, 144, 160, 167, 193, 195, 216, 220 (see also, employment, hustling, income, prostitution, pushers, unemployment)
Ohio, addicts in, 100-1
onset of drug abuse, 78, 96-7, 101, 101-2, 109-10, 114, 130, 143-4, 153-4, 168, 173, 175, 179, 182, 184, 215; peer relationships and, 22, 24, 32-3, 81, 88, 91, 109-10, 127, 130, 134, 137, 166, 169, 173, 175, 215, 217 (see also, adolescent drug use, age, diffusion, family, medically-induced addiction, psychological factors, social factors, subculture)
opiate use, 10-11, 28, 77, 78, 85, 89, 91, 93, 103, 121, 130, 137-8, 146, 147, 150, 152, 169, 170, 187, 202, 216, 220

Orientals, 28, 29, 78 (see also, Chinese, Asian American)
overdose, 54, 125-6, 139, 182, 190 (see also, death)

paregoric, 38, 103, 141
passivity of addicts, 83, 97, 136, 160, 166, 174, 176, 185, 197-8 (see also, aggressiveness, homosexuality)
Pennsylvania, addicts in, 168 (see also, Philadelphia)
personality of addict (see, aggressiveness, alienation, anxiety, aspirations, attitudes, authority, cautiousness, homosexuality, identity confusion, immaturity, mental illness, passivity, psychiatric diagnosis, psychological factors, psychopathic personality, rigidity, schizophrenia, self-esteem, time perspective, violence)
peyote, commercial control of marketing, 206; physiological effects, 204, 207, 208, 210; relation to narcotics, 206; therapeutic use, 206, 207, 209, 210, 211, 212-3
peyote cult, as adjustment to acculturation, 204, 205, 209, 211, 213; as combination of Christianity and native religion, 209, 210, 211, 212, 213; as developing unity, 209, 210-1; economic factors, 204, 206; history of, 204, 205, 208, 211, 212, 213; relation to nativistic movements, 204, 205, 209; as revivalist movement (anti-Christian), 211, 213; as response to cultural and social disorganization and oppression, 204, 205, 206, 207, 209, 211; ritual, 204, 206, 208, 210, 212; Sioux Way (Western Slope Way), 210, 213; Tipi Way, 210, 213
Philadelphia, addicts in, 94, 168 (see also, Pennsylvania)
Phoenix Houses (New York City), 43, 83, 106, 107 (see also, group therapy, therapeutic communities)

physicians (see, medically-induced addiction)
Plains Indians, peyote cult and, 208, 210
police detection of addiction, 87, 110, 126, 129, 132-3, 140, 156-7, 161, 165, 190, 194; bias in, 4-6, 40, 104-5 (see also, arrests)
political problem, drug abuse as a, 8-10, 90, 56-7, 125, 150, 162-3
poverty, 37, 86, 96, 97, 101-2, 115, 123, 124, 135, 137, 145, 159, 194, 203, 206, 220, 226, 228 (see also, social factors)
prevalence of drug abuse (see, incidence, number, rates)
prison, addicts and (see, arrests, incarceration)
prostitution, as addict occupation, 88, 91, 92, 144, 149, 202 (see also, crime, female)
psychedelics (see, hallucinogens)
psychiatric diagnosis, 73, 76, 82-3, 91, 97, 100, 101-2, 115, 116, 117, 120, 120-1, 126, 148, 176-7, 205, 208, 213, 226 (see also, psychological factors, psychological traits)
psychological factors in onset of drug abuse, 72, 73, 82-3, 84-5, 88, 95, 97, 100, 101-2, 103, 107, 109, 112-3, 114, 115, 116, 120, 120-1, 122, 126, 134, 136, 139, 140, 148, 149-50, 160, 166, 168, 169, 170, 174, 175, 176-7, 177, 182, 183-4, 185, 187, 190, 193, 196-7, 202-3, 205, 208, 209, 210, 217, 226, 228; curiosity, 97, 113, 134, 168, 169, 175; dependency on mother, 83, 97, 115, 123, 136, 165, 185, 226; emotional attachment to other addict, 109; escape, 101-2, 114, 123, 139, 170, 196-7, 198, 210, 217, 226; existential anguish, 114; freedom from restraint, 210; frustration of high aspirations, 22-3, 37, 55, 72, 115, 123, 169, 171; inability to communicate, 88; inability to

residence house treatment (see, therapeutic communities)

retention in treatment, 74-5, 86, 90-1, 104, 118, 134, 151, 161-2, 167, 169, 170, 184, 192, 202-3, 223; rates, 43, 74-5, 118, 118-9, 129, 170, 180, 192, 202-3, 231 (see also, relapse)

retraining, 158, 202

rigidity of addicts, 114, 140 (see also, psychological traits)

rural addiction, 77, 79, 101, 102, 147, 181, 193 (see also, Southern addicts)

St. Louis, addicts in, 33, 87, 165

sale of drugs, 39-40, 92, 93, 144, 158, 167, 182, 190, 231 (see also, arrests, crime, pushers, source of drug supply)

Salt Lake City, addicts in, 161

San Antonio, addicts in, 196, 201

San Francisco, addicts in, 124, 152, 161, 170 (see also, California)

San Jose, addicts in, 197

schizophrenia, 83, 100, 121, 126, 176 (see also, mental illness, psychiatric diagnosis, psychological traits)

sedatives (see, barbiturates)

self-esteem, deprivation of, 97, 110, 115-6, 121, 148, 169, 172, 185, 190, 194, 197-8, 205, 207 (see also, psychological factors, psychological traits)

sequence of events in addict lives (see, arrests, death, diffusion, education, maturing out, onset)

sensitivity training (see, group therapy, therapeutic communities)

sex, differences among addicts, 36, 71, 78, 98, 99, 101, 102-3, 109-10, 112-3, 113-4, 124, 125, 130, 140, 143, 144, 147, 149, 153-4, 156, 174-5, 179-80, 181, 183, 190, 195, 216; ratio among addicts, 35-6, 78, 92, 109-10, 112-3, 113-4, 130, 134, 137, 141, 143, 161, 174-5, 179-80, 180, 183, 190, 193, 202, 217

sexual behavior of addicts, 106-7, 134, 138, 148, 174, 177, 184

Shoshone, peyote cult and, 210

skin-popping (see, methods, subcutaneous)

Sioux, peyote cult and, 208

Slavs, 76

slums (see, ghettos)

social factors in onset of drug abuse, 37, 72, 83, 84-5, 95-6, 96-7, 101-2, 103, 114, 122, 123, 137-8, 139, 141, 146-7, 150, 159-60, 161, 165, 166, 168, 171, 173, 176, 183-4, 185, 187, 190, 194, 195, 197-8, 201, 202-3, 204, 205, 208, 210, 211, 213, 215, 220, 228, 231 (see also, adolescent drug use, alcoholism, availability, counterculture, crime, discrimination, education, family, ghettos, hustlers, hustling, income and class, juvenile delinquency, marital status, mobility, occupation, onset, poverty, rural, socioeconomic status, subculture, suburban unemployment, urban)

social problem, drug abuse as a, 6, 8-10, 21-4, 54-7, 84-5, 96, 110, 122, 123, 137, 139, 143, 158, 160, 164, 183, 185, 187, 190, 194, 198, 201, 202-3, 204, 206, 209, 210, 211, 213, 216, 220, 228

socioeconomic status of addicts, 36-7, 72, 83, 84-5, 103, 109, 112, 120, 121, 123, 124, 135, 139, 141, 145, 146, 154, 160, 168, 184, 192, 197, 201, 204, 216, 226, 228 (see also, family, income, occupation, mobility, in status, poverty)

solvent sniffing (see, gasoline, glue)

source of drug supply, illegal, 7, 54, 78, 91, 94, 103, 112, 143, 159-60, 181, 195; legal or quasi-legal, 7, 18, 25, 78, 91, 103, 139, 141, 181 (see also, medically-induced addiction, sale of drugs, subculture)

Washington, D.C., addicts in, 85, 86, 108-9, 124-5, 135-6

West Indians, 32, 33, 136-7, 145, 146

White addicts, 14-15, 24, 28, 33, 38, 39, 40, 89-90, 131, 137, 152 (see also, race, comparison with whites)

withdrawal, 27, 54, 169, 176, 192; barbiturate, 54, 72; methadone, 192

wives of addicts, 100, 174

ABOUT THE EDITORS

PATTI IIYAMA was Research Assistant at the Metropolitan Applied Research Center, Inc. (MARC). She holds a B.A. and M.A. from the University of California at Berkeley.

SETSUKO MATSUNAGA NISHI is Associate Professor of Sociology at Brooklyn College and at The Graduate Center of The City University of New York and a Fellow at MARC. He was awarded a Ph.D. by The University of Chicago and is the author of books and articles on race relations and social welfare.

BRUCE D. JOHNSON, Assistant Professor of Sociology at Manhattanville College, has his Ph.D. from Columbia University. He has written books and articles on drug subcultures.

CORRECTIONS: Problems of Punishment and
Rehabilitation

> edited by Edward Sagarin and
> Donald E. J. MacNamara

CRIME AND DELINQUENCY: Dimensions of Deviance

> edited by Marc Riedel and
> Terence P. Thornberry

CRIME PREVENTION AND SOCIAL CONTROL

> edited by Ronald L. Akers and
> Edward Sagarin

DEPRIVED URBAN YOUTH: An Economic and Cross-
Cultural Analysis of the United States, Colombia, and
Peru

> John P. Walter, William H. Leahy, and
> Arthur G. Dobbelaere

IMAGES OF CRIME: Offenders and Victims

> edited by Terence P. Thornberry and
> Edward Sagarin

A SURVEY OF PUERTO RICANS ON THE U.S. MAINLAND IN THE
1970s

> Kal Wagenheim